Indians on the Move

Critical Indigeneities

J. Kēhaulani Kauanui and Jean M. O'Brien, *series editors*

SERIES ADVISORY BOARD

Chris Anderson, University of Alberta

Irene Watson, University of South Australia

Emilio del Valle Escalante, University of North Carolina at
    Chapel Hill

Kim TallBear, University of Texas at Austin

Critical Indigeneities publishes pathbreaking scholarly books that center Indigeneity as a category of critical analysis, understand Indigenous sovereignty as ongoing and historically grounded, and attend to diverse forms of Indigenous cultural and political agency and expression. The series builds on the conceptual rigor, methodological innovation, and deep relevance that characterize the best work in the growing field of critical Indigenous studies.

Indians on the Move

Native American Mobility and Urbanization
in the Twentieth Century

· ·

DOUGLAS K. MILLER

The University of North Carolina Press Chapel Hill

This book was published in association with the William P. Clements Center for Southwest Studies at Southern Methodist University by the University of North Carolina Press.

© 2019 The University of North Carolina Press
All rights reserved
Set in Charis by Westchester Publishing Services
Manufactured in the United States of America

The University of North Carolina Press has been a member of the Green Press Initiative since 2003.

Library of Congress Cataloging-in-Publication Data
Names: Miller, Douglas K., 1976– author.
Title: Indians on the move : Native American mobility and urbanization in the twentieth century / Douglas K. Miller.
Other titles: Critical indigeneities.
Description: Chapel Hill : University of North Carolina Press, [2019] | Series: Critical indigeneities | Includes bibliographical references and index.
Identifiers: LCCN 2018036571 | ISBN 9781469651378 (cloth : alk. paper) | ISBN 9781469651385 (pbk : alk. paper) | ISBN 9781469651392 (ebook)
Subjects: LCSH: Indians of North America—United States—Social conditions. | Indians of North America—Government relations—History. | Indians of North America—Urban residence. | Migration, Internal—United States.
Classification: LCC E98.S67 M55 2019 | DDC 970.004/97—dc23
LC record available at https://lccn.loc.gov/2018036571

Cover illustrations: Photographs from BIA Relocation Records, Edward E. Ayer Manuscript Collection, Newberry Library, Chicago.

For Christopher

Contents

Illustrations

Acknowledgments

Where to begin. So many remarkable people have provided me so much support, guidance, perspective, trust, and encouragement. It's an honor to acknowledge them here.

The late Erskine Carter, my English literature professor, was my first great academic influence, as well as an early film, literature, and Dylanology guru. He taught me that it's important to "spend some time with it." I didn't get a chance to express my adoration and appreciation prior to his passing. Before I ever would have guessed that I would end up in this profession, he showed me that it's okay to be unconventional (myself).

At the University of Minnesota, Jeani O'Brien's class changed my life course. "You should go to graduate school, Doug," she said one afternoon in her office, where I used to linger with so many questions. "What's graduate school?" I replied, quite seriously. She saw something in me that I could not see. On her advice, I broke up my band and moved to Chicago. And she was right. Here I am today. Unbelievable.

At the University of Illinois at Chicago, my thesis adviser, Brian Hosmer, coached me up from a musician posing as a history student to a history student posing as a musician. He created so many opportunities for me over the years, and he remains a loyal advocate and caring mentor to this day.

At the University of Oklahoma, my doctoral adviser, Warren Metcalf, provided outstanding guidance, perspective, and support. He was the calm but confident mentor I needed for such an ambitious research project at a challenging time in my life. Also at OU, I appreciated generous support and advice from David Wrobel, Josh Piker, Robert Griswold, Bob Rundstrom, Terry Rugeley, Steve Gillon, and Sterling Evans.

I remain so fond of my time at Southern Methodist University's Clements Center for Southwest Studies, where I joined a new family. Sherry Smith believed and invested in my project, my future, and me. She listened carefully and kept the faith. Andy Graybill became and remains a great friend, professional adviser, and champion of my work. Ruth Ann Elmore was the first person I met upon arriving in Dallas. What a great ambassador! More than that, she became my dear friend. My fellow fellows—Rachel

St. John, Andrew Offenberger, and Gavin Benke—made my fellowship year an especially enjoyable experience. At my Clements Center manuscript workshop, I received unparalleled and truly inspiring instruction on the crafts of writing, conceptualization, and analysis from my workshop invitees Phil Deloria and Robert Self. As well, I benefited from thoughtful critiques and encouragement from fellow workshop participants Ed Countryman, Louis Warren, Neil Foley, Todd Kerstetter, Max Krochmal, Margaret Neubauer, Steve Denson, Sami Lakomäki, and Lisa Barnett. Such a fine group of scholars; I truly miss the Clements Center.

I am so grateful for Oklahoma State University providing me the opportunity to harness all of this support, inspiration, and mentorship in service of my own career, colleagues, and students. From this side of the profession, I now try to pay things back and forward. But then I'm just accumulating more debt here. I sincerely appreciate my wonderful students and faculty colleagues here in Stillwater. In her capacity as history department head, Laura Belmonte offered reliable and extensive support for my book project, my teaching, and my general role within the department. I am indebted to my faculty writing group colleagues—Jim Huston, Rick Rohrs, Laura Belmonte, John Kinder, Yongtao Du, Holly Karibo, Thomas Carlson, Emily Graham, Anna Zeide, Matt Schauer, Richard Boles, Louise Siddons, and Laura Arata—for providing critical feedback on my work. I thank my entire department for the friendship, generosity, enthusiasm, and support they have demonstrated since my arrival.

At UNC Press, I am especially grateful for my editor Mark Simpson-Vos's strong support for my project. Mark did an outstanding job shepherding this book through publication. He listens patiently and carefully, and takes my ideas and concerns seriously. He has been the nurturing presence I needed. At UNC Press, I also thank Jessica Newman and Cate Hodorowicz for their hard work bringing this book to fruition. As well, I sincerely thank my two anonymous manuscript reviewers for providing careful and encouraging feedback that made this a much better book. Finally, I thank J. Kehaulani Kauanui and Jeani O'Brien for inviting my book into their series.

I owe a special mention of gratitude to the people who took time to share with me their personal insights and reflections on the urban relocation program and urban Indigenous communities. Father Peter Powell was instrumental in setting this project in motion when he invited me to Chicago's St. Augustine's Center for American Indians and opened his personal archive to me. Ada Deer graciously spent an entire day with me in

Wisconsin sharing her experiences with the relocation program. The late Matthew Pilcher spent an entire day with me discussing his urban experiences in Los Angeles and Chicago, and his return to his Winnebago, Nebraska, home. At the Urban Inter-Tribal Center of Texas, Angela Young and Mike Frazier spent the afternoon reflecting on their experiences as proud members of the Dallas–Fort Worth Indian community. Most recently, the great singer-songwriter John Angaiak took time to share some personal reflections on his song "I'm Lost in the City."

So many more people have lent their time, friendship, feedback, advice, and professional support along the way. Thank you Kevin Whalen, Coll Thrush, Colleen O'Neill, Boyd Cothran, Dan Cobb, John Troutman, Malinda Maynor Lowery, Kasey Keeler, Nick Rosenthal, Kent Blansett, David Beck, Albert Old Crow, Steve Blake, Carter Meland, Kristen Shedd, Justin Castro, Jeff Fortney, Rowan Steinekker, Brian Rindfleisch, Brandi Hilton, Dustin Mack, Jim Sack, Jenna Nigro, Michael Goode, Perry Clark, Tom Dorrance, Robert Johnston, and Corey Capers, among many, many others.

Now I turn to family. Christopher, Mary, AJ, and Seth von Alt welcomed me into their family, made me feel like I belong, and continue to provide needed love, support, music, joy, and laughter. My little brother, Nick, has been a great friend, confidant, and model of strength and determination; I look up to him. Maggie and Holland curled up next to me many late nights while I wrote this book. They reminded me that a grand adventure begins with each new and never dull day.

When I search for some psychoanalytical, autobiographical explanation for what drew me to this book's subject, I tend to think of my mother. My mother worked from the bottom up, against the odds. She taught me to let our family's hardships drive me but not define me. She worked tirelessly to provide for my brother and me. She held us together in the eye of a hurricane. I owe her my life.

Finally, I marvel at my wife's stunning beauty, and I revel in her infinite love. A great friendship and sense of adventure has underscored our relationship from the outset. I could not have written this book without her feedback, support, and assistance. My love for her is pure and true. And now, as I let go of this project, I am excited to turn to our new project—our amazing baby boy, Christopher.

Introduction

Painting a New Landscape: Native American Mobility
in the Twentieth Century

• •

Abandoned at birth in a garbage can in Gallup, New Mexico, Tom Bee survived a tough childhood as a Dakota boy far removed from Dakota country. Reaching adulthood in the late 1960s, he adopted the course of so many
aspiring young musicians anxious to break into the rock-and-roll business
and receive from fans the adoration their parents failed to provide: he
boarded a bus bound for Hollywood. After several rounds of knocking on
record company doors, Bee finally found work as a songwriter in the Los
Angeles office of the legendary Motown Records. Having successfully composed hit songs for Michael Jackson, to whom he gifted a turquoise ring,
and Smokey Robinson, Bee finally scored his own album deal and formed
an intertribal Indian rock band from Albuquerque dubbed XIT (an acronym
for "Crossing of Indian Tribes"). During its peak in the 1970s, XIT opened
its live shows with the voice of western film icon John Wayne reciting a pre-
recorded Pledge of Allegiance over the audio system while a spotlight
homed in on front-man Bee, draped in a rhinestone-sequined upended
American flag—a traditional Native American distress symbol.[1]

Indian people in distress emerged as a central motif within the group's
music. For example, despite operating out of Albuquerque and touring metropolitan America with marquee artists such as Three Dog Night, Joe
Cocker, and the Beach Boys, XIT condemned cities for their punishing treatment of Native peoples. The group's third album, *Relocation* (1977), took
specific aim at the federal Bureau of Indian Affairs' former pet program,
the Voluntary Relocation Program, which between 1952 and 1972 provided
programmatic support for the movement of roughly one hundred thousand
Native Americans from rural Indian Country to what increasingly became
urban Indian Country.[2] XIT's appraisal of the relocation program is best captured in a cutting lyric from the album's title track: "Relocation / taking
me far away / relocation / taking my roots away."[3] Perhaps Bee's indictment
of the big city, which he depended on for his livelihood as a musician,
stemmed from his own catastrophic urban beginnings. "Entering the world

the way I did, just left in a garbage can, is not a thing to be proud of," he disclosed. "For years I felt betrayed."[4]

A similar betrayal explains not only musicians' but numerous Native peoples' enduring memory of urban America as a "place made of sorrow."[5] Many urban Indians felt abandoned by a paternalistic federal government that raised expectations for a better standard of living and often failed to meet them. In her autobiography, the late Cherokee Nation chief Wilma Mankiller portrayed relocation participants as unwitting victims, "lured" from their ancestral homelands into urban traps. Recalling the fear she experienced as a child witnessing an elevator for the first time after her family relocated to San Francisco, she claimed, "No one had bothered to even try to prepare us for city living."[6] Likewise, at one point the main protagonist in Kiowa author N. Scott Momaday's Pulitzer Prize–winning novel *House Made of Dawn* (1969) falls under the disorienting spell of colorful Los Angeles lights, store windows filled with "shiny things," and old men selling newspapers who are "always yelling at you, but you can't understand them."[7] "You know that relocation program," Momaday explained, "I think it was bad for most of the tribes . . . because they just weren't equipped . . . to leave the reservation and make their way in the city. It was just too much of an adjustment."[8] Consider too the suggestion by Russell Means—famed Lakota actor and leading figure during the American Indian Movement's early-1970s heyday—that the federal government's primary agenda had been to "integrate Indians into urban ghettos so that in a few generations [they] would intermarry and disappear into the underclass. Then the government could take the rest of [their] land and there would be no one left to object." Concluding there, Means's summary captures the prevailing appraisal of the program. But he had more to say: "I didn't quite grasp all that at the time. I understood only that reservation Indians were being offered transportation to several cities around the country, plus job training, and housing and employment assistance."[9]

Consider a second, less ambivalent counternarrative. The title of Yupik singer-songwriter John Angaiak's 1971 album *I'm Lost in the City* ostensibly seems to agree with the reigning memory of urbanization as an adverse experience for Indigenous people—a place where one becomes lost, isolated, endangered, alone. But he employed a different meaning of "lost" in his album liner notes on the title track: "To many Natives that have never experienced a city life, city is a place where they can escape the norms of the village life. City is a place where no villager watches him any longer; that is, he is able to do things that he normally does not do in the village. So he gets lost in

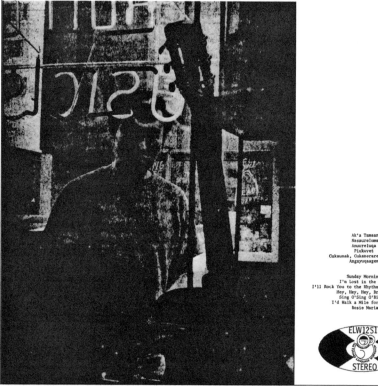

I'M LOST IN THE CITY
John Angaiak

Ak'a Tamaani
Nassureluma
Anuureluqa
Piukuvet
Cukaunak, Cukanerareluten-Ilu
Angayuqaagema

Sunday Morning
I'm Lost in the City
I'll Rock You to the Rhythm of the Ocean
Hey, Hey, Hey, Brother
Sing O'Sing O'Birdie
I'd Walk a Mile for My Girl
Rosie Maria

John Angaiak (Yup'ik), *I'm Lost in the City* album cover (1971, reissued in 2016). Courtesy of John Angaiak and Light in the Attic Records/Future Days Recordings.

the city, as it is kind of a pioneering all the way." From Angaiak's perspective, cities were not burial grounds for Indigenous cultures; rather, they were places of opportunity, where one could escape surveillance, be anonymous, and do things one "does not do in the village." Angaiak *wanted* to get lost in the city, to remove his mask or wear a new one. He wanted to reflect on life beyond his daily cultural context. Such an experience was not distressing but enriching: "Amazing city / I found it to be / And the skies are full of mystery / And the streets are full of many people / And people I don't know."[10]

Cities do, after all, project timeless auras as places of reinvention. This book explores this dimension of the urban Indian experience. It casts

Indian mobility and urbanization, especially through the federal Voluntary Relocation Program, as a larger story of survival—or, more appropriately, *survivance*, to borrow Anishinaabe writer Gerald Vizenor's term—through transformation.[11] It argues that urban relocation could be just as regenerative as degenerative, that Native people bent relocation to their own purposes and influenced its outcomes in unpredictable ways. While being mindful of power differentials between Native people and the American settler-colonial state, this book seeks to accentuate the fortitude urban Indians demonstrated in making the difficult and consequential decision to achieve socioeconomic stability through spatial mobility. While taking seriously the traumatic legacies that became the story of relocation, this book attempts a richer history of not only Native people's winding paths to cities but also their circular paths *through* cities, "mainstream" systems of settler-state power, and their viable position within increasingly global communities. This is not to implicate Native people in the program's failures but to emphasize their ingenuity and resolve in spite of those failures. Indeed, this book considers not just the fraught effects of urbanization but also the dynamic causes.

A personal statement that self-identified "full-blood" Northern Cheyenne oil painter Dennis Field, submitted as part of his Adult Vocational Training program application in 1963, is revealing. "If I am given half the chance I will make it pay off," he promised. "I feel it in my blood. . . . I want a chance to learn what the schools of art have to offer and a chance to learn more." At home in Lame Deer, Montana, Field was barely getting by selling oil paintings of western landscapes. In fact, just two years prior, he had checked himself into the Montana State Hospital for alcoholism treatment. As he stabilized, friends and family impressed by his artistic talents began encouraging him to aspire to something greater. Finally agreeing, Field submitted his application for training in fine art at a studio based in Chicago, over one thousand miles from home. "The one and only reason that I signed up for AVT is to further my knowledge of my trade, 'The pallet and the paint brush,' and to develop my talents as an artist," he disclosed. "No man can know to [sic] much or enough." Suggesting the premium he placed on lifting himself above any restrictions on how and where he could belong in the wider world, Field concluded, "I deeply respect teachers because they are men who started from the bottom and worked up. . . . I have learned that once started on a trail, never turn back."[12]

Stretching canvases, selecting tools, blending colors, fashioning a vision, refining an aesthetic, sharpening a skill, chasing inspiration—these particulars of Field's painting practice form a fitting metaphor for a substantial portion of the Native American population's entry into America's social, cultural, economic, and political mainstream during the twentieth century. Through a series of complementary programs, the Bureau of Indian Affairs (BIA) promised to provide Native people with steady jobs and desirable housing in various western and midwestern metropolises. Program architects predicted that movement into the "mainstream" of American life would offer Indians an escape from socioeconomic despair while providing the Cold War–era Congress an opportunity to "get out of the Indian business," which had become dangerously distended during the New Deal, critics charged. For the most part, however, this did not unfold according to plan. Unanticipated outcomes resulted from Native people bringing their own experiences—their baggage—along for the ride.

With that, twentieth-century urban Indian migrations amounted to more than a consequence of BIA machinations. In their collective refusal to be starved and stereotyped into reservation margins, Native people not only adapted to changing historical currents but also moved into the belly of the settler-colonial beast and, paradoxically, achieved a degree of decolonization by harnessing a historically Indigenous survival strategy: mobility.[13] In the process, they negotiated the terms of relocation while shaping its outcome in profound and unexpected ways.

The postwar urban Indian generation significantly expanded the previously restricted potential for Indians to become not just welders and hairdressers, in gendered fashion, but also doctors, lawyers, actors, athletes, politicians, college professors, and more. Through that determination, they incorporated such futures into, and not outside, Indigeneity. Moreover, numerous urban Indians gained important skills to improve their respective nations' ability to exercise self-determination and sovereignty in a changing political arena. On one hand, "the master's tools will never dismantle the master's house," as Audre Lorde cautioned.[14] Before Native Americans could dismantle the settler's house, however, they had to rebuild their own. In the context of recent traumas perpetrated by the settler state, physical and cultural confinement, and economic desperation, Native people innovated to survive. One way they survived the settler state was by "mainstreaming" into it. Indeed, discussing the Makah people's survival on their ancestral Pacific Northwest lands and seas, historian Joshua Reid calls this a "traditional future," explaining that they "succeeded because they engaged the settler-colonial world, but on their own terms and for their own reasons."[15]

Native Americans who urbanized in the twentieth century attempted something similar. They practiced what historian Eric Hobsbawm might have referred to as "working the system . . . to their minimum disadvantage."[16] Through this process, they became a racialized minority in the settler state's imagination and legislation. Yet they were also the only racialized minority either welcomed or forced into an Anglo-American culture and society that barred other racialized minorities from equal belonging in the body politic. Thus, while participation reified settler-state power, it also created a unique opportunity for Native American people to mobilize the colonizers' idiom of "progress" in service of decolonization. As migration historian James Gregory notes, "Conquest may not be the only basis through which moving masses can redirect the flow of history. Infiltration can also be powerful."[17]

This approach began well before the BIA's postwar urban relocation program, or even before Native peoples' autonomous foray into urban war production industries during World War II. It began, however (in)visibly, with the ambitions of a generation of young Native people who, during the late nineteenth and early twentieth centuries, entered boarding school and work outing programs that removed them from reservations—at times through categorical abduction—and exposed them to remedial versions of market capitalism and Western education epistemologies. Rather than return to reservations upon completion of their studies (a process federal officials derisively termed "going back to the blanket"), numerous government boarding school graduates carved out space in urban industrial centers, where they could advance their educations and deploy their vocational skills for gainful employment. Convinced of their capacity for competing in modern American society on their own terms, they established burgeoning Indian communities in such places as Chicago, Los Angeles, and Tulsa. Some socially savvy Indians formed national Indian rights organizations, such as the Society of American Indians, which sought to "uplift the Indian race" from the supposedly dehumanizing effects of reservation life. These "Red Progressives" decried federal paternalism and advocated socioeconomic mobility as the most viable path forward.

During the 1930s, this racial uplift movement of Indian intellectuals yielded to a broader social movement of Native people who incrementally fanned outward from reservations as they participated in New Deal programs, such as the Civilian Conservation Corps. Subsequently, during World War II, upward of sixty-five thousand Native men and women either enlisted for overseas military service or secured employment in the new war production industries that dotted the American West. After the war, discharged soldiers and a contracting war industry forced many Indian workers back home. Those who had enjoyed steady wages and cosmopolitan life for the first time were understandably distraught when they returned to their reservations and witnessed the further deteriorating socioeconomic conditions and diminishing acreage. Facing such moribund circumstances, thousands of American Indians applied for urban relocation and vocational training programs.

Joining the overarching trend toward postwar sociocultural consensus, the Bureau of Indian Affairs designed its Voluntary Relocation Program as a solution to the United States' enduring "Indian problem." Federal policymakers hoped that steady employment for adult Indian males, domestic lessons for adult Indian women, and public schooling for Indian children would finally "emancipate" Indians from cultures they deemed inherently at odds with capitalism. Notwithstanding program officials' aggressive campaigns, however, Native people, whenever possible, attempted to negotiate the terms and goals of relocation for their own purposes. As it turned out, not all succeeded according to the government's plan; thousands of Native people landed on skid row and suffered the consequences of entrusting their lives to the program. Some became lost in labyrinthine urban metropolises. Meanwhile, the old urban industrial centers decayed during the national shift to a service economy, the American dream relocated to the suburbs, and deindustrialization undermined the potential for an urban Indian middle class. Those who lived the failure of relocation's promise connected through a shared experience across tribal lines and joined other racial and ethnic groups in a wider condemnation of the deindustrializing Cold War urban landscape. Importantly, such disaffection fueled not only the rise of the Red Power movement but also a process of reverse relocation, in which a significant number of urban Indians migrated back to Indian Country and played pivotal roles in tribal leadership.

· · · · · ·

In 1952—the Voluntary Relocation Program's inaugural year—the Pulitzer Prize committee honored Oscar Handlin's *The Uprooted* (1951) with its annual award given to an outstanding new work of history. Handlin fashioned his analysis around rural European peasant communities within which members nurtured a relatively homogeneous existence and from which they derived their primary sense of being. According to historian Rudolph Vecoli, however, such communities never actually existed. He argued that

Handlin's study assumed "idealized" peasant communities that on closer examination demonstrated far more stratification than Handlin understood or acknowledged. Diversity, Vecoli insisted, mattered. A truly satisfying interpretation of human migration, he implied, must appreciate the protagonist as much as the process. Moreover, he reasoned, treating immigrants as faceless masses does little to reveal the vibrancy, dynamism, and sheer importance of their individual journeys.[18]

A comparable historiographical oversight applies to the first wave of scholarship on urban American Indians, of course with the important distinction that American Indians are not immigrants. Most foundational interpretations position Native people who ventured beyond their reservation limits within a binary analytical framework that considers rural space inherently antimodern and urban space inherently modern. It follows that within this framework, Indians who moved to cities were always moving deeper into assimilation. Effectively, assimilation, or the lack thereof, became the overarching analytical problem for scholarship that ultimately did not advance much beyond Handlin's antiquated assertion that the "history of immigration is a history of alienation and its consequences."[19]

While most of the extant literature on Indian urbanization succeeds in explaining how Native people managed metropolitan life while cultivating a unique brand of urban sociocultural space, it often fails to explain why they accepted the urban challenge in the first place, or how the relocation program fit within larger patterns of Indian social, economic, and spatial mobility during the twentieth century. It also tends to emphasize a narrative in which Indian people only accepted relocation assistance out of sheer economic desperation and then fell prey not only to a poorly administered program but also to technological puzzles. Numerous works of both fiction and nonfiction privilege accounts of Indians who fumble with modern gadgets and struggle to cope with the future. Such works perhaps inadvertently perpetuate what Ned Blackhawk sees as the pathological urban Indian trope, or what Coll Thrush terms the "primitive rube" in the city trope.[20] Take, for example, an informant in Stan Steiner's popular book *The New Indians* (1968), who claimed that some urban relocatees could not figure out when to eat lunch.[21]

Dakota scholar Vine Deloria Jr. indicated that he was not impressed by such literature when, during his introduction to a panel discussion on urban Indians at Princeton University in 1970, he pointed to the "old statistics-type" of literature that was then available. Citing a study that asked how a Navajo homemaker in Denver calculated her family's weekly budget, he concluded, "I think the literature regarding off-reservation Indians is incredibly bizarre."[22] Deloria was on to something. For numerous Native people, urban relocation was indeed alienating, frightening, and challenging. The impersonal face and breakneck pace of urban life could be incredibly isolating and overwhelming. And new modes of technology could be quite befuddling. But this was true for most rural people new to city living. As the following study will stress, Indian urban migrants were more than a monolithic group of "disadvantaged newcomers and chronic underachievers," to borrow James Gregory's language.[23]

Telling a more complicated story, then, is about more than locating human agency or rescuing urban Indians from victimhood. It is about depathologizing and demystifying urban Indians' struggles with urban adjustments. It is about removing them from the realm of caricature. It is about a determination to tell this story without unwittingly reproducing the idea that Indigenous peoples do not belong in cosmopolitan urban space. It is about seeing urban Indians as practitioners of competing modes of modernity, mobility, ingenuity, and even anonymity, but not at the expense of Indigeneity.

A recent movement of more nuanced and satisfying scholarship on internal United States migrations and Indian urbanization supports this approach. This study embraces James Gregory's challenge to migration historians to dismantle the "maladjustment paradigm."[24] In addition, it heeds historian Coll Thrush's challenge to move beyond discourses of urban Indian poverty and dislocation that "mask more complicated experiences: the surprising opportunities offered by urban life, the creative struggles to carve out Indian spaces in the cities, and, most importantly, the ways in which Native women and men have contributed to urban life."[25] This book therefore explores the wages of Indian urbanization. By that I mean it focuses less on statistics, organizations, policies, and program mechanics, and more on Native peoples' lived experiences migrating from Indian Country to mainstream urban America and back—the complicated costs and benefits of mobility and urbanization, if you will.

Moreover, this is a story not only about beginning and end points but about the spaces in between. It is about the general patterns of mobility Native Americans practiced and how that mobility affected their relationships to their kinship systems and to their Indigenous nations while creating new relationships to urban space and culture, the American body politic, and the settler state. Even as they maneuvered across the protean landscapes of liberal capitalism and settler cultural space, Indian urban migrants actively resisted and transcended the traditional-versus-progressive and primitive-versus-modern two-world tropes.[26] They instead moved through three of anthropologist Thomas Biolsi's four "imagined geographies," which comprise a system of graduated sovereignty: sovereign tribal space on reservation homelands; *national indigenous space*, where "pan-Indian" people cultivate a supratribal ethnicity and exercise portable Indigenous rights within inclusive and legally protected settler space, such as the San Francisco Bay Area in 1969; and *hybrid political space*, where Native people practice three modes of citizenship: tribal nation citizenship, United States citizenship, and citizenship within multicultural and global social communities. Throughout the twentieth century, Native people sought to reconcile these fraught and paradoxical relationships between Indigeneity and mobility.[27]

New sources consulted for this book add complex and surprising dimensions to the urban relocation story. On several reservations, there were waiting lists to go on relocation. Many Native Americans actively solicited information about the program. Many tribal governments officially supported relocation, and some even developed their own relocation support networks. During the relocation program's first four years of operation, a majority of the participants were war veterans with prior off-reservation experiences.[28] Some relocation officials at the local level were quite sensitive to program participants' needs and often encouraged Native Americans to find and help one another in cities. Numerous Native people went on relocation for transitory purposes, without ever intending to stay. Many went on relocation more than once. In some cases, it was members of the older generation, not the younger generation, who were more determined to stay in cities and make relocation work. Most importantly, far more Native people self-relocated and migrated to and through far more destinations than scholars typically acknowledge when focusing on the BIA's midcentury program and its limited range of official destinations. Native people urbanized in far greater numbers, to many more places, for many more purposes, and much earlier than the prevailing narrative indicates.

This book ultimately strives for a panoramic view of Indian urban migrations in the twentieth century. It encompasses migratory push and pull factors, programmatic goals and results, the complicated relationship between rural and urban Indian communities, and federal policy making and tribal governance. In adopting a wide-angle view, it looks beyond any one urban destination or chronological period. While it began as a focused study of the BIA's midcentury relocation program, a topic that still occupies its narrative center, it argues that relocation's importance—or relative *unimportance*—cannot be satisfactorily understood in isolation from its wider contexts. Therefore, this study begins in the late nineteenth century, when the American settler state resolutely denied Indian social and spatial mobility on a national scale, with the expectation that Indian peoples and culture were either doomed to extinction or destined to fully assimilate into Anglo culture and become white, somehow without actually leaving reservations unless to attend remote boarding schools.

It is perhaps also important to mention how this book does *not* function. I confess two principal shortcomings that I hope future scholarship can help elucidate. First, with some worthy exceptions, this book tends to flatten space. I concede that Chicago in the 1950s was not Los Angeles or Denver or Dallas. But this is a sacrifice I make in order to achieve a comprehensive study of Indian urbanization from a national perspective. Besides, we already have excellent books on urban Native North American peoples in Chicago, Los Angeles, San Francisco, Detroit, Albuquerque, Boston, Seattle, and, most recently, London.[29] Additionally, I am determined to focus more on human beings and the human condition. Certainly this is not to suggest that self and space are not mutually constitutive. However, a deep exploration of, say, Salt Lake City's housing demographics in the 1960s would produce a rather unwieldy volume. Second, with some exceptions, this book does not deeply explore urban Indians' relative position within urban racial hierarchies and participation in race making and unmaking. As much as I strived to achieve this, that topic might require a volume of its own. Moreover, it reflects a source problem. It is quite difficult, for example, to access conversations that a Lakota worker might have had with a black American worker to his right and a Mexican American worker to his left on a factory line in 1950s Chicago.[30]

In addition to clarifying what this book does not do, it is worth stating clearly and firmly what it does not say. This book does not champion the BIA's relocation program. Rather, it champions Indian survival, ingenuity, and aspirations for a better future. Similar to recent scholarship that has added great complexity to the histories of boarding schools and the Dawes Act, this book refuses to cast a generation of Native people—many of them grandmothers and grandfathers to young Native Americans today—as pathetic pawns of federal programs.[31] To be sure, many Native people who went on relocation suffered from racism, unemployment, substandard housing, cultural isolation, loneliness, homelessness, and incarceration. But they also demanded the fruits of their labor and military service, sought better education and social opportunities, developed new job skills, gained leadership experience, enjoyed cosmopolitan life, raised their standard of living, returned home to lead tribal governments and businesses, expanded the parameters of Indian Country, expanded their presence and importance beyond Indian Country, and proved Indigeneity's resiliency across space and time.[32]

· · · · · ·

General renderings of contemporary Indian Country are often framed within statistics concerning alcoholism, premature mortality, rampant poverty, and widespread malaise. Even the success of tribal gaming incurs significant wrath from critics who, when not dismissing the enterprise as some sort of undeserved Indian entitlement, brand it a failure by asserting that casinos are inherently detrimental to societal health.[33] Without question, such accounts of pain and suffering matter, at times as an explicit effect of urban relocation. After all, the substantial number of homeless American Indians currently occupying U.S. cities such as Minneapolis, Seattle, and Phoenix points to one poignant legacy of urban relocation.[34]

But what good is another story of Indians in defeat? My sources compel me to tell a different story. In particular, handwritten letters from Natives to their respective reservation superintendents asking, sometimes begging, for an opportunity to work and try life somewhere else captured both my imagination and my heart. To hold original copies of these letters is humbling. Was this letter written at the kitchen table? Did the family gather around to discuss the opportunity? "Should we do this? Should we go on relocation?" Was the family afraid? Excited? The decision must have been agonizing. The gravity under which academics agonize over what it all means can never compare to the gravity under which an Indian family made such a decision. To begin to try to appreciate that decision is to see past yet another example of the federal government pulling a fast one on Indian people. This book ultimately seeks to recast that decision as an empowering one that, above all, reflected Native Americans' determination to work, fight, and survive.

1 The Bear and How He Went over the Mountain

Confinement and the Boarding School Generation

· ·

I do not wish to be shut up in a corral. It is bad for young men to be
fed by an agent. It makes them lazy and drunken.

—Sitting Bull (Lakota, 1881)

Recalling his experiences as a child enrolled in California's Fort Yuma Indian School during the second decade of the twentieth century, Quechan–
Mojave tribal elder Lee Emerson disclosed, "If [there] were . . . repeated
runaway[s], they'd catch them and put shackles on them, ball and chains. I
always think that, perhaps, they got the idea from the territorial prison right
next to us." He was hardly being melodramatic. Such punitive measures reflected prevailing turn-of-the-century assertions that coercive assimilation
into "the main stream" of America would emancipate Indians from their
supposedly uncivilized cultural patterns and doomed destinies. So not only
did Catholic nuns and federal authorities physically shackle young Indians
to distant off-reservation boarding schools, but they also figuratively incar-
cerated them within a colonizing state's relentless impositions on how and
where Native people could and should belong in the now firmly entrenched
United States. It is not surprising, then, that mobility, in its many forms,
proved so important to the boarding school generation.[1]

Yet Native American social mainstreaming and spatial mobility in the
early twentieth century can be appreciated less as historical innovations and
more as recoveries of historical practices. While the contexts and stakes
have changed over time, the urban relocation program, as large as it looms
in both this book and recent Native American history, is but one stage among
many in Native peoples' longer history of engaging urban space and maneuvering within and beyond the confines of settler colonialism. Historical
examples of North American Native peoples embracing mobility in anticipation of, or in response to, external pressures or internal ingenuities are
so ubiquitous in scholarly studies and tribal histories that a series of examples could easily fill one volume.

There is perhaps no better example of precolonial Native American urbanization than the Mississippian city of Cahokia, which two scholars call the "great Native American metropolis." During its twelfth-century peak, Cahokia was home to over twenty thousand Indigenous people. In the resource-rich Mississippi River valley, near its confluence with the Missouri River, Cahokia functioned as an urban center made possible and shaped by its farming and timber hinterlands, not unlike Chicago in the nineteenth century.[2] Cahokia's five square miles offered planned neighborhoods, temples, space observatories, and—most notably—a grand plaza that functioned as a downtown. The city depended on a complex labor and economic system that exhibited social and class stratification, from manual laborers, to middling skilled artisans, to academics who practiced geometry, astronomy, and calendrics, to a class of royal elites. Its trade networks reached as far north as present-day Minnesota and Wisconsin and as far south as Oklahoma and Louisiana. According to anthropologist Timothy Pauketat, Cahokia provided its inhabitants and area neighbors with peace, religion, food, friends, allies, order, and security. At its peak, the city's central population eclipsed ten thousand, with somewhere between twenty to thirty thousand more residing in the surrounding area of satellite towns and suburban farming districts. Until the year 1800, then, when New York's and Philadelphia's metro populations first eclipsed the thirty thousand mark, Cahokia, to the best of scholars' knowledge, had been the largest city in North America. By the 1350s, possibly as a result of floods and droughts related to climate change, deadly illnesses, violent internal strife, violent external threats, or some combination thereof, Cahokia's urban Indigenous people had entirely abandoned their city for better lives somewhere else.[3]

Iroquoian history explains how the ancient *onkwe:honwe*, who lived on the turtle's back, eventually turned to mobility as a survival strategy when "their resources were becoming depleted." They traveled far. And their journeys to new lands in present-day upstate New York became a formative experience for the Iroquois people, as their migrations ultimately created the Six Nations we recognize today.[4] Jon Parmenter's scholarship on the Iroquois emphasizes mobility as central to their Indigeneity prior to and during the colonial encounters period. Parmenter suggests that the Iroquois people practiced extensive spatial mobility in order to build reciprocal relationships and for political, ceremonial, and economic purposes. Throughout the sixteenth and seventeenth centuries, Iroquois people regularly traversed hundreds of miles in every direction from their homeland and, by the end of the seventeenth century, "possessed an unsurpassed level of geographical knowledge of northeastern North America." Rather than compromise or destroy Iroquoian cultural values, Parmenter argues, mobility strengthened and spread them.[5]

Facing military defeat at the hands of the Iroquois Confederacy during the seventeenth century, the Wendat (Huron) people in the northeastern Great Lakes area turned to relocation as a survival strategy within a dramatically and traumatically changing world. According to historian Kathryn Magee Labelle, "The Wendat uprooted their population, packed up their material and cultural capital, and re-established themselves in far-off lands according to Wendat customs."[6] In contrast with the Wendat, who resorted to mobility in order to escape overwhelming external power, the Jicarilla Apache in the eighteenth and nineteenth centuries depended on mobility from northeastern New Mexico to the Rio Grande River valley to exercise power within a self-regulating regional exchange system dating back five centuries. "The Jicarilla relinquished this position only when the foundation of their adaptation began to erode under American control and ultimately was cut short by reservation confinement," archaeologist B. Sunday Eiselt writes.[7]

By the late nineteenth century, Indian nations across the continent were reeling. Reservation confinement tightened its grip, the total Indigenous population dropped to its historical nadir of roughly a quarter of a million, and scars from recent tragedies such as the Wounded Knee Massacre continued to both hurt and heal. Against this harrowing backdrop, several Indigenous communities migrated to survive, while others looked for distant resources to improve life at home. To the northwest, Columbia River Indians fashioned a tribal identity inextricably linked to movement and a collective resistance against being corralled into one externally controlled space. The river, and not a reservation, became central in their evolving criterion for tribal belonging.[8] In one final example, late nineteenth-century Ojibwe men in the northern Great Lakes region embraced off-reservation work in the lumber industry to fill the economic void created by land and resource dispossession. "Although they worked in some of the most dangerous jobs, many of them found that this work afforded them a measure of separation from Indian agents, valuable skills, and even a degree of prestige," historian Chantal Norrgard explains. "Many Ojibwes used new forms of transportation, such as trains and ships, to access resources, begin new economic ventures, invigorate their connections to territory ceded in the treaties, and sustain relationships with one another outside of reservation boundaries."[9] Ojibwe people had been migrating since as long as they could remember. There was great precedent for mobility as a survival strategy. "Migration has always been a key component in Anishinaabe adaptation strategies," historian Melissa Meyer argues.[10]

Challenging the American settler state's long project to remove Indians from the land and erase them from existence, a veritable "infinity of nations" for centuries consistently thought of themselves as peoples of the world and acted accordingly. Indeed, as historian Michael Witgen asserts, Indians have always been an essential part of modernity, at least up until the nineteenth-century era of removals, at which point "the cultural and political space for this sort of multidimensional Indianness was gone." In the imagination of the colonizers, Witgen explains, "Indians became traditional people, socially and culturally primitive beings incapable of participating in a democratic society, or becoming part of a new nation."[11]

Paradoxically, however, federal policy architects never envisioned reservations as permanent solutions to their enduring "Indian problem." Rather, they conceived reservations as temporary laboratories within which Native people could be dispossessed of the tribal cultural and commercial patterns that were central to their Indigeneity.[12] For their part, neither did most Native people value reservation confinement as a solution to their own interpretation of the "Indian problem"—a misnomer, many among them insisted. It is a grand understatement to suggest that they understood the value of land, even when the land for which they negotiated title did not fall into the category of historical homeland. But they never asked for a future existence exclusively bound within reservation limits. As journalist Robert White astutely observed, "The lands reserved for Indians in treaties with federal and state governments became their prisons, and their resulting destitution inaugurated an era of utter dependency."[13] Ultimately, while the goals Native people hoped to achieve through mobility both converged and diverged with those of federal policy makers, what remained consistent was Indians' determination to direct their own mobility. Gripping the reins of what most outsiders assumed were forlorn futures, Native people defiantly worlded within a world that steadily closed in on them.[14]

· · · · · ·

In April 1878, Civil War veteran Richard Henry Pratt supervised the transfer of seventeen prisoners from Fort Marion in St. Augustine, Florida, to the Hampton Institute in Virginia, established ten years prior as an industrial training school for black freedmen. The prisoners that Pratt escorted to Hampton were not former slaves, however. Most were Kiowa and Cheyenne men who had fought against reservation confinement in Indian Territory on the southern plains. While still in Florida, Pratt developed an educational program that embraced his prisoners' industrial and intellectual capacities, as he imagined them, while jettisoning their cultural value as Indians. If anyone at Hampton felt particularly apprehensive about the prospect of two supposedly inferior races working together, Pratt proved quick to soothe their fears. "There will be no collision between the races here," he promised. "These Indians have come to work."[15]

As a result of Pratt's apparent success at Hampton, funding poured in from northeastern humanitarian and missionary societies. Secretary of the Interior Carl Schurz then asked the school to accept forty Sioux boys and nine Sioux girls from the Dakota Territory, while the federal government offered to contribute $157 per student to help offset travel and enrollment expenses. Building on his success with the pilot program and seeking greater autonomy in his mission, Pratt departed Hampton the following year to found his own Indian training program in Pennsylvania. His new Carlisle Indian Industrial School quickly became the most prominent Indian boarding school in the nation, providing an education for such Native luminaries as physician and Indian rights activist Carlos Montezuma (Yavapai) and world-class athlete Jim Thorpe (Sac and Fox).[16]

Meanwhile, Pratt's program at Hampton only grew in his absence. During Hampton's first ten years of hosting Indian students, 320 Native boys and 147 Native girls from twenty-seven different tribes passed through its doors. The training school pursued three primary goals for its Indian students: to build character ("stimulate the mind"), learn marketable skills, and become financially self-sufficient. If successfully met, administrators assured, these goals would provide a path away from tribalism and toward "civilized" American life. School officials mostly fretted over the third goal. Because the federal government subsidized the Indian students' education, officials decried the "loss to him of a valuable means of true education and progress." Notwithstanding many young Native people's inability to pay for their own education, school officials believed these young people could only truly appreciate an opportunity born from their own hard efforts; they had to want it.[17]

Rather than return home to the distant West for summer vacation, especially ambitious students could voluntarily, or often through coercion, participate in the school's summer outing program. This typically occurred from June to October in Berkshire County, Massachusetts—itself a veritable crossroads of the nation's traditional puritanical past and modern industrial present. Roughly twenty-five to thirty students advanced through the outing program each summer. Students' wages varied, if they were remunerated at all. But some received "gifts" in the form of clothing, money, and other items. Outing-program sponsors believed that such gifts, alongside the general work experience, would help boost Indian students' morale and intelligence.[18]

Hampton program architects also hoped that Indian graduates would continue to pursue opportunities away from their tribal homes. As one instructor wrote, "They are, and are encouraged to feel, free to choose their own homes where they will." Susan La Flesche—sister of famous Indian rights advocate Susette La Flesche (Bright Eyes) and Smithsonian anthropologist Francis La Flesche—charted such a course when she advanced from Hampton to the Woman's Medical College of Pennsylvania in Philadelphia. In a letter updating her former teachers on her progress, she discussed how graduates such as herself could serve as beacons of "civilization" for "non-progressive" Indians, and how their example could provide a "stimulus" for other Native people to "go and do likewise."[19] At times, Native elders embraced the same message. For example, a Brule Lakota man expressed his support for the Hampton Institute to the Reverend J. J. Gravatt of Philadelphia's Indian Rights Association. "I am sick and cannot live long," he confided. "I want my children to go to school, that they may be able to take care of themselves after I am gone."[20]

Still, school officials predicted that most students would inevitably return home. They therefore tried to mold them into sociocultural "missionaries" capable of converting their fellow tribespeople. As Hampton matron Cora Folsom put it, "The idea of Hampton is that its students should be fitted for leaders of their people at just this crisis in their history, when earnest, intelligent men are so much needed." Indeed, the first Shawnee person to take an individual land allotment was a Hampton graduate who, in Folsom's estimation, understood the "wisdom" of owning and developing private property. After graduating from Hampton, a third La Flesche daughter, Marguerite, returned to her Omaha tribe and then wrote to her Hampton teachers with an update on her fellow graduates. As far as she could discern, all of the Hampton graduates she knew were doing well except for Milton Levering, whom she disparaged because he was "off with a show"—a "Wild West" show, his only source of sufficient income. Most graduates had taken up farming or were advancing their education in area mission schools. Also, many attended reservation night school, where Marguerite landed a teaching position. "My Hampton schooling has been of the greatest value to me," she confided. "God bless both those schools [Hampton and Carlisle], for only through them and by them can the 'Indian problem' be solved." The school did not result in socioeconomic uplift for all pupils, however. From 1878 to 1888, thirty-one Indian students died at Hampton, in most cases well over a thousand miles from home. A majority of the deceased succumbed to consumption. Also within that time, the school prematurely dismissed 111 Indian students, many of whom school physicians deemed too unhealthy to stay.[21]

Back in Indian Country, many students struggled to put their new skills to use. In February 1888, as part of a study to determine Hampton graduates' potential for positively influencing their reservation communities, Harvard ethnologist Alice C. Fletcher ventured to the Omaha and Winnebago reservations. She expressed frustration over her observation that Indian students gained exposure to an "enlightened community" out East but suffered from the "vast inertia of reservation life" upon their return, and often needed to relocate to more populated areas in order to find work that matched their skill sets. According to Fletcher, some Indigenous people who had not been educated in Anglo schools became convinced that the Hampton graduates had been taught to "look into the future." If we translate the foregoing phrase to mean planning for the future, then clearly Fletcher was confused, ignorant, or willfully advancing stereotypes on this. Indian people, of course, have always planned for the future. Nevertheless, Western epistemologies and capitalistic goals could drive a wedge between returning boarding school graduates and those who remained with their people. In order to safeguard their own financial stability, those who did not receive a boarding school education occasionally banded together to bar Hampton graduates from local employment opportunities. We might surmise that the problem was not one of looking into the future but one of looking into the future in a way that was not conducive to the holistic health of the tribal community.[22]

Within this fraught context of both internal and external pressures, Native people gradually normalized urban working and living as viable Indian futures. Reservation push factors certainly played a role in their decision to leave, but an increasing desire to practice economic and social mobility drove Native people to succeed with more than just pure survival at stake. Indeed, Indian boarding school vocational training programs created a problem in that they prepared students to deploy their new skills in a market that either proved apprehensive about embracing them or simply lacked opportunities commensurate with their talents. Raising expectations and then failing to meet them caused disappointment and distress among a generation of young Native people. Regardless of whether or not they asked for vocational instruction, many now wanted and needed to use their new skills, which in some cases came at the expense of compromising their position among fellow tribespeople who lamented potential culture loss.[23]

Albert Cobe's life is representative of the ennui that both frustrated and fueled thousands of young Indians who saw no future in their parents' painful pasts or in reformers' remedial roles for their generation. Born in 1904 and raised among his people on the Lac du Flambeau Chippewa reservation in northern Wisconsin, Cobe wrote about his first attempt at running away from boarding school, years before he would emerge as a professional golfer on the PGA tour and a leader of Chicago's Native American community during the 1950s. He pleaded with his logger father not to make him return, primarily because he dreaded learning English and reading books. "The school is very hard on our people," his father granted. "But you have to learn to read and write. Times are changing, and you must be ready." Young Albert's obstinacy persisted, but so too did his father's commitment to a Western education for his son. "Someday, you'll be glad they made you look at books," Albert's father declared. "I wish someone had made *me* look at books!" When Albert protested that his father had never participated in the white man's world, his father countered: "Of *course* I did. How do you think I learned to run the sawmill? How do you think I raised enough money to buy a car? By selling lumber! Believe me, my Indian heritage didn't teach me anything about *that*. And what do you think I do when they call me to meetings in Washington?"[24]

His father's directive prevailing, Albert made his way to the Haskell Institute in Kansas, where he looked forward to traveling as a member of the school's basketball and baseball teams. After graduating, he spent two years in nearby Kansas City, where he played semi-pro basketball while nurturing an interest in golf. In 1930, he relocated back to his reservation in Wisconsin. "I had been outside the sphere of Indian life," he explained. "I once would have accepted any identification other than Indian." After initially focusing his attention on his sick mother, Cobe began developing an interest in tribal politics and national Indian affairs. Distraught over his perception of social, economic, and political apathy on the part of his tribal elders, he began touring other reservations in an old Chevy coupe, hoping to rouse fellow Native people from what he perceived as a state of inertia. "I could see that things hadn't improved on the reservation; the poorer people were poorer, worse than they had ever been," he recalled.

"I realized that I still had the interest of my people inside me." Recognizing a need for talented young minds, Albert's father recruited his educated son into the tribe's political fold. "We need young people like you around here," he reasoned. "People who aren't afraid to speak up."[25]

After playing a brief but influential role in tribal political debates over the Indian Reorganization Act, Cobe again departed his reservation. He spent the rest of his adult years as a PGA tour pro and as a golf instructor at a downtown Chicago YMCA, where he mentored young Indian children whose families had relocated to Chicago during the 1950s. Still, however far away he ventured, he kept memories of his reservation home close to his heart. In 1970, reflecting on the sum of his experiences, he shared his dream of one day retiring in the Northwoods of Wisconsin. Indeed, his brief autobiography concludes with a picture of him standing at a forest's edge, arms folded, gazing pensively across an open expanse of a tallgrass prairie.[26]

Mirroring Cobe's experiences and perspective, Leroy Wesaw (Potawatomie) recounted how, after graduating from Michigan's Harbor Springs boarding school in 1939, he "just kind of worked at whatever was available at the time." Elaborating on his wider experiences, Wesaw explained that from childhood onward he embraced freedom of movement and opportunity, a value embedded in a story his father used to tell: "And seeing my share of the country at this time, and dad always, he used to like to tell me this story about the bear and how he went over the mountain—finally came back home and figured that's where he's going to stay and I kind of remembered that and dad had no real disagreement with my traveling at the time, so I traveled all over the United States when I was quite young, furthered my education this way. I always been a real heavy reader." In 1952, after working for years as an interstate truck driver, Leroy and his wife, Patricia (Mohawk), eventually made their way to Chicago after Patricia stressed that she could no longer live life like a "yo-yo." In 1978, Leroy graduated from Chicago's Native American Educational Services College. Commenting on his college degree, he suggested, "It's just like a key that opens up a door and everything becomes wide."[27]

· · · · · ·

Progressive Era national Indian leaders, many of them members of the Society of American Indians (SAI), most visibly promoted a rhetoric of socioeconomic uplift for Native people while paving the way for the more widely acknowledged process of Indian urbanization during the 1950s and 1960s.

As founding SAI member Laura Cornelius Kellogg (Oneida) asserted in 1911, "I am not the new Indian; I am the old Indian adjusted to new conditions."[28] Many progressive Indians championed the prospects of urban life while demonstrating a degree of contempt for rural life. This generation of boarding school and college-trained Native people helped clear paths to the city. Eventually, subsequent generations of Indian people would pursue those same inroads to urban space while sometimes echoing the sentiments of Progressive Era national Indian leaders.[29]

There was perhaps no greater paragon of turn-of-the-century Indian self-help and racial uplift than Dr. Carlos Montezuma, who unabashedly exploited Chicago's cosmopolitan space for social, educational, and economic benefit. When missionaries asked Dr. Montezuma why he did not go back and practice medicine among his Apache people, he coolly responded, "Thank you, but I believe I can do more good for my people by being their voice in civilization and their missionary in Chicago." Several decades later, numerous urban Indians would express an obligation to return to their respective reservations in order to share their knowledge of the wider world on behalf of their people. Montezuma was diametrically opposed to any such agenda. Pointing to himself, he championed the capacity of the Indian individual while decrying the larger structural system that bound Indians in chains. A staunch assimilationist, Montezuma believed that Indian children "should have their privileges beyond the tribe, the privilege of seeing and knowing what the United States is. Reservation for Indians means the reservation from experiences and from opportunities for education and betterment in industry."[30] Writing in 1918, he intensified this position: "Reservation life is not freedom. It is bondage."[31]

Writing in 1913, Montezuma argued that the very term "reservation" contradicted the purpose for which it was designed. Reservations were supposed to be training venues for "civilization." As far as Montezuma was concerned, however, they only succeeded in keeping civilization out.[32] Writing in 1914, he could not have been more explicit in his disdain for reservation space. "Reservations are prisons where our people are kept to live and die, where equal possibilities, equal education and equal responsibilities are unknown," he proclaimed. "For our people to know what freedom is they must go outside of the reservation and in order for them to harmonize with it and get used to it, they must live outside of the reservations."[33] It was therefore especially vital that his readers understood that he was not a reservation Indian. "The world was my sphere of action and not the limitations, nearly as binding as a prison, of a strictly Bureau-ruled reservation," he insisted. While he admitted the cruelty in being torn away from "paternal love, care and protection" at a young age, he concluded that a childhood many would characterize as a tragic misfortune had ultimately "proven the greatest blessing." At least where his own life was concerned, his attitudes toward reservations and Indian service paternalism were legitimate. Experiences in the wider world raised Montezuma's expectations for his own capacity as a modern person. Kidnapped as a child, he did not request removal from tribalism, but when that fate unfolded, what was he to do?[34]

Montezuma's close mentor and confidant Colonel Richard Henry Pratt shared his former student's sentiments. "I want to emphasize the position you know I have always occupied, that the place for Indians is as a real part of our people," Pratt wrote to Montezuma. "They must quit being Indians and become citizens. . . . The tribe offers them actually nothing worth thinking about." As Montezuma and Pratt exemplify, Indian "uplift" in the early decades of the twentieth century typically meant an absolute severance from tribal life. In subsequent decades, however, the meaning of Indian uplift created room for the achievement of skills necessary to preserve Native peoples' choice to pursue whatever goals they set for themselves, whether that meant walking the "Red Road" or embracing non-Indian ways.[35]

Carlos Montezuma's convictions did not necessarily reflect the most economically or socially expedient course for all Native people during the progressive era. Nor did his perspective encapsulate the sociocultural values of numerous Native people who believed that the survival of Native culture depended on protecting it from non-Indian corruption. Still, Montezuma certainly was not alone in his likening of reservations to prisons. As Yale graduate and future prominent Indian education reformer Henry Roe Cloud put it, "The reservation, confining the people as it did, tended to narrow and circumscribe the thought-life of the race." He argued that isolation from outside cultures and societies produced a "conservative spirit" among Native people, which rendered them "too much contented with things as they were." Cloud, like Montezuma, argued that reservation confinement sapped Indians of their human ambition and barred them from meaningful participation in both the American and the worldwide community. Not only were Native people not free to participate in society at large, he stressed, but they were not free to manage their own lives within reservation boundaries. "Our dependency was made complete and emphasized by a vast, cumbrous machinery of government," he concluded. "Its tentacles reached from Washington to all the reservations."[36]

SAI president Sherman Coolidge (Arapaho)—like Montezuma, an adopted son of white parents—also argued for uplift of the Indian race. He advocated Native people's settling in towns and communities where they would be less of a "burden" and could instead "become productive, useful men and women" capable of shouldering what he considered their fair share of responsibility for national and world affairs.[37] Coolidge argued against any notion that Native people suffered from an inherently limited intellectual capacity. He instead maintained that Indians' contemporary second-class citizenship was mostly the result of having been kept in the dark about "enlightenment."[38] Likewise, an article authored for SAI's *Quarterly Journal* by Charles H. Kealear (Yankton Sioux)—a former student of both the Carlisle Indian school and the Hampton Institute—implored readers to look forward, not backward. "You may go all over the country, on different reservations, and who are the boys and girls that are making steady progress?" he prodded. "You will not find among them one who is always looking in the past." He challenged his readers to "put themselves side by side with the white man—our pale-face brethren—and [say], 'We can do as much; we can do as well.'"[39]

Such convictions were not limited to Indian adults who had ample experience to draw on when selling their message to fellow Native people. Numerous Indian boarding school students continued to emphasize the importance of achieving a higher education and gaining experience in the off-reservation world. In her prize-winning essay "The Value and Necessity of Higher Academic Training for the Indian Student," Hampton Institute student Lucy E. Hunter (Winnebago) argued that her ability to even conceptualize such an essay title was evidence that Indians are capable of a "great awakening, which is no other sign than that of progress." In her essay, she predicted that "the time is soon coming when we shall be thrown upon our own resources; and without government aid we shall have to look after our rights and interests and transact our own business concerning personal and real estate property, and now is the time to prepare ourselves." With that assertion, Hunter's essay anticipated the eventual arrival of a federal termination policy, in which the government-to-government relationship between Indian tribes and the United States would be dissolved, thus leaving Indians in the political and economic lurch. Whether or not Hunter personally welcomed such a policy shift is unclear. What *is* clear is her conviction that Native people should waste no time in preparing themselves to manage their own affairs. In this respect, she anticipated the

Indian self-determination movement decades in advance of the 1960s, when it firmly gained traction throughout Indian Country and slowly convinced a handful of Washington bureaucrats of its merit.[40]

Similar to Lucy Hunter, a growing chorus of young Indian voices increasingly spoke to education's capacity for awakening within Native students a cross-cultural curiosity that years of conflict and confinement had seemed to erode. "The time has come when the Indian must have an education, that he may help in uplifting his race to a higher standard of civilization," Choctaw student Bennett Lavers declared in 1913. "The future hope of the Indian depends on the boys and girls who are striving in this age to take advantage of all that is given them." Tohono O'odham student Joe Ignacio agreed: "The current of civilization is slowly but surely bearing down upon [the Indian], and will shortly engulf him if he has not learned to swim out of it." Chippewa student Mary LeJeune elaborated on a burgeoning competitive spirit among Native students who firmly rejected second-class citizenship. "The Indian people will not always remain in back of the people who have taken the Red Man's country for theirs," LeJeune signaled, "but they are coming to the front and will one day show the white man that an educated Indian can do as much good as any man belonging to the white race, but to do this they must first receive as good an education as their competitors."[41]

Tribal epistemologies endured during the late nineteenth-century period of military conquest and reservation confinement, often in clandestine fashion. Yet those who advocated for Westernized education could find common ground with keepers of tribal culture on the idea that a limited, isolated worldview did not correspond with Indigenous education and knowledge systems. Prior to the removal and reservation eras, Native people had demonstrated a long history of cooperative cultural change and exchange. In the final decades of the nineteenth century and the early decades of the twentieth, Indian students increasingly advocated a return to those cosmopolitan practices. Some among them were quite dismissive toward the value of tribal epistemologies in a rapidly changing world while still embracing Western education as a tool of uplift—a new technology that could help their families and nations survive. After all, they did not ask to be thrust into the tutelage of government boarding schools. When such events transpired, they fell into the unenviable position of having to choose between two approaches to life that authority figures from both sides of the spectrum argued were correct and mutually exclusive. Those who hoped to blend their experiences as the most expedient means toward socioeconomic up- lift for Indian people faced a difficult challenge as they worked to tran- scend that two-worlds binary.[42]

$$\cdots\cdots$$

Dynamic survival strategies proved essential for the relative health of In- dian economies at the turn of the century. But for some Native peoples, free- dom of movement proved difficult to achieve as a result of interference from the settler state, which encouraged mobility only insofar as it accorded with its own agenda. In his career-reflecting treatise on the Indian service, former commissioner of Indian affairs Francis Leupp revealed how, during the early reservation period, Indian service agents typically played the role of "despot." "Like the captain of a ship on the high seas," Leupp imagined, "he was in command of a company of human beings mostly ignorant and irresponsible; in charge of a large quantity of his employer's property; iso- lated from the rest of mankind, and remote from any place where justice could be regularly administered." Despite his use of the term "despot," Le- upp's assessment positioned Indian agents as brave men at the edge of civi- lization, tasked with keeping supposedly primitive and dangerous people under control. He elaborated on how Indians during that period needed per- mits and papers to leave their reservations. Such papers would typically describe the bearer physically, state the destination and reason for the jour- ney, and "assure every one that he was worthy of confidence." At times, reservation agents even exploited traveling papers and some Indians' En- glish illiteracy as an opportunity to practice bigoted bureaucratic pranks at Indian people's expense. "TO WHOM IT MAY CONCERN. The bearer of this paper is a Ballyho Indian named Ah-wo-ke or High Feather, com- monly known as Lazy Jake. He is without exception the worst fraud and petty scoundrel it has ever been my misfortune to meet," one note read. "NOTICE. Lazy Jake, to whom this paper has been issued, is a thoroughly worthless and unreliable Ballyho Indian. R. Van Winkle, *U.S. Indian Agent*," a second example besmirched.[43]

According to Leupp, travel permits had been necessary for deterring "the wanderings of an element who were merely restless without evil intent." In his words, the measure almost sounds benevolent. But in reality, permits primarily contributed to population surveillance and control. Indeed, the Office of Indian Affairs barred Indians from visiting other reservations on the grounds that such practices were "injurious." At the same time, some obedient Indians received travel passes as a reward for good behavior, especially when they demonstrated industriousness. However, Indians granted travel passes were routinely subjected to police escorts. Leupp eradicated the permit rules when he assumed the helm of the BIA in 1905, but he also confessed that it was difficult to phase out the practice and that he was "not sure that a remnant of it does not lurk there still."[44] If not the permits themselves then at least the idea behind them certainly did continue to "lurk." "Their instincts are purely nomadic," the Pine Ridge Agency superintendent complained about the Lakota people under his surveillance in 1922.[45] In 1907, even Leupp himself demonstrated this brand of thinking with his troubling handling of a group of Ute Indians who protested and then fled from unsatisfactory living and working conditions on their assigned reservation in Utah.

During the 1907 annual meeting of the Lake Mohonk Friends of the Indian social reformers club in upstate New York, Leupp discussed how the federal Indian service had been busy developing a plan for "getting the Indians away from the reservations, trying to mix them with the white people, and having them work just as white people do." Leupp advocated an integrationist program to "mix" Indian people with white people through urbanization and work to essentially make them white. He also laced his message with paternalism by insisting that such an agenda could succeed only under Indian service oversight.

Leupp then proceeded with a story about how, during the previous year, between three and four hundred aggrieved Ute Indians abandoned their reservation and headed toward the Sioux reservation in South Dakota, where, convinced that the land was part of their shared "Indian Country," they assumed they would gain refuge.[46] Commissioner Leupp berated the Ute people, insisting that they were trying to escape their destiny as white people while clinging to "primitive" ways. More accurately, the Ute people were resisting coercive pressure from the federal government to allot their lands, relocate to remote areas of Utah to work on the Santa Fe railroad, and sell off their large pony herds. As Ute leader Red Cap put it, "The white men have robbed us of our cattle, our pony grass and our hunting ground."[47]

No longer willing to submit, the Ute people fled. On their journey to the Sioux reservation in 1906, farmers in Wyoming and South Dakota fell into panics and fanned fears of an Indian uprising. Perhaps they were emotionally stoked by haunting memories of the brutal Wounded Knee Massacre that stained South Dakota's ground with hundreds of Lakota people's blood just sixteen years prior. That story, after all, bore some resemblance to this one: prior to being intercepted by a military detachment and then annihilated the next morning alongside the Wounded Knee Creek, Chief Spotted Elk and his Miniconjou people fled for their survival from the Standing Rock reservation, where Sitting Bull had been assassinated, to the Pine Creek reservation.

Before hysteria over the approaching Ute people totally boiled over, however, President Theodore Roosevelt ordered a military detachment to intercept the Ute people and force them back to their reservation. Ute party leaders negotiated a meeting with the president in Washington, during which they stressed their desire to practice their "traditional" culture and live among the Sioux people. Finally relenting, Roosevelt helped orchestrate a contract with the Cheyenne River Sioux to allow the influx of Ute people. But the president had one condition: that they support themselves through wage work.[48]

Back at Lake Mohonk, Commissioner Leupp, frustrated with Roosevelt's compromise with the Ute people, assured his audience that Indian people would need to choose between working and starving, and on the Indian service's terms, no less. "Now the pinch of hunger is one of the greatest educators for any race of people," Leupp surmised, before adding, "*We sometimes say that we reach the American mind and heart through the purse; with the aboriginal American we reach it through the stomach.*"[49] In this new condition for settler mercy and then compulsory incorporation into the settler society, only Indian people would receive physical punishment as a form of discipline. The disciplinarian commissioner had effectively resorted to starving the displaced Ute people into submission, assuring his audience that should the Utes attempt a revolt, they will be "suppressed, and, if necessary, with an iron hand." And on that menacing note, Leupp's audience erupted with applause.[50]

Certainly by 1907 the Ute people needed no introduction to the relationship between work and hunger. Leupp seemingly failed to realize this when he equated the Ute people's desire to live in their "traditional" way with idleness. In truth, the Ute people were not so much resistant to work as they were to federal coercion and control that denied them the fair fruits of their labor. Leupp punished the Ute people for not relocating to the job site he arranged. Their apparent crime rested in their determination to control their own labor and mobility.

Transitioning to an example of softer Indian service power, commissioner Leupp then introduced his new supervisor of Indian employment, Charles Dagenett, to the Lake Mohonk audience. Leupp had instructed Dagenett to go wherever railroad tracks were being laid or irrigation ditches were being dug and to "drive the best bargain he could for furnishing so many Indian workmen."[51] A member of the Peoria tribe, married to a Miami Indian from Oklahoma, Dagenett provides a rare example of a Native American who ascended to the Indian service's upper ranks during the early twentieth century.[52] The Indian service promoted him as a model federal boarding school graduate and paragon of Indians' capacity for assimilation. For his part, Dagenett, too, advocated a transformative program capable of catapulting Indians into the capitalist American labor market. "Of course we do not expect or desire that the Indian will always remain a day laborer," Dagenett assured the Lake Mohonk crowd. "The quickest way to get him beyond the day-labor stage is to hurry him into it." From Dagenett's perspective, Indians were worthy of an Anglo-American home and a lucrative job. The Indian service's responsibility, he believed, was to teach Indians to desire such things.

Dagenett then gave weight to rhetoric by turning attention to the new Indian Employment Bureau's recent successful arrangement for six hundred Indian workers to labor in beet and cantaloupe fields near Lejunta, Colorado. "What they learned there is bound to be of use to them in their ultimate home building," Dagenett ventured. "That, I believe, was as good an education as could have been given them."[53] During its inaugural year of 1905, the Indian Employment Bureau (IEB) placed roughly six hundred Indians, including both adults and schoolboys, in profitable employment. The following year, the total number of Indians working in IEB programs spiked to over five thousand, with roughly eleven hundred working on a dike project around the Salton Sea in Southern California, near the Mexican border. The roughly two hundred Indians who worked for the Santa Fe railroad that year earned a combined total of $25,101, while the Salton Sea workers earned a combined $115,784. Later reflecting on the IEB's achievements, Commissioner Leupp expressed pride in how the Santa Fe railroad and Salton Sea workers took anywhere from 60 to 93 percent of their earnings back home with them to their respective reservations.[54]

Dagenett touted the Colorado job program as a smashing success. This was more than job creation for Indian people, he suggested. From his perspective, this was cultural mentorship through labor, education, and subsistence intertwined, the kind of thinking that would guide the Bureau of Indian Affairs' urban relocation program decades later. Yet among the first wave of six hundred Indians who went to pick beets in Colorado, five hundred were current boarding school students or recent graduates from the

Southwest. These were young people being promised that cutting their hair, learning English, separating from their communities, and developing industrial vocational skills would raise them up from their supposed doomed and limited culture. And here they were, practicing intensive hands-in-dirt, backbreaking labor. The people needed the work and the wages, but then what was the point of enduring the traumas of boarding school? After all, Dagenett claimed that the best education was in the fields. Either way, in both the schools and the fields, Indian service officials saw Indigenous people more as workers than as students.

After elaborating on the IEB's partnership with the Santa Fe railroad, Dagenett offered his own appraisal of the recent Ute protest and flight to Sioux country. He revealed that he had met with the Ute people and offered to take them all to Rapid City, South Dakota; secure steady work for each able-bodied male; and enroll the Ute children in Rapid City schools. The proposal never came to fruition. Dagenett blamed its failure on the Ute people's supposed "disinclination to work hard." "They are not lazy, but, like many whites, they do not work for pure love of it," he ventured. "It is generally prompted by necessity." This provided an easy segue to his concluding remarks, which essentially echoed Leupp's threat to cut off rations to those who refused to submit.[55]

Penning his memoir in 1910, one year after finishing his tenure as commissioner of Indian affairs, Leupp began his author's preface to *The Indian and His Problem* by declaring, "The Indian problem has now reached a stage where its solution is almost wholly a matter of administration." From Leupp's perspective, Indians were wholly prepared to merge into the American mainstream and make a contribution to the national economy. Both Congress and the Indian service needed to curtail their tendency toward "mere sentiment" and "mawkishness" when thinking about Indians, he insisted. Moreover, he noted, federal guardians needed to raise their socioeconomic expectations for Indians and replace their tentative approaches with a "steady hand." Even in his attempt at sympathy for his former Indian charges, Leupp betrayed a paternalistic and patronizing tone when he promised readers "a message of friendly counsel from a white citizen of the United States, proud of his country, and anxious to see the members of our dominant race do their full duty toward a weaker element in the population who were Americans long before we were."[56]

Given its basic contours and rationale, we might locate the roots of the BIA's post–World War II urban relocation program in Leupp's Indian Employment Bureau. Not unlike the architects of postwar relocation, Leupp proved prone to lofty thinking, and his program for Indian employment was conceptually narrow, imposing just as many restrictions as innovations. Yet his potential precursor diverged in one essential respect. Writing on Indian education, he warned against urban employment as a solution for the "Indian and his problem." He argued that Indian youths who graduated from boarding schools and landed in New York City, Boston, and Philadelphia would only succumb to the threat of homesickness and a dependence on handouts. But what about cities situated closer to the former "frontier zone": Chicago, St. Louis, Minneapolis, and Omaha? "I have seen it tried," Leupp demurred, before providing three examples of Indians who resorted to hustling their survival on city streets. "One experimenter is today subsisting by his wits, borrowing from every chance acquaintance upon whose kindness he can impose, and never paying," he claimed. Ultimately, Leupp's strategies for educating young Indians involved exposing them to white ways and even the white world, albeit without the promise of higher education, professional employment, and urban mainstream living. He lectured against teaching Indians "from above downward," instead arguing that educators should be "starting with him on the ground from which he must be raised."[57]

Despite his resistance to Indian urban employment, Leupp did admonish the federal government for not supporting off-reservation employment projects in the rural West. Why should a substantial number of Indians not be employed to till western farmlands, dig ditches, clear forests, open mines, and build railroad embankments? he asked. "Because," he prodded, "he must be kept on a reservation and away from his white neighbors, lest he should learn to drink and gamble and use bad language." Given the combative commissioner's tendency toward contradiction and condescension, it is no wonder Cherokee historian Tom Holm christened this period in Native American history "the great confusion in Indian affairs."[58]

· · · · · ·

Such confusion notwithstanding, Native people did not wait around for a clearer policy picture to emerge or for some sort of survival manual to descend from the federal Indian service. They pursued their own agendas. During the early 1930s, largely in response to the 1928 Meriam Report's advocacy of better work opportunities for Native people, the Office of Indian Affairs gradually introduced off-reservation employment programs at several reservation agencies. Indians who benefited from the programs were mostly young boarding school graduates. They successfully established burgeoning Indian communities in Chicago, Detroit, Los Angeles, and the Pacific Northwest. In time, however, the program withered as a result of the Great Depression, federal work relief projects that kept people closer to home, and the Indian New Deal—a significant transformation in Indian policy that sought to revive Indian self-government and encourage economic rehabilitation and development of reservations. By 1940, the Indian office had officially abandoned the program.[59]

A collection of interviews conducted in 1940 with former Flandreau Indian School students illustrates how federal boarding schools continued encouraging a process of Indian uplift predicated on steady vocational employment, typically beyond the parameters of rural Indian Country. For example, Emmett Jones, who graduated from the South Dakota boarding school in 1936 with an auto mechanic license, was busy driving a diesel grader for $110 per month as part of a Civilian Conservation Corps–Indian Division (CCC-ID) construction team operating out of Fort Yates, North Dakota. He had previously worked in Pierre and then Sioux Falls, South Dakota, as a mechanic for Chevrolet dealerships. Because he was now qualified as a "specialist," he was one of the highest paid among his Fort Yates construction team and worked a steady nightshift. He was also a proud owner of his own tool set and claimed to lead a "clean, moral life." Despite his busy work schedule, he still found time for dancing.[60]

Not all Flandreau students enjoyed the same good fortune as that of Jones. Still, even among those who struggled to find firm footing in the off-reservation economy or achieve boarding school administrators' idea of success, mobility remained a consistent theme in their lives. The great grandson of two Yanktonai Sioux chiefs, Hobart Gates moved between rural and urban America in perpetual pursuit of labor and social opportunities during the 1930s. He left the Flandreau Indian School in 1936 and "wandered about"—from Santa Fe to the Haskell Institute in Kansas to Pine Ridge and back to Flandreau. While in New Mexico, he first found work in oil fields before moving on to a CCC-ID rural electrification project. From there, he migrated to the Haskell Institute to join the school's boxing program. In 1940, he enlisted in the United States Army and eventually received assignment to the Ninety-Eighth Coastal Artillery Division in Hawaii, where he survived the Japanese attack on Pearl Harbor. In 1943, he transferred to the Thirty-Fifth Infantry field artillery battalion in Europe and saw action in the Battle of the Bulge on Christmas Day 1944. He emerged from that catastrophic battle as one of 17 survivors from among his division of 120 men. Upon his honorable discharge, he bounced back and forth between

New Mexico and the Dakotas as a federal officer on various Indian reservations. Finally, his career arc arrived at the major Great Lakes metropolis of Cleveland, where he worked as a job counselor.[61]

Boarding school graduates such as Hobart Gates often preferred urban employment, but many urban employment directors hesitated over hiring Indian workers. In 1936, a letter from an Indian education agent to Potawatomie Agency superintendent H. E. Bruce illustrated the challenge some Indian agents faced in obtaining urban employment positions for young Indian graduates. In the letter, the Indian agent explains the agency's failure in convincing either the general secretary of the Topeka YWCA or the Topeka employment secretary to help locate domestic work for two Potawatomie girls from Mayetta, Kansas. Both employment agents rejected the girls for two primary reasons: they were already busy helping a small group of Mexican girls, whom they claimed were at a similar level of preparedness, and the capital city's large transient population of political "hangers-on" offered too many hazardous social opportunities for the uninitiated.[62]

Parents of Indian girls who sought employment in Kansas City as part of Haskell's work-outing program expressed similar concerns about keeping their daughters away from harmful elements. For example, the mother of a Kickapoo girl from Powhattan, Kansas, wrote an education official to express her concerns about Haskell's plan to send her daughter to Kansas City for work. She insisted that her daughter attend church every Sunday, limit visits to the movie theater to once per week, and make a weekly deposit of one dollar into a savings account in order to purchase new clothing for the next school year. Despite agreeing to the arrangement, the student's mother did not express much confidence in the program. "[The children] have too much liberty regardless of what we say or want them to do," she wrote. "This idea of sending our children to town has caused our children to drift away from us, disobey us and go where they please," she protested.[63]

· · · · · ·

Recent scholarship reveals rather dynamic and stratified communities of urban Indian people in places such as Chicago and Los Angeles. In those cities and elsewhere, urban Indians increasingly became distinguished not by the absence of Indigeneity but by a new characteristic of Indigeneity, as urbanization, off-reservation work, and education resulted in shared experiences across tribal lines and new dimensions of what it meant to be Indian in "mainstream" America.[64] Moreover, such burgeoning communities established a precedent that a majority of American Indian people would eventually replicate in post–World War II America, and not just under the auspices of the urban relocation program. Early-twentieth-century urban Indians maintained connections to their people and tribal homelands. They frequently worried about those they left behind. Their reasons for moving to cities were myriad, unpredictable, and sometimes empowering, even against the backdrop of colonial pressures. In seeking to consolidate their collective influence and expand their methods of survival, they understood that Indian social, cultural, and economic patterns could not stagnate if Indian people were to survive in a world constantly remaking itself.[65]

The first generation of urban Indians with some degree of visibility to the general non-Indigenous public emerged from turn-of-the-century boarding school programs that forced them to think, act, and survive as individual capitalists, rather than practitioners of tribal communalism. Many among them formed burgeoning urban Indian communities in numerous cities, which could be quite hostile in their reception.[66] In 1876, for example, a group of Pima and Maricopa Indians established a small neighborhood in Phoenix—at that time an unincorporated city of almost two thousand people that catered to copper miners. Local non-Indians portrayed the Native people residing in their midst as lazy vagabonds who subsisted on "melons, pumpkins, and other cheap vegetables." In 1889, reflecting southern black codes that regulated African American behavior in the Jim Crow South, a city ordinance made it illegal for Indian people to appear on city streets without proper clothing or to be out after dark if they lacked proof of employment and sponsorship by a non-Indian citizen. A context of racial segregation notwithstanding, the Phoenix Indian community expanded centrifugally from the Phoenix Indian School, centrally located in the city's Encanto Village. One member expressed pride in the "real community," replete with a drug store, beauty shop, and tavern.[67]

In 1924, a cohort of Indian professionals and progressive reformers formed the Society of Oklahoma Indians in Tulsa. Founding members included prominent Creek Nation leader, Bacone College graduate, and oilman Joseph Bruner, and Osage lawyer and state senator Sylvester Soldani, who served as the group's first president. In 1926, they began pressing their own newspaper under the banner "A Publication That Reflects the True Character of the American Indian." The "Indian Capital of the World," the paper proclaimed about its Tulsa home.[68] For the November 1930 issue, Choctaw editor Lee Harkins reserved the lead spot for a reprint of an article titled "Emancipating the Indian," which foresaw the rhetoric terminationist U.S. senator Arthur Watkins would peddle two decades later.[69]

The article perhaps provides a window into Society of Oklahoma Indians' thinking. It called Chicago Indian community leader Dr. Carlos Montezuma a hypocrite, who begged for the Indian Bureau to "Let My People Go!" despite never truly being confined by a reservation. It then urged readers to realize that no Indians are confined—that they only fail to exercise their freedom: "Our readers are assured that the men and women of [Montezuma's] band of Apache are urged by their present superintendent to go wherever their interest or fancy may dictate and remain as long as they wish." The article concluded by likening the Indian to the prodigal son of biblical verse, who will never succeed in the larger world as long as he knows the safe arms of his father await him at home.[70] These wealthy and educated Tulsa Indians called for racial uplift through capitalism, education, and community engagement; they represented the relatively rapid social and economic class expansion and stratification taking place in twentieth-century Indian Country.

Looking eastward to a similar example, Native people in 1926 Manhattan established the American Indian Association, which doubled as a mutual and travelers aid society and entertainment outlet. Created by and for Indians, the club was relatively unique for its time. Its launching was attributable to Mary Newell, a full-blood Cheyenne woman who for fifteen years had been teaching courses in "the great out-of-doors" at area schools and museums. Born and raised in Oklahoma and better known by her stage name, Princess Chinquilla, Newell was among the first Cheyenne students to attend the Carlisle Indian Industrial School in Pennsylvania. After graduation, she toured with Buffalo Bill's Wild West show to Canada before forming her own vaudeville team, which toured the United States and Europe. Eventually putting down roots in New York City, she believed the roughly three hundred Native people residing in Manhattan would benefit from an organized meeting place where they could bond with other Indians navigating the Big Apple. In addition to local Indian residents, the club assisted visiting Native people with everything from sightseeing to locating friends and relatives.[71]

Plumbers, electricians, mechanics, ministers, college professors, and opera singers populated club ranks. Some even landed regular positions as Indian extras in New York's film industry. Others had migrated to New York City for World War I industrial jobs. Likewise, shipyards in nearby Philadelphia employed over fifty Indians during the war. Native people also labored in various munitions factories and motor plants in both cities. "These young braves were not unprepared for work in a great metropolitan center," one journalist stressed before summarizing America's appreciation for Native people's war effort: "The great war has made us co-discoverers with Columbus; it has helped us to rediscover the Indian—his individuality, his bravery, his worth as a citizen. Let us put forth the right hand of fellowship and welcome him as he deserves, as a citizen of the twentieth century—a real American."[72]

Included among the American Indian Association's roughly two hundred members were numerous single and married World War I veterans who had experience managing their own lives and embraced the "whirl of city life." Historian Thomas Britten discusses how some Indian veterans sought a more profitable life away from their reservations and Indian communities upon their return. Despite a dearth of reliable statistics and narrative accounts, Britten agrees with fellow historian Donald Parman that "World War I set a minor precedent for the more sizeable off-reservation exodus Indians made after World War II." Moreover, Britten suggests that many returning Indian veterans both suffered from and perpetuated a sociocultural divide between those who had ventured away from the reservation and those who remained at home, a divide not unlike that experienced by boarding school graduates at the time and World War II and Voluntary Relocation Program veterans in later decades. Finally, while many Native World War I veterans—such as Choctaw hero Joseph Oklahombi—returned to impoverished homes and struggled with alcoholism and unemployment, others joined the national fight for Indian civil rights. Many among them appreciated their experiences overseas as an opportunity to expand their worldview and participate in larger off-reservation communities. Thomas Britten quotes one Indian veteran as stating, "In my travels with the army I have seen a great world. I did not know till then that I had been living in a reservation wilderness."[73]

In New York City, American Indians embraced popular cultural trends of the day, most notably heterosocial dancing, something that many Native people did not historically practice. Unchaperoned soirées, which gained popularity in progressive Greenwich Village circles during the 1910s, were a relatively new phenomenon among Americans intent on challenging Victorian social mores.[74] Importantly, however, club members, who otherwise reflect their Progressive Era Anglo counterparts, expressed support for the continued teaching and preservation of Indian culture and history. Similar to clubs that would soon appear in Chicago and Los Angeles, on the second Friday of each month members of the American Indian Association hosted public lectures that employed the latest "magic lantern" technology to capture non-Indian audiences' attention and correct their deficient understanding of Indian history and culture.[75]

Native people gradually fanned outward toward urban spaces during the first half of the twentieth century, with the total percentage of Native American people living in urban areas rising from less than 1 percent in 1900 to just over 13 percent by 1950, the decade in which the relocation program began. As they developed urban Indian communities, however, they did not necessarily do so at the expense of loyalty to their tribal economies, cultures, and communities. For example, the Mohawk high steel workers who made weekly migrations to Brooklyn regularly sent a significant portion of their earnings back home to their Kahnawake reservation, located within Quebec, just across the Saint Lawrence River from Montreal. Relatives then directed the earnings toward reservation projects, including housing developments and a new church. Several scholars have discussed how relocated Indians actively constructed Native spaces of belonging—especially through organizations—within new urban locales during the 1950s and 1960s. Despite emerging well ahead of that trend, the Brooklyn Mohawks certainly belong in that discussion.[76] But they also unambiguously mined cities to strengthen tribal institutions back home. Moreover, they kept up regular appearances in Kahnawake, undeterred by the twelve-hour drive along Route 9. The Mohawk commuters even established popular dining spots along the way, and the repetitious road trips evolved into an important feature of their worker identity. As Brooklyn Mohawk community church leader David Cory put it in 1955, "Perhaps Caughnawaga (Kahnawake) and Brooklyn have indicated in both economic and ecclesiastical terms a technique for conserving the values of the reservation and adjusting to the modern economy."[77]

Beginning in the 1920s, the Brooklyn Mohawks frequently shuttled back and forth not just between reservation and city but also between three nations—Kahnawake, Canada, and the United States—in pursuit of steady work. They also established visible communities in Philadelphia, Buffalo, and Detroit. According to journalist Joseph Mitchell, "[The men] roam from coast to coast, usually by automobile, seeking rush jobs that offer unlimited overtime work at double pay. . . . A gang may work in half a dozen widely separated cities in a single year." Likewise, Brooklyn Mohawk women often ventured to state and county fairs in Connecticut, New Jersey, Pennsylvania, and New York to sell dolls, beaded handbags, and belts.[78]

By the end of World War II, roughly three hundred Mohawk people had taken up residence near a busy shopping district in Brooklyn's North Gowanus neighborhood. Across several decades, the bilingual, transnational Mohawk men of steel constructed American modernity in the form of iconic New York City landmarks—the World Trade Center, the Empire State Building, the Chrysler Building, Madison Square Garden, the George Washington Bridge—while simultaneously constructing their own version of modernity, which depended on a resolute tenacity for engaging capitalism head on in the most treacherous of professions. And their dramatic feats of labor were not contained within New York, as many answered the call to help construct Chicago's Sears Tower and San Francisco's Golden Gate Bridge, among other national architectural marvels. The Brooklyn-Kahnawake Mohawks were resourceful people, earning money by virtue of daring labor skills in the most dynamic cities in the United States.[79]

Not only did the Brooklyn Mohawks fashion inroads into America's largest labor market and associated unions, but they also formed cultural bonds with fellow North Gowanus residents. Single Mohawk men occasionally found marriage partners among local Filipino, German, and Italian immigrants. Mohawk children no doubt struggled to adjust to their new surroundings, as any child would, but they made friends in the neighborhood public and parochial schools, where, alongside other students, they read comics, shot marbles, listened to the radio, played stickball, and caught double features. On a typical evening, Mohawk women and men could be seen gossiping or talking sports in front of the brownstone and redbrick apartment buildings they shared with Italian and Irish immigrants. When a journalist took a walk through the Brooklyn Mohawk neighborhood with the Reverend David Cory, the community religious leader pointed to a young Mohawk boy playing baseball in the street with Polish and Italian boys. "Quite a little melting pot out there," Cory remarked.[80]

Perhaps the Mohawks' strongest presence in the community radiated from the Cuyler Presbyterian Church, where Reverend Cory embraced them with open arms. On Sundays, numerous Mohawk families who did not elect to drive back to Kahnawake for the weekend flocked to the church to hear Cory deliver songs and sermons in the Mohawk-Oneida language he gradually mastered. To assist him in that endeavor, two Mohawk women translated several hymns into their own language. Cory in fact had a deep familiarity with Native people, having previously worked as a missionary to numerous Indian reservations. In this case, however, Indians came to him.[81]

None of this should suggest that the Mohawk migrants were necessarily determined to sever their tribal cultural and kinship connections. Still, some Mohawk people likely felt uncertain about how powerfully they wanted to amplify their Indian identity while gaining their socioeconomic footing. For example, when a journalist visited community leader Josephine Schmidt, he noticed that her apartment offered no visible indication that she was Indian—save for a beaded doll resting inconspicuously on the mantel. It turned out, however, that she kept several Mohawk cultural items in her apartment, including headdresses and moccasins. Tucked away in a storage closet, they were simply out of visitors' view. But she proved quick to retrieve them from storage and reveal their significance. "You see, we are all very proud to be Indians," she stressed.[82]

Across subsequent decades, Mohawk people persisted as important members of New York City's cosmopolitan cityscape. They also have not been alone in reclaiming the New York City area as a Native place, a place that has long reigned in American mythology as one in which Indians were swindled out of their land in exchange for a handful of glass beads. According to the 2000 Census, New York City officially counted 87,241 people who identified as American Indian, thereby surpassing Los Angeles as the largest urban Indian population in the country. This is especially interesting in light of the fact that the Bureau of Indian Affairs never designated New York City as an official relocation center as part of its postwar urban relocation program. In a city so densely populated and culturally diverse, Native American people's physical and cultural presence can be easily overshadowed. Yet Native American people built many of the very buildings that cast literal angular shadows across New York City's people and streets.

Indeed, they were there throughout the twentieth century and remain so into the next. On September 11, 2001, in the immediate aftermath of the most catastrophic terrorist attack in American history, roughly fifty Mohawk steelworkers rushed to the site of the toppled World Trade Center to help search for survivors buried under the rubble of the towers that Mohawk workers once proudly constructed. Working ten-hour shifts for three months, they blasted through twisted steel with magnesium-rod torches. New York City mayor Michael Bloomberg praised them as "ground zero heroes" and officially designated April 25, 2002, Mohawk Ironworkers Day.[83] In May 2013, Mohawk workers helped raise the spire on the new One World Trade Center "Freedom Tower." "It was a great honor to bring back the height to New York," Mohawk ironworker John McGowan expressed.[84]

The Mohawk workers who built, and then rebuilt, the World Trade Center in New York City might have identified with Mohawk ancestors who just over one hundred years prior cleared the wreckage of a Mohawk steel spectacle. In 1907, what would one day be the world's longest cantilever bridge, the Quebec Bridge straddling the Saint Lawrence River in Canada, buckled and twisted into a deadly trap before plunging seventy-five men—including thirty-three Mohawk steelworkers—to their deaths in the river below. Back on the Kahnawake Reserve today, a memorial monument to the fallen steelworkers observes, "These Kanien'keha:ka did not strive to be heroes. Instead, they traveled and worked because it was their responsibility to provide for their families."[85]

· · · · · ·

To be sure, reservation out-migrations came at a cost for an Indian Country already reeling from the settler state's divide-and-conquer-and-contain strategy. Yet the first postcolonial generation of urban Indians, however inconspicuously, gained something in exchange.[86] Their efforts were not inconsequential, as an increasing familiarity with American social, political, and economic institutions that off-reservation sojourns facilitated helped lay the intellectual and experiential infrastructure for exercises in self-determination during subsequent decades.[87] Indeed, Native people who cleared paths to mainstream America often were not so much courting assimilation as they were eluding settler-colonial state surveillance.[88] More than that, they sought to escape what influential Cherokee intellectual Bob K. Thomas, writing in the context of the 1960s, explained as the deprivation of *experience*—a cause and effect of *classic colonialism*, which resulted in reservation poverty, an inability to meaningfully engage with other cultures, and an inability to confront the imperial state on anything resembling an even playing field.[89] They perceived value in acting *cosmopolitan*, which historian Steven Conn defines as someone who moves comfortably in unfamiliar and diverse space.[90] Historian Philip Deloria has identified the turn of the twentieth century as a "moment when Indian people had effectively reached the bottom: population severely reduced; land effectively stripped; cultural and religious practices under restriction; children often removed in the interests of a kind of colonial reprogramming; lives under government surveillance."[91] Therefore, while entering mainstream America held negative potential for advancing colonization and accelerating the destruction of Indian culture, it also held positive implications for freeing Indian people from confinement and for decolonization—or, perhaps more accurately, what Kevin Bruyneel terms *postcolonial resistance*.[92]

Native American people, for myriad subjective reasons, braved urban space decades before the Bureau of Indian Affairs conceptualized its urban relocation program and at a time when federal officials like Francis Leupp firmly rejected metropolitan life as a viable future for Indian people. This should encourage historians to think critically about where the urban relocation narrative begins, and about the implications for wresting that narrative away from the midcentury urban relocation program's grip. From the turn of the century forward, the limits of Indian Country expanded in numerous directions while Indian people practiced new social formations and self-representations. Within that setting, urbanization was not just a cause but also an effect of incremental transformations and stratifications in Indigeneity. This would remain true during the post–World War II period, when the American settler state subsidized Indian urbanization. Ultimately, the first postcolonial generation of urban Indians pursued a socioeconomic uplift impulse that centered on mobility. Soon, tens of thousands of Native American World War II industrial workers would turn that burgeoning impulse into a concrete new form of belonging in America. As firebrand Oneida activist Laura Cornelius Kellogg put it during a talk she delivered to the 1911 inaugural meeting of the Society of American Indians, "Whether he is a citizen or not, or whether he has lands or not, whether his trust funds continue or not, whether he is educated or ignorant, one thing remains unchanged with the Indian: he has to have bread and butter, he has to have a covering on his back, he has to live."[93]

2 Who Can Say They Are Apathetic and Listless Now?

War Industry Work and the Roots of the Relocation Program

• •

My experiences in the army came along just at the right time for me.
I got to do a lot of things and be a part of the excitement. At least I
made it back . . . with a lot of knowledge, good and bad.
—Hollis Stabler (Omaha)

In May 1942, the quaint village of Seneca, Illinois, nestled along the Illinois
and Michigan Canal ninety miles southwest of Chicago, began experiencing a dramatic wartime transformation. Over the next eight months, workers converted undeveloped pastureland into a bustling industrial machine
as the "clang of steel on steel" rang forth and welding torches lit the evening skies. In return for their construction of the U.S. Navy's massive new
tank-landing ships, skilled Seneca shipyard workers, under the aegis of the
American Federation of Labor, earned $1.20 per hour working nine-hour
shifts, six days a week. By June 1943, the shipyard was producing one boat
per week.[1]

Among Seneca's first wave of 10,900 migrant war-industry workers were
two hundred Cherokee men, whom shipyard chair of labor and management
Tom Greenwood recruited from Oklahoma. It was certainly relevant that
Greenwood himself was a Cherokee man, especially during a time when
most employers would not have imagined America's surviving Indian population as an industrial workforce, if they thought of Indian people at
all. After migrating to the Windy City in 1923, Greenwood worked for two
decades as a job recruiter and general booster for Chicago's emerging Indian community. In Seneca, however, he and his Indian labor cohort did not
simply join an established urban industrial network. Rather, in the shadow
of the second-largest city in the nation, they helped convert a village of twelve
hundred into a temporary industrial satellite town of over twelve thousand.[2]

Roughly twenty-seven thousand total workers passed through Seneca
during World War II. In their wake, they created an overnight demand for

housing, waterworks, sewerage, streets, schools, police officers, firefighters, and a movie theater to accommodate workers and their families. Circuses and rodeos passed through town, too, and the community even hosted a "Shipyard Queen" contest. Before long, however, the demand for tank-landing ships plunged as rapidly as it had spiked. Practically a ghost town by 1946, Seneca's wartime whirlwind of activity faded into memory. "You close your eyes and you think about the sounds and the lights and the smells that would have been here at the time and all the people and how they had to manage this little society," one shipyard welder's grandson imagined.[3]

Gone too, of course, were the two hundred Cherokee workers. They must have either returned home or moved on to new industrial work opportunities, perhaps to nearby Chicago. Yet while their faces and names remain a mystery, the spirit of their hard efforts at the "prairie shipyard" match those of thousands of fellow Native Americans who, during World War II, made deliberate, self-navigated strides from rural to urban space and back. In various industrial worksites, they manufactured opportunities for significant but often fleeting socioeconomic transformations.

There is a paradox here worth exploring. Why would Indian workers build weapons of war for the very settler state that militarily overwhelmed Indigenous nations during the previous century? The simplest answer is that numerous Native people were both desperate and determined to improve their standard of living and gain a foothold within that same settler state's overwhelming economy. It is perhaps fair to suggest that Indigenous Americans who embraced wartime work opportunities were more ingenious than idealistic. After all, fretting over the ultimate product of one's labor is a luxury that most impoverished people cannot afford. In addition to simply surviving within the settler state, Native people also practiced profound patriotism during the war. Fighting on behalf of democracy and their home-lands, they purchased more war bonds, grew more victory gardens, and enlisted for service in higher proportional numbers than any other racial or ethnic group within the United States. This amounted to an Indian version of a "Double-V" campaign for continued socioeconomic advancement after the war's conclusion.[4]

Both during and after World War II, American Indians generally saw no reason to choose between American patriotism and tribal nationalism. Rather, they practiced a hybrid identity that manifested in patriotism to both the United States and their respective tribal nations. According to

historian Paul Rosier, the experience of fighting for "two linked geographical spaces" resulted in Native Americans developing "a sharpened sense
of themselves as Native and as American." In exchange for their service,
many American Indian veterans hoped that the United States would honor
treaty rights and finally decolonize Indian Country in accordance with
larger international trends. At the same time, those who offered their lives
or forged their livelihood in service of the nation's war effort thought of
themselves as Americans and sought access to mainstream American society, but on their own terms. They shared their own vision for the nation's
postwar demographic composition while forcing non-Indian people to acknowledge their capacity for contemporary belonging and economic pro-
ductivity. In Rosier's words, Indian people tried to "reform America as a
pluralist society even as non-Indians coercively pushed for a homogeneous
society."[5]

The changes World War II wrought also substantially reshaped tribal
communities back in Indian Country. "During the 1930s," historian Alison
Bernstein writes, "Indians had remained largely isolated from the social and
economic forces which shaped white society."[6] For the roughly sixty-five
thousand Native American people who either enlisted for military service
overseas or filled vacancies in the defense industry, the sudden onset of war
ruptured this trend and provided an economic escape from not just the Great
Depression but also decades of tribal economic privation. It is perhaps too
melodramatic to suggest that their lives would never be the same, but certainly their expectations were fundamentally changed.

This chapter illuminates what Native people hoped to gain by migrating to urban war-production centers and serving both the United States
and their respective tribal nations on the World War II domestic front. In
doing so, it situates Indians' wartime migrations within a larger story of
socio-spatial mobility that stretched back to the late nineteenth century
and forward to the BIA's Voluntary Relocation Program. Native people's
motives for supporting the United States' war effort were complicated
and their paths circuitous. If their gains depended on compromise, they also
remained self-generated. Meanwhile, the federal government paid close attention to Indian wartime mobility and patriotism and began devising a
plan for new postwar Indian policies and programs. The federal government did not, however, attempt to dictate Indian survival strategies—at
least not yet. Throughout the war, Indian urbanization remained an Indian
initiative. Indeed, as this chapter demonstrates, American Indians' own

actions played a significant role in shaping both tribal communities' and federal policy makers' visions for possible postwar Indian futures.

· · · · · ·

Experiences during World War II familiarized thousands of American Indians with urban industrial work and the off-reservation world at large. New Deal commissioner of Indian affairs John Collier called the Native men and women who either joined the armed forces or worked in wartime industries the "greatest exodus of Indians" from reservations at that time. Just over half of all able-bodied Indian men between the ages of eighteen and fifty either donned a military uniform or clocked in at war-industry plants, a figure that does not include the thousands of Indian women who supported the war effort at home and abroad.[7] Writing in 1970, Dakota scholar Vine Deloria Jr. recalled, "The war dispersed the reservation people as nothing ever had. Every day, it seemed, we would be bidding farewell to families as they headed west to work in the defense plants on the coast."[8]

As the United States lunged into war, Native people funneled into defense industry centers that ranged from small towns within reservation proximity to major metropolises hundreds or thousands of miles away. In the Great Lakes region, 129 men from the Bad River Chippewa reservation left home for regional jobs in tank, gun, and shipbuilding factories. Many headed to the Walter Butler shipyard in nearby Superior, Wisconsin, where they worked alongside white welders and shipwrights. "They are making a record for industry and loyalty in the Butler yards," one supervisor noted. Others entered training in a War Power Commission program in Duluth, Minnesota, just across Lake Superior's southern tip. At the nearby Lac du Flambeau reservation, ten Ojibwa women earned Red Cross pins for the 150 hours of sewing and knitting they conducted from home on behalf of the armed forces. While sewing materials for the United States military, these Native women figuratively sewed a place of new importance into the larger American social fabric. For both the men who practiced industrial labor in military factories and the women who nurtured and nursed, their culturally acceptable, permissibly gendered brand of labor likely made their contributions to America's war effort all the more welcome by non-Indian people.[9]

Nearby Minneapolis and St. Paul received a significant influx of job-seeking Indians during the war, ultimately pushing the cities' Native population to just over six thousand—roughly half of the state's total Indian population.[10] In the Twin Cities, Indian men found work as machine operators, welders, assembly linemen, truck drivers, and auto mechanics. Further reflecting gendered work patterns, Indian women worked as sales clerks, waitresses, typists, nurses, and telephone operators. After the war, many moved home only to quickly return after confronting their respective reservations' poor economic conditions. Others never left the Twin Cities; they established stable lives in urban America years before the Indian Bureau officially sponsored relocation.[11]

The new Twin Cities urban Indian community blended tribal traditions with mainstream American social practices. In her popular book *Night Flying Woman* (1983), Ojibwe migrant Ignatia Broker recalled her wartime experiences in Minneapolis. In 1941, she moved to the Twin Cities, found work in a defense plant, enrolled in night classes, and took up residence in a nine-by-twelve-foot room with six fellow Ojibwe women. Together they established a food, clothing, and housing support network. "This is how we got a toehold in urban areas—by helping each other," she recalled.[12] In 1950, that toehold expanded into a footprint when members of the Twin Cities Indian community formed American Indians, Inc., a group that held weekly gatherings where Native people danced, made baskets, played on ball teams, and planned Christmas parties.[13]

Although Indian men were typically the first to enlist for overseas duty and the first to take war industry jobs in distant cities, Indian women like those in the Twin Cities played just as significant a role in the national war effort. Work opportunities were typically gendered, but Native women, not unlike Rosie the Riveter and thousands of fellow American women, occasionally overcame such restrictions and landed positions in typically male industries. On North Carolina's Eastern Band of Cherokee reservation, seventy-nine Cherokee girls drove tractors, repaired automotive equipment, and worked farm fields in order to replace more than one hundred Cherokee men who had joined the armed forces. Over one hundred additional Cherokee women sewed vast quantities of material for the Red Cross. The Eastern Cherokee tribe as a whole contributed thousands of feet of timber to the war effort, while the tribal council allocated $150,000 from the tribal fund for the purchase of war bonds.[14]

Native women's industrial contributions were also not confined within reservation space. For example, Juanita Pacheco (San Juan Pueblo) made milk runs between Indian training programs in Santa Fe and Albuquerque using a truck that she both operated and repaired. Marjorie McCovey worked the overnight "MacArthur" shift at Douglas Aircraft in El Segundo, California. "I like my job very much and am quite contented here," she wrote to her reservation superintendent. Ada Old Bear and Marie Jefferson (Musquakie) inspected ammunition in a Des Moines, Iowa, plant; a group of female Indian graduates from the Sherman Institute found work at Solar Aircraft in San Diego; and numerous Navajo women worked as silversmiths, truck drivers, and chemists.[15] According to Kurt Peters, the roughly thirty-five hundred Indigenous women who worked in Richmond, California's rail yards during World War II did "everything" men did, including skilled industrial labor tasks such as locomotive repair and drill press operation, while vocally demanding the same pay as men.[16]

Not all Native workers needed to migrate to the nearest city for war-industry work. Native people who were already established in urban metropolises before the war stayed where they were and exploited their local war industry as an opportunity to earn better pay and extend their employment network. For example, the Brooklyn Mohawk steelworkers added battleship construction to their collective résumé when they filled shipwright positions at the Brooklyn Navy Yard in Wallabout Bay. The Mohawk men could boast their talent and reliability as high steel workers when contracting with the Brooklyn Navy Yard. After all, in addition to buildings and bridges, they had by that point built a reputation.[17]

Statistics concerning Native people who secured employment away from reservations ranged from as few as fifty from the Standing Rock Sioux reservation to twenty-five hundred from the Tohono O'odham reservation to thirty-five hundred Navajo from the Window Rock agency.[18] Not all, however, moved to urban areas. At the Tohono O'odham reservation, for example, 60 percent of the adult males were working off-reservation in cotton fields, in mines, and on railroad gangs. Among them, two hundred held positions in the copper mines in Ajo, Arizona. The mining company wanted to hire thirty more men, but none were available.[19] The Tohono O'odham reservation was not unique in this respect. A *New York Times* article claimed that on an unspecified number of reservations, as many as half of the total male population had volunteered for military service.[20]

The Blackfeet Agency in Montana reported that between three hundred and five hundred Blackfeet Indians had obtained work away from the reservation. In fact, the Blackfeet Tribal Council Defense Committee played the most productive role in securing positions for its tribal base. The tribal council helped provide transportation, food, lodging, and union dues for members who sought off-reservation work.[21] Similarly, Washington State's Colville Agency reported that roughly seven hundred Indian workers had secured employment away from the reservation, and mostly through their own networks. They typically approached local unions and the state employment bureau for job leads, and some landed positions after attending defense industry training programs in Seattle. Likewise, the superintendent of the Hopi Agency in Arizona reported that the roughly one hundred Hopi who found work away from the reservation did so by pursuing their own leads through Phoenix's public employment agency.[22]

The superintendent of the Pine Ridge Agency in South Dakota did not know exactly how many of his subjects were currently working away from home. He did, however, know that the figure typically registered at roughly nine hundred among the approximately nine thousand enrolled members, but because of available war-industry opportunities, that estimate was almost certainly too low. Still, compared to other agency reports, far fewer Pine Ridge Indians pursued positions in the war industry. According to the superintendent, this was because upwards of fifteen hundred tribal citizens had for many years undertaken seasonal employment positions as potato pickers in various fields around Nebraska and did not want to lose leverage within that system. This can be appreciated as an example of how wartime Indian workers made calculated decisions about their current employment prospects in light of future job security.[23]

The Turtle Mountain Agency in North Dakota reported that approximately seven hundred of its enrolled members had obtained employment away from the reservation. These Indians typically secured their own positions as farmhands within a two-hundred-mile radius and traveled to work sites as large groups in their own automobile caravans. The reservation superintendent also explained that his subjects for the most part had not made inroads into defense industry positions. Again, rather than reflecting a lack of ambition, this was attributable to the reservation's especially remote location and lack of information about possible war-industry openings.[24]

The superintendent of the Cherokee Agency in North Carolina claimed, "Our Indians are anxious for employment, get same pay as whites." He explained that while most landed jobs through their own efforts, the Tennessee Valley Authority had recruited many of them to help construct the Fontana Dam. While almost certainly a reflection of the nation's demand for wartime labor, he closed his report by insisting that the Indian people he represented had no more difficulty than anyone else when it came to getting jobs.[25]

These employment trends for Native people continued throughout the war's duration. In 1944, the Fort Belknap Agency in Montana reported that fourteen of its people were employed with Geo Brooke Beet Fields in nearby Savoy, twelve were working hay fields in nearby Harlem, and twelve more labored in the Anaconda Copper mines just outside Butte. Farther away, thirty had landed positions in Portland, Oregon's Kaiser Shipyards, and ten had found work in the Puget Sound Navy Yard in Washington State.[26]

That same month, Nebraska's Winnebago Agency superintendent shared a similar set of data in his survey response when he claimed that "our people are pretty well scattered all over the nation, however the majority of them have gone to nearby towns and secured jobs for themselves and no attempt has been made to try and keep any track of them because they are coming and going all the time." Likewise, the Forth Berthold Agency superintendent mentioned in his report that "quite often these people go direct to a certain point because they have friends there. They then get work, how they secure it, we do not know."[27]

In July 1944, Minnesota's Red Lake Agency superintendent Tom White wrote Commissioner of Indian Affairs John Collier to update him on the employment situation for the Ojibwe people in his care. Several Red Lake men had elected to take positions close to home at the airport in nearby Bemidji. Red Lake girls—who, according to White, "are always running off to the Twin Cities"—had also been working as waitresses and domestic workers in Bemidji. Farther away, more ambitious Red Lake workers had taken positions in the Department of Defense's ordnance plant in Hastings, Nebraska. Farther still, a handful of Red Lake men filled positions at the Kaiser Shipyards in Portland, Oregon. Finally, and most remarkably, numerous Red Lake men had spent the last three years working at an unspecified job site somewhere in the distant Alaska Territory.[28]

The fact that Native people pursued wartime job opportunities on a national scale should not be revelatory. Notwithstanding stereotypes, Native people have never championed idleness. What is interesting, however, is how far they were willing to travel for jobs, and how aggressive they were in pursuing their own opportunities. In virtually every example, the superintendent of record mentioned that Indians found off-reservation work as a result of their own efforts, typically through partnering with employment agencies. Most reports also mention that relocated Indians found their work experiences satisfactory and that they were being paid the same wages as white employees for the same work. The fact that these were Indian-generated work opportunities is best reflected in the clear degree of uncertainty among reservation agents about exactly how many of their Indian charges were finding employment away from the reservation, and where exactly they were going. Put bluntly, reservation superintendents were clueless. Indian people were going everywhere—and in greater numbers than previous scholarship on this topic has acknowledged. When the war ushered in a surplus of jobs, they did not sit and wait for the Indian service to lift them from economic despair. They calculated and considered their options, hoping for work at home but willing to take it wherever they could find it. In this respect, they advanced a precedent set by tribal elders who in previous decades showed them how to survive during trying times. To be sure, the war produced unprecedented opportunities. But Indian initiative, above all, deserves credit for maximizing those opportunities.

· · · · · ·

Born just west of Anadarko, Oklahoma, in 1919, Carl Kickingbird must have felt pressure to match the example of his Kiowa forebears. His great grandfather, Chief Kickingbird, signed the important 1867 Medicine Lodge Treaty, and his grandfather served in the Seventh Cavalry's L Troop prior to becoming an influential Methodist pastor. Continuing his grandfather's trend of traversing the spaces between Kiowa and Anglo worlds, Carl Kickingbird hoped to land a job with the Indian service after graduating from business school. When the war suddenly interrupted his plan, however, he enrolled in a sheet-metal training program at the Chilocco Indian School in Ponca City, Oklahoma. "These war industries were hollering for people," he recalled. "Of course my ambition was to get into some kind of government service but it never happened. I went to a war plant, an aircraft plant and started working there." Upon completion of his course at Chilocco, Kickingbird first worked for Boeing in Seattle before relocating to Boeing's plant in Wichita, where he met aircraft wing maker and future wife Kay Sue Burnette (Potawatomi) and enjoyed closer proximity to his family and tribal home. Rather than return home after the war's conclusion, however, he took a job with an oil company in Illinois for several years before finally returning to Oklahoma to work as a newspaper copyeditor. In addition to a career in journalism, he ran his own printing business in Oklahoma City during the 1960s and led his people locally, regionally, and nationally as a member of the Kiowa Constitutional Revision Committee, the El Reno Civil Defense Program, the Oklahoma Indian Rights Association, and the National Congress of American Indians.[29]

Kickingbird's experience is one example of how numerous World War II–era boarding school graduates blended local, regional, and national work experiences while embracing wartime education and industry as a means toward a multifaceted career founded on mobility and flexible labor. Unlike thousands of wartime adult Indian workers who did not want or receive much help from reservation superintendents, thousands of young Native American boarding school students faced immense pressure from school officials and fellow students alike to go forth and serve their country. Six of the nation's leading Indian vocational schools introduced war-industry training programs that by 1942 had already placed twenty-five hundred graduates in national aircraft, tank, and shipbuilding factories.[30] Before the war's outbreak, these schools had already practiced a long history of exposing Indian students to a certain brand of cultural assimilation steeped in racial uplift rhetoric. It is therefore not surprising that boarding schools became stepping-stones for patriotic young Indians to make their way toward war jobs and the armed services.[31]

In 1941, Oklahoma's Chilocco Indian School instituted the aircraft-production training program that changed Carl Kickingbird's life course. The program not only taught the fundamentals of aircraft production but also assisted graduates in job placement. This elevated, or reduced (depending on one's perspective), Chilocco to a veritable labor mill. After successfully placing 83 inaugural graduates in war-industry jobs, the program's second year produced another 170 graduates.[32] Their destinations included San Francisco, Tulsa, Providence, San Diego, Chicago, Phoenix, New Orleans, Seattle, Kansas City, and Burbank. In November 1942, a Chilocco graduate wrote the school journal to share his experiences working at the Richmond Shipbuilding Corporation in California. "The wages are very good and the work not too hard especially when you think of what the other boys are doing for us," he expressed. With a patriotic stroke of the pen, his letter concluded, "I could write more but Uncle Sam says, 'Keep your mouth shut.'"[33]

In early 1942, Los Angeles Office of Indian Affairs job recruiter Katherine Mahn traveled to Chilocco to deliver an address on tips for landing a job in the big city. "When you go for an interview you should be appropriately dressed, mindful of your manners, and confident," she advised. A visit to the school by two agents from Ponca City's employment bureau just one week later further indicates the degree to which some employment coordinators combed Indian schools for factory workers. The two agents spent the day interviewing senior boys who boasted advanced skills while making records of their home address, height, weight, and social security number. They also verified birth certificates and took notes on prior work experience before promising to return in one week for a second round of interviews.[34]

Further illustrating Chilocco's explicit connections to thriving job markets and war production industries, during March that same year the school introduced a new aircraft sheet metal instructor to teach overflow night courses. Jack Meixner had trained at the Boeing School of Aeronautics in Oakland and had previously worked at Lockheed Aircraft in Burbank and Beechcraft of Wichita before taking a position at Chilocco. He arrived just in time. According to a report from Washington, defense plant directors across the nation were "clamoring for the Indian workers" that had trained at the Haskell Institute and Chilocco. "We want more of them if possible," one personnel director announced.[35]

In fact, it was becoming less possible. By early 1943, Chilocco's Vocational Training for War Workers program had been so successful that the school was running out of Indians to enroll. In February of that year, school superintendent L. E. Correll sent an internal memo to his staff urging them to find Indian men or women between the ages of eighteen and fifty with at least one-quarter degree Indian blood to enroll in the program. "It costs nothing," he pleaded, before reminding them that they were allowed to recruit "slightly physically handicapped" students as long as they made certain to coordinate such enrollments with the state director of vocational rehabilitation. In addition to capturing how badly workers were needed to keep America's war industry running, this directive perhaps best illustrates the significant degree to which the war allowed otherwise marginalized American Indians to enter and play a key role in the surrounding society.[36]

It is not surprising that by 1943 Chilocco faced a shortage of desirable enrollees. At the program's outset in 1941, hundreds of Native people jumped at the opportunity to gain admission for themselves, their spouses, their children, or any combination thereof. For example, in August 1941, Stella Norman from Ada, Oklahoma, sent a handwritten note to Superintendent Correll to see if she could "put my boys in that Sheet Metal foundry training." She assured Correll that "one like mechanic work + one like Electricity [sic]," before concluding, "Write and let me know at once if you can take them I will bring them over hoping to hear soon [sic]."[37] Likewise, that same year Chilocco class of 1924 graduate and current Indian service nurse Mrs. Benge wrote Correll from the faraway Cheyenne River Agency in

South Dakota to request enrollment for her Cherokee husband, Tim, in "the course for young men of Indian blood." "My husband is very anxious to get work in some government plant but due to the lack of the proper training he is unable to do so," she wrote. Taken together, Stella Norman's and Mrs. Benge's letters demonstrate how enthusiasm among Native people for industrial training and employment transcended both generational and educational boundaries as parents and children, educated and uneducated alike, pursued the new wartime economic opportunities.[38]

Alongside Chilocco, the Haskell Institute to the north in Lawrence, Kansas, also prepared students for participation in the war industry. For example, a brochure advertising the school's aircraft-production training program announced the following:

WAR EFFORT AROUND THE CLOCK AT HASKELL

15 ½ HOURS — WAR TRAINING

8 ½ HOURS — SCHOOL TIME

100 PER CENT TIME FOR THE ALLIES[39]

Answering Uncle Sam's call, six Haskell graduates found work at Standard Steel Works, and four more took jobs at Columbian Steel Works. Both factories were based in Kansas City, which had a population of more than 120,000 in 1940.[40] An eleventh graduate, Harry Clement (Creek), was busy building bombers in Wichita. According to Haskell superintendent G. Warren Spaulding, finding work for graduates was key: "Training the students is only half the job. Unless we can find positions for them in government or private industry, we consider our job only half done."[41]

Out west, dozens of young Indian men from the Sherman Institute in Riverside, California, had already been working at various shops in Los Angeles for several years before the war broke out. Ben House (Navajo) arrived in Los Angeles with only a pair of overalls, but within three years he owned a car and regularly put money away in a savings account. In 1941, he left his factory job to join the armed forces.[42] Also representative of a new generation of young Indians hoping to gain economic independence during the war was Joe Saluskin (Yakima). Having once donned beaded regalia while straddling "wild-eyed ponies," Saluskin now dreamed of working for Seattle's Boeing Corporation. At the time, he was one of two dozen Indians among a total of 450 young men working in shops as part of the Seattle Resident Project. Students who graduated from this program successfully landed jobs in aircraft factories around Puget Sound. Saluskin balanced a night shift from 4:30 P.M. to 1:00 A.M. with a five-day class schedule while learning to build warplanes for $30 a month. Knowing he could make $30–$40 a week at Boeing helped him concentrate on his studies.[43]

Alas, while thousands of Native American people chased new futures during the war, thousands of ignorant non-Indian bystanders clung tightly to ideas about Native people that were firmly fixed to their imagined pasts. Just up the road from the Chilocco Indian School, a reporter for the *Wichita Beacon* offered a cringeworthy but revealing window into how some observers simultaneously championed and fetishized Indian wartime labor. "It's too bad one of the Wichita-made planes isn't called the 'Tomahawk' or 'Tepee,' or something equally as Indian," the reporter quipped. While Chilocco's program appeared to be a great success, such sentiments reflected the stereotypes with which Indian laborers were forced to grapple. In this example, the reporter suggests that inanimate objects—weapons of war, no less—could be "equally" Indian. Did the reporter care, or even know, that Wichita's Indian workers did not wield tomahawks or return home to tepees after an arduous factory shift?[44]

. . . . . .

World War II had a profound impact on Native people's social, economic, cultural, and political relationships to and positions within the United States. A central product of that impact was a raised set of expectations among Native people for how and where they could belong in a changing America. Those paying close attention to this phenomenon began writing and thinking critically about the potential crisis that could manifest if the federal government failed to meet those expectations. Writing in 1944, Dakota scholar Ella Deloria explained, "The war has indeed wrought an overnight change in the outlook, horizon, and even habits of the Indian people—a change that might not have come about for many years yet." Echoing the concerns among boarding school graduates and Society of American Indians members discussed in chapter 1, Deloria predicted, "They will want to participate in the larger thought and life of the land and not be given special work scaled down to their abilities, as if those abilities were static, or to their needs, as if those needs must always be limited to tribal life."[45]

In 1944, former Navajo Business Council chair and current Navajo Tribal Council chair Henry Chee Dodge communicated a similar confidence that, in the midst of World War II, Native people were "looking forward to a new and better life in which all their unique inherited gifts, supplemented by the best of the white man's way of life, will equip them to meet the complications of the future world." As far as Dodge was concerned, Indians had *not* arrived at "the End of the Trail."[46] By summer 1944, roughly twenty-five hundred Navajo men had enlisted for service, and approximately ninety-five hundred Navajo men and women had labored in war production industries. Upon their return to the reservation, Dodge predicted, they would bring "increased needs as well as increased knowledge." He also cautioned that postwar adjustment would be especially difficult for the Navajo because, more so than most tribes, they were largely uneducated and unassimilated according to contemporary American standards. Moreover, many resided in extremely remote areas of a vast reservation. Still, despite the BIA's vision for a reservation-based work program for the Navajos, including plans for tourism development, Window Rock Agency field representative Floyd W. La Rouche insisted that many Navajo people would need to begin looking for employment opportunities away from the reservation. The general American public, he concluded, would have to overcome race discrimination and realize that Indians had made significant contributions to America's victory overseas.[47]

In 1951, Harvard anthropologist Evon Z. Vogt conducted a study of Navajo World War II veterans who returned to an anonymous community in the Rimrock region of New Mexico. As part of his study, he surveyed fifteen Navajo veterans' attitudes toward "white" culture as represented by housing, clothing, food, personal hygiene, and interest in radio programs, among other topics. Vogt's reading of the impact of radio among the Navajo community proved inconclusive because, unlike nearby Pueblo communities in the Rimrock area, the Navajo had not yet benefited from an expansion of electricity to their remote locales. Battery-powered radios were too expensive, and few radio stations could be picked up in the Rimrock area anyway. On the subject of food, Vogt found that virtually all the Navajo veterans and their respective families still preferred the traditional Navajo diet of wheat-flour tortillas and roasted mutton. Some had introduced eggs to their families' diet and taught their wives how to prepare them. As for automobiles, Navajo people wanted them, but most could not afford them. On the topic of clothing, Vogt's research team found that most of the men had fully adopted Anglo clothing. This, however, cleaved along gender lines. But it did so according to a specific caveat: the men insisted that the "uneducated women should keep their own Navaho clothes."[48]

Concern with personal hygiene and general appearance proved to be the cultural adaptation that Navajo veterans felt strongest about, even if a dusty climate and scarcity of water mostly rendered extreme standards of cleanliness difficult to maintain. One veteran remembered how his sergeant would shout, "YOU CLEAN SHAVE, CLEAN SOCKS, WASH YOUR FEET!" Many also became particularly anxious about the cleanliness of their homes. "Everything was so dirty inside the hogan," one veteran remarked. Others took umbrage with the lack of fly screens on their old homesteads. Moreover, where housing was concerned, eleven of the fifteen returning veterans preferred to occupy new "white-style" homes, even though such homes proved impractical during cold winter nights and heavy summer rains. It is important to note, however, that in all cases of Navajo veterans either dwelling in or constructing Anglo homes, they also maintained a Navajo hogan for ceremonial purposes. This suggests that, as with the Navajo veterans' attitudes toward food and clothing for women, the returnees blended their cultural preferences according to personal tastes. Moreover, it suggests that a predilection for white American material goods did not necessarily reflect a rejection of Navajo culture, and vice versa.[49]

Anthropologist Ruth Underhill also conducted fieldwork among the Navajo during the 1940s–50s and subsequently wrote on World War II's significant impact on the Diné people. According to Underhill, as a result of wartime employment and overseas service, "the People were beginning, at last, to see what the whites worked for and what could be had." Many adopted popular American names and began working eight-hour days. With their new earnings, they installed showers, beds, and wood floors in their homes. Some exchanged moccasins for athletic shoes, and numerous Navajo men began dressing in "cowboy costumes." "Send my little brother to school," one Navajo soldier wrote home from the war. "I've just found out what I could do if I was educated."[50]

The Navajo veterans' reports suggest that returning veterans were initially more concerned with improving the quality of life on their own reservation than critiquing the structural race and labor issues that complicated easy access to mainstream America. Their tribal reservation homeland still mattered. Yet, according to Underhill, when wartime prosperity ended, many became disillusioned with the limited socioeconomic potential of reservation life. They had experienced the wider world while enjoying an improved degree of social equality. After a succession of terrible blizzards during 1947 and 1948 temporarily destroyed the Navajo tribe's agricultural prospects and plunged thousands into starvation and despair, many Navajo people embraced the opportunity to seek refuge in Denver, Salt Lake City, and Los Angeles as part of the Indian Bureau's special Navajo relocation program. Ultimately, though quite hyperbolically, Underhill concluded that World War II "shook the Navaho out of the Middle Ages."[51]

Some observers were less optimistic about World War II's potential for producing Indian social advancement. Writing years later on the "profound reentry shock" returning Indian veterans faced after "heady years of freedom and equality," former Rosebud Lakota tribal chair and firebrand activist Robert Burnette explained, "When they went to banks off the reservations to borrow money on guaranteed GI loans, the bankers told them to go back to the reservation, that the white bankers couldn't deal with Indians." Concluding his thoughts on how it must have felt for Indian veterans who had offered their lives in service of America's war effort, Burnette poignantly declared, "Hatred replaced the pride that many veterans had felt in serving their country." He ultimately suggested that military service could only do so much to produce goodwill among non-Indian Americans and combat racism and ignorance. Indian war veterans had every right to feel disappointed and scorned.[52] Yet while Indian people seeking off-reservation acceptance could be met with jarring hostility, reservation life often introduced its own share of problems. After the war, it became evident that numerous reservations were generally incapable of supporting the brand of economic advancement and class mobility that thousands of Native people practiced during the war. As one social expert put it, "Sooner or later, Indian migrations would have been inevitable."[53]

For their part, it did not take long for federal Indian policy makers and social theorists to realize that Indian people's willingness—and, in some cases, desire—to work off-reservation held the potential to both solve and complicate their Indian problem. First and foremost, Commissioner of Indian Affairs John Collier advocated rehabilitation of reservation economies and the development of reservation resources. Yet while he wanted Native people to be able to support themselves at home, he also understood that federal loans from a revolving credit fund and a partial restoration of the tribal land base would not be enough to lift some tribal nations out of economic despair. Moreover, Collier appreciated that some Native people wanted to move freely and find their own work opportunities, especially when World War II increased their availability.[54]

In September 1941, just months ahead of Japan's attack on Pearl Harbor, Collier sent a directive to each reservation superintendent outlining a program of support for Native people who sought urban industrial labor positions away from their tribal communities. He explained to reservation superintendents how important it was for Indians to take copies of their social security cards and birth certificates with them when migrating to cities. He also encouraged his subordinates to help their Indian charges acquire the right clothing for their prospective jobs. Further, he stressed that Indians leaving the reservation should have a sufficient amount of cash to survive until their first paycheck and should receive transportation and lodging assistance to help them make it to their respective destinations. Next, he instructed reservation superintendents to phone ahead to urban YMCA offices and church groups and ask them to be prepared to help Native people adjust to their new communities. Finally, Collier implored reservation superintendents to convey to departing Indians the importance of both paying their bills on time and putting some earnings into a savings account each month. He stressed the importance of each Indian saving money not only to be prepared for future needs but also "to assist his people or family at home."[55]

Collier's final point implies that he recommended off-reservation employment less as an opportunity for Native people to sever their connections to tribalism and more as a path toward generating income that could improve reservation life. Not unlike numerous Native people who pursued their own paths to urban space during the first half of the twentieth century, Collier appreciated the city more as a means than an end. Similar to the Mohawk people who migrated to Brooklyn during the 1920s and sent a substantial portion of their wages back to their Kahnawake reservation, Collier did not believe that urban relocation had to come at the expense of tribalism and reservation development. As an advocate for cultural pluralism, he supported urban work and social opportunities only insofar as they served the health and legitimacy of Indian culture, his paramount concern. Indeed, it is not surprising that he championed the spread of Indian culture into new American frontiers and trusted that it could withstand such a process. During his formative years as an Indian expert, he idealistically likened a Pueblo community in New Mexico to a "Red Atlantis" that held the antidote for all of industrial America's socioeconomic ills.[56]

Ultimately, Collier suggested exploiting cities in a manner that can be appreciated as an inversion of what the federal government would eventually sell to Native people. He imagined that urban wages could contribute to tribal economic rehabilitation and preserve Indian culture. Subsequent federal Indian policy architects, by contrast, imagined a permanent brand of relocation—one that would engineer Indian culture's eradication. Interestingly, then, not only did Collier essentially outline the relocation program ten years in advance of its official unveiling, but he also managed an Indian perspective on urban relocation's value and promise.

Collier was not alone in his thinking. In 1942, Sacramento Indian Agency field representative John Rockwell wrote Collier for his opinion on the extent to which the federal government should develop industrial labor initiatives for Indian people. Rockwell mentioned that Indians in the Sacramento area were hearing about the good wages industrial workers were earning and wanted to know how they could gain access to similar opportunities. "I believe also that the range of individual differences, in abilities as well as interest, is as great with Indians as with whites," Rockwell imparted. "Believing this, I cannot close my eyes to the fact that many young Indians are eager to enter industry." But he also stressed that those seeking industrial work were not necessarily interested in surrendering their tribal culture as part of the deal: "Instead, I would say, they will cling tenaciously to those values which they know are good, and which are a very real part of them. (In this we should give them every encouragement.)" Rockwell continued, "The capacity of the Indian to believe in himself is great."[57]

In the aftermath of Native people's strong support for the United States' war effort, several non-Indian social theorists joined federal policy makers in entertaining debates over how best to solve the nation's enduring Indian problem, and the role that reservations should or should not play in that solution. Writing for the Association on American Indian Affairs (AAIA) in 1944, Columbia University professor Gene Weltfish suggested that Indians should attend strong agricultural colleges, such as the University of Iowa and Cornell University, and then return to their tribes with "something of white American culture at its best, to be spread among their tribesmen. This process of bringing the surrounding culture to the surrounded people is one of encouraging the merging of two cultures; but it calls for careful direction," she continued. "More often than not, under the present haphazard way, only the worst of white American culture gets back to the tribe."[58]

In a second, more cynical, example, AAIA president Haven Emerson wrote a rejoinder to a 1945 *Reader's Digest* article extolling the emancipation of Indians from reservation confinement. Emerson cautioned against drawing such hasty conclusions about the weak value of reservations and the ease with which Native people could leave them behind. Such myopic "*Set the Indians Free!*" philosophies, Emerson argued, had only resulted in catastrophic tribal land dispossession during the last fifty years. "Set the Indian free?" Emerson interrogated. "Free to what? Free to sink to the bottom and die away, hopeless and discouraged, in an economy and a society which he is not, as yet, equipped to handle?" Emerson then suggested that those who wanted to dissolve reservations mostly embraced that belief as a result of their own selfish plan to sweep in and claim title to vacated land. "A *reservation* is not in any sense a restriction upon Indians who hold rights on it," he insisted, before admonishing those who invoked tribal land as some sort of "outdoor prison." Emerson also made certain to point out that reservations could continue to be of value even to those who elected to migrate away for better employment, educational, or social opportunities. "For those who leave, it is always there to return to in hard times," he reasoned. "It is a priceless asset, a rock of security in a complex world, a base from which those who are beginning to learn how to compete in our society may go forth with the confidence that, if they fail, they have something to which to return."[59]

In a separate essay for the AAIA's quarterly newsletter, Office of Indian Affairs education director Willard Beatty predicted that Native people would be less sentimental about their reservation homes. He suggested that prior training in vocational schools and CCC camps had made a difference in Indians' ability to advance in technical positions with the armed forces during World War II. Because many reservations lacked necessary resources, and a great portion of the tribal land base had been leased out to non-Indians, he worried that those who had learned and practiced technical skills in shipbuilding and aircraft factories during the war would become frustrated by a lack of similar opportunities at home upon their return. In particular, Beatty pointed to Indians from Arizona and New Mexico, whose states denied them the right to vote, as being particularly frustrated by discrimination and denial of socioeconomic opportunities. "Many an Indian boy reports that, sharing a foxhole on Guadalcanal or Bourgainville with a white buddy, he has been asked searching questions as to the handicaps and advantages of being an Indian," Beatty wrote. He also suggested that numerous Indian servicemen and servicewomen resented laws that prevented them from imbibing alcohol on their reservations. Finally, he mentioned that many Indians who migrated to war production centers disliked the substandard housing in undesirable areas to which they typically found themselves relegated. Ultimately, Beatty predicted that the number of Indians who would attempt to return to urban industrial work would depend on the national economy's ability to succeed in reconversion. If the jobs were there, he believed, then Indians would gravitate toward them. "The postwar trend of Indian employment, therefore, *is largely beyond the control of the Indian Service* and will not be influenced greatly by what the Service believes to be desirable or undesirable," he concluded.[60]

Ultimately, arguments concerning reservation versus city living cut in numerous directions. Some Native people were less concerned about where they were living than how they were living. Similar to turn-of-the-century boarding school graduates, many Native military and war-industry veterans sought freedom from surveillance, alcohol prohibition, and voting restrictions. Such individuals wanted to escape paternalism and use educational and military experience as a springboard to a better life but one still fundamentally Indian. Most importantly, the federal government did not dictate these goals, even if previous federal government crimes against Indian people made such goals necessary. Rather, they were self-generated through Indian people's recent experiences around and away from Indian Country. This perhaps explains why so many Native people from the World War II generation were initially enthusiastic about the BIA's relocation program, and also why so many among them were disappointed when, however voluntary, the program eventually appeared to be another tool of paternalism and assimilation.

· · · · · ·

During the war, the Office of Indian Affairs kept its collective eye on President Roosevelt's Executive Order 9066, which mandated the relocation of Japanese Americans to various labor and detainment camps throughout the West—some of them within Indian reservation borders.[61] Inspired by that program's results, some Indian service leaders began promoting the relocation of Japanese Americans as a potential postwar model for relocating Native people to urban centers. Interestingly, they were apprehensive about broadcasting that connection. For example, in September 1943, Indian service welfare director Fred Daiker wrote Assistant Commissioner of Indian Affairs William Zimmerman to express his approval of just such an agenda. In doing so, however, he advised Zimmerman that if he could reword the report outlining such a program and "omit any reference to the Japanese or evacuees," it might be "very helpful." Daiker was otherwise on board and shared his conviction that Indian laborers who worked away from reservations during previous years could "lay the groundwork for other Indians" to do the same.[62]

In August 1944, during a meeting at the United Pueblos Agency to discuss work opportunities for returning Indian veterans, BIA representative Walter Woehlke promised to deliver points so important that he ordered an assistant to immediately transcribe his speech and send it via airmail to William Zimmerman in Chicago. Woehlke exaggerated the urgency of his message, but as a window into the thinking that eventually culminated with the BIA's relocation program, it deserves some quoting at length. "In the discussion about re-employment of veterans we touch on a problem that has been confronting the Indian Service since the Year One," he opened. The problem, he elaborated, concerned the lack of sufficient economic resources on tribal bases and the rapidly increasing Indian population that rendered resource deficiency especially critical. Woehlke then provided some background on the Indian service's decades-long support for boarding school vocational training programs designed to help young Native people find opportunities in off-reservation industries. Those efforts, Woehlke claimed, had repeatedly been thwarted by two primary factors: unavailability of jobs and racial discrimination against Native people.[63]

Addressing the first problem, Woehlke defended the Indian service against accusations that it had perpetually confined Indians within reservations, kept them "in the blanket status," and denied them opportunities to maneuver freely within capitalist America. This, he assured his audience, was a "perfectly silly accusation." He likened the second problem to one faced by Japanese Americans, including doctors and engineers, who were "rejected by white society and forced back into the Japanese ghetto equivalent of the Indian reservation, but in these they did not have proper basis for self-support." What the Indian service needed to do, Woehlke argued, was help Native workers overcome their typical economic status of "last to be hired, first to be fired." Moreover, it needed to help employers conquer their skepticism over hiring Indian workers. Woehlke reminded his audience that this objective was especially crucial because thousands of Native people, he predicted, would return to reservations at war's end and quickly become disenchanted with rural life and the lack of socioeconomic opportunities.[64]

Woehlke closed by advocating the recent relocation of 130,000 Japanese Americans to work camps as a model for a successful Indian relocation program. The War Relocation Authority, he explained, had succeeded in mobilizing churches, Rotary Clubs, Kiwanis Clubs, and other organizations "so as to minimize community resistance to the acceptance of Japanese." Woehlke seemed to suggest that through sponsoring the migration of Native people to bustling labor markets and recruiting urban allies capable of facilitating their sociocultural adjustment, the Indian service could rehabilitate the public standing of a second marginalized group whom many

Americans remembered as playing the part of mortal enemies in the nation's imagined past.[65]

In 1944, Assistant Commissioner of Indian Affairs William Zimmerman expressed support for a BIA-sanctioned off-reservation work program for Indians. "I believe that we may be forced to consider both temporary outside employment and permanent relocation," he reasoned. At the same time, he warned that the BIA should not be too hasty in its policy making and outward support for such a program. Referring to various government officials' nascent discussions about the relative wisdom in abolishing the Indian service and terminating tribal sovereignty, Zimmerman confided, "I am somewhat fearful of the effects of a circular—following the various recommendations to abolish the service. Would many people conclude that we saw the handwriting on the wall?"[66]

Zimmerman also shared with welfare director Fred Daiker the precious notes on Japanese American relocation that Walter Woehlke had recently airmailed to the Indian service's temporary wartime headquarters in Chicago. They must have made an impression on Daiker. Two weeks later, he wrote fellow BIA Welfare Division agent and future Billings area relocation director Paul Fickinger to request reports on Japanese relocation and ideas for a similar Indian relocation program. Daiker also mentioned that he had been reading a copy of *The Use of Japanese Evacuees as Farm Labor*, which, in his opinion, reflected "some of the same problems that involve employment of Indians." Finally, Daiker expressed his firm conviction that the Indian service needed to reestablish some sort of off-reservation job placement service for prospective Indian workers. To head such an initiative, he felt that the Indian service would need to rely on social workers, the type that helped American employers "overcome prejudice and place Japs in communities for employment." In his estimation, Indians faced a similar brand of discrimination. "What we learn during the next year . . . should prove most helpful in showing whether this type of service is necessary and should be reestablished," he concluded.[67]

Writing in 1971, anthropologist and former associate commissioner of Indian affairs James E. Officer argued, in a subtle analytical departure, that while the relocation program was the "brainchild" of John Collier's Indian service administration, it was more a "progeny" of the 1928 Meriam Report than a reproduction of the Japanese American internment program. He arrived at this conclusion based on the fact that during the Collier administration, Indian service officials conducted extensive studies that revealed how reservation resources could not support the growing Native population. Therefore, some sort of off-reservation living and employment solution was needed. After World War II, this sentiment gained even greater traction among federal policy makers. Moreover, Officer pointed to the importance of an Indian youth training program enacted in the fall of 1946, which offered a five-year basic and vocational training education at the Sherman Institute, as yet another model for Indian relocation. Officer ultimately argued that relocation became confused with the termination policy in the minds of both Indians and policy makers. "From a careful examination of the record," Officer wrote, "the conclusion drawn is that except for a temporal relationship, these two major tenets of federal Indian policy during 1946–1958 were not, in fact, the offspring of the same parent."[68]

To a degree, then, federal policy makers laid the foundation of the 1952 relocation program almost ten years in advance of its official launching. Relocation certainly functioned as an accomplice to the era's more ominous and cataclysmic termination policy, but the foregoing evidence warrants a more nuanced interpretation and suggests the value in divorcing relocation from the termination policy and appreciating it as a discrete historical phenomenon that produced its own particular set of consequences for Native people. Moreover, while the Truman administration and Commissioner of Indian Affairs Dillon S. Myer were central in the development of the wide-scale federal urban relocation program and partly responsible for its worst outcomes, they were not the sole architects of the program, especially the ideas behind it.[69]

Interestingly, Dillon Myer came from the very War Relocation Authority that Indian New Dealers adopted as a procedural model for Indian relocation. A major distinction between Indian New Dealers' and Dillon Myer's support for relocation, however, rested in the former group's embrace of relocation as a strategy to improve the health and sustainability of reservation economies and communities. Thus, they adopted the process but not necessarily the goals. Upon taking office in 1950, Myer, by contrast, moved full-speed ahead with a policy to terminate tribal sovereignty and break apart tribalism once and for all. Unlike James Officer, Myer appreciated relocation as a complement to the termination policy. Symbolizing his break from the previous administration's path, he immediately dismissed personnel from Collier's administration, including Assistant Commissioner of Indian Affairs William Zimmerman, who promoted relocation but resisted Myer's pursuit of a termination policy. If considered from multiple angles, then, relocation as a federal program initiative, not unlike the federal termination policy, unfolded in fits and starts, with no discernible rhyme or reason. Moreover, while Myer's eventual leadership on relocation proved callous and quite deserving of vilification, the driving forces behind Indian urban relocation both predated and transcended him.[70]

· · · · · ·

On the afternoon of August 28, 1951, a military burial to honor the body and memory of Sergeant First Class John Raymond Rice was underway at Memorial Park Cemetery in Sioux City, Iowa. Flanked by an Army color guard and an American Legion honor guard, the funeral procession passed the cemetery gates and advanced toward Rice's final resting spot. Suspended six feet above a freshly dug grave, the flag-draped coffin was ready to be lowered into the earth when, panicking at the sight of numerous American Indians in attendance, cemetery manager Ben Willey interrupted the service. Citing a Caucasian-only policy, Willey informed Sergeant Rice's widow, Evelyn, that the cemetery would only accept her husband's remains if an army official signed a form swearing that the body was white. She summarily refused the offer. Willey then cut her a refund check for her $100 deposit. She refused that offer, too.

Before its rejection by the Memorial Park Cemetery, Sergeant John Rice's body had been relocated several times. Servicemen first moved it from a bloodstained Korean War battlefield to a hospital in Tabu-dong, where Rice died from wounds sustained during the Battle of Pusan Perimeter. From there, his body passed through the Graves Registration Service to a military warehouse, a cargo ship out of Japan, and finally a stateside train that delivered it to his Winnebago reservation home in Nebraska. During World War II, Rice himself had supervised the movement of bodies when he served with a regiment in charge of escorting fallen soldiers from Japan back home to the United States.

Catching wind of the cemetery's refusal to accept Sergeant Rice's body, President Harry Truman made arrangements to have the slain soldier buried in Arlington National Cemetery. A funeral procession then escorted Rice's body from Winnebago to a Sioux City railway depot, where it was loaded onto a train bound for the nation's capital. Finally, one day short of a year after Sergeant Rice's body fell in Korea, it was lowered into the ground in Arlington while a band played "Just as I Am without One Plea," "Our Fallen Heroes," and "Nearer My God to Thee." As the Truman administration's official representative, Commissioner of Indian Affairs Dillon S. Myer looked on in mourning.[71]

As the shameful cemetery incident indicates, the great wartime expansion of socioeconomic opportunities for Native people was not permanent, and it did not solve their collective problems overnight. Writing in 1944, Dakota anthropologist Ella Deloria cautioned, "There are countless families in the remote pockets of reservations still in great poverty. Anyone who drives through their country can see it." She acknowledged that many Native people had "made a success that is outstanding and are now out working and receiving incomes commensurate with those earned by young people of other races for similar work." But for the most part, she concluded, the results of Native people's hard efforts had not yet amounted to a comprehensive transformation in socioeconomic opportunity. She also admonished social critics who concluded that persistent reservation poverty stemmed from Indian indolence. Going forward, she argued, stronger effort was needed not from Indians but from non-Indian Americans who had largely failed to understand the structural nature of tribal poverty and that being poor was not some noble Indian social tradition. "As soon as our country became involved in war, the Indians of all tribes got into action. They did it in 1917 and they did it again and in fuller measure in 1941 and the years following," she proclaimed. "Who can say they are apathetic and listless now?"[72]

Indeed, thousands of Native people embraced America's war engagements as opportunities to simultaneously advance within mainstream American society and produce better living conditions within an expanding Indian Country. Those who migrated to urban war-production industries or served their country overseas practiced a well-traveled path toward upward socioeconomic mobility through spatial mobility. In their first war as citizens of the United States of America, Native servicemen and servicewomen fought against not only reservation economic poverty but also an impoverished social position within a nation for which they offered their lives. This evolving and enduring uplift impulse would underscore the next decade's urban relocation program. During 1953—the relocation program's second year of operation—63 percent of program participants were war veterans. In 1959, Assistant Secretary of the Interior Roger Ernst claimed that at least 50 percent of all urban relocated heads-of-household were veterans of either World War II or the Korean War.[73]

Still, Indian efforts at socioeconomic mobility could not succeed in the absence of greater support. Tens of thousands of Native people demonstrated ingenuity and tenacity during the war and, in the process, began demanding from the non-Indian American citizenry a new perspective on Indians' capacity for belonging in American society. And yet, a desperate need for defense-industry workers notwithstanding, the cultural and economic exclusion of Native American people persisted. On the one hand, the war created a temporary opportunity for Indian workers to experience higher wages and off-reservation life. As Carlo Rotella notes, however, the end of the war also marked the beginning of the urban manufacturing sector's gradual decline, which lasted from the 1950s through the 1980s, after which a service economy emerged in its place, automation increased, and business leaders relocated their factories to new areas both within and beyond the United States in pursuit of higher corporate profit margins. This would increasingly impact not only urban American Indian people's fate but also that of thousands of urban black Americans who migrated to "October cities" such as Chicago and Detroit during the war.[74]

Native American people who self-migrated to urban defense industries were also too often met by non-Indian people who had failed to update their own thinking and a federal government that refused to cede paternalistic control over Indians, even those that seemed quite capable of managing their own futures. Their opinions of Native people were still wedded to lingering notions of Indians as an inferior race—a people who could achieve equal stature only if they agreed to become white. And if enlisting for service in the U.S. military and dying in battle was not white enough to be buried in a particular cemetery, then imagine how much hope and pressure was riding on a possible urban relocation program as a panacea for America's "Indian problem."

World War II marked a discernible shift in who commanded the reins of Indian mobility and who controlled the viable paths to urban resources. Not long after the war, the federal government would throw its weight behind urbanization as part of its larger plan to "get out of the Indian business," as numerous politicians were putting it. When the federal government began subsidizing Indian urbanization during the late 1940s, it initially provided some help and many promises. More importantly, and more problematically, it also began undermining and overmanaging an Indian-driven process that had unfolded organically among tribal communities across previous decades and perhaps reached its peak efficacy during the war.

3 These People Come and Go Whenever They Please

Negotiating Relocation in Postwar Native America

· ·

We must make him feel just a little bit special. We must cushion the
impact of a strange new city upon him. . . . We must prepare him to
solve his own problems within the community just as anyone else does.
—Denver Field Relocation Office Operating Manual

They need to feel that they "belong."
—Commissioner of Indian Affairs Dillon S. Myer (1951)

In March 1952, Montana area relocation placement officer George Barrett
and his team of assistants arrived at the Crow Indian Agency armed with
two film canisters. They were on special orders to arouse Crow people's interest in the BIA's new urban relocation program. The two films did not, as
one might expect, include propagandist portrayals of Native American
people working, living, and playing in sprawling metropolises. They were
not exactly popcorn films either. They were odd choices. Summarizing
the national Social Security system "as it applied to the average citizen,"
the first film was likely informative but probably dull. The second film—
certainly the main attraction, though likely just as monotonous—was a
Ford Motor Company production titled *6,000 Partners*, which discussed how
auto manufacturing depended on interagency cooperation.[1]

These films probably did not lend much excitement to the suspiciously
titled Voluntary Relocation Program. According to George Barrett, the films
delivered an important message about cooperative labor and living arrangements in present-day America. Reporting back to Montana area relocation
director Paul Fickinger, Barrett expressed confidence that the films had successfully "brought out many very fine points that our Indians need to consider, that living in a very complex world, how dependent we have become
on each other." As far as Barrett and his colleagues were concerned, the time
had arrived for "our" Native American people to play a productive role not
only in the nation's manufacturing of goods but also in the maintenance of
America's supreme position in a "complex world."[2] Four years later, Barrett

possibly had in mind his visit with the Crow people when he warned, "As long as we continue to subsidize people who are willing to accept relief instead of going on relocation we will perpetuate an impossible situation. Our reservations have become sanctuaries for people who wish to continue a pattern of seasonal work and relief as a program for living."[3]

It is not surprising that Barrett used the term "sanctuaries" to describe tribal homelands. State officials did tend to think of American Indian people as endangered animals, biding their time in nature preserves. The Truman administration's comprehensive Voluntary Relocation Program was supposed to provide an escape from those sanctuaries, while Congress's concurrent termination policy, designed to dissolve tribal sovereignty and bring Indigenous nations under the jurisdiction of state governments, quietly destroyed them. Despite the BIA's energetic promotion leading up to the relocation program's introduction, however, it did not initially unfold according to plan. This is because Native people were active players in the process, not just victims of the latest state machinations.

Federal policy makers and Native people alike sought socioeconomic solutions in the promise of urban life, but mostly for a different set of problems and with a different ultimate effect in mind. Federal policy makers sought to remove Native Americans from their familiar cultural contexts and ultimately preclude their futures as Indian people, all in an effort to prune federal expenditures, support Cold War cultural consensus, and solve their perpetual "Indian problem."[4] By contrast, when Native Americans entered the city, they were determined not only to survive as Indian people but also to expand the possibilities for Indian culture in new contexts while commanding the terms of movement in, around, and away from Indian country. This was a risky proposition in that it meant grounding Indigeneity in new places while hoping to preserve important connections to ancestral homelands and kinship systems—a gamble that Native people well understood. Therefore, while many Native Americans, especially military and urban war-industry veterans, were primed to make that leap, others were understandably hesitant to surrender their commitments to seasonal work cycles, which for many were not only relatively reliable but also inextricably linked to what it meant to be a member of a particular Indigenous nation.[5]

In this respect, there is continuity between urban relocation and other major federal Indian policy initiatives—such as allotment, boarding school education, and termination—whose eventual outcomes indicated Native people's ability to critique and shape their form and implementation.[6] This chapter focuses on this important theme as it manifested in critical actions and conversations that unfolded between the aftermath of World War II and the national relocation program launch in 1952. Once Native people began maneuvering within and around the relocation program, they both frustrated BIA efforts at selling its new program and played a decisive role in affecting its efficacy. Indeed, as this chapter demonstrates, relocation amounted to more than another example of the federal government unilaterally acting on Native people. Relocation instead reflected a negotiated process that eventually arrived at ends as unpredictable and multifaceted as its beginnings.

· · · · · ·

As part of the BIA's relocation program launch, the Chicago Field Relocation Office disseminated a brochure titled *The Indians Are Coming!* designed to enlighten the American people about migrating Indians' needs. Positing relocation as a solution for most reservations' inability to support more than 50 percent of their respective residents, the brochure suggested that "Fairness and Justice require that we help the American Indian improve their standard of living through their own individual efforts." Further elaborating, it explained that Indian veterans from two wars had experienced the city, learned about urban work opportunities, and now desired better housing and a brighter future. Moreover, the brochure made clear that many Indians, through their own efforts, had already staked out a future in various metropolises, although those were typically the "more venturesome" or better educated people. "American Indians want to get into the stream of American life and swim," it concluded. "They don't want to sink in the idleness of submarginal reservation lands."[7] Such assertions, steeped in the language of the era, provide prime examples of the quantitative and qualitative analyses that played a key role in rallying the Bureau of Indian Affairs and Congress around urban relocation's potentially mitigatory power. More than that, they served as sales pitches not only to prospective Indian enrollees but also to any federal government representative—from the commissioner of Indian affairs down to local program office staffers—or average American taxpayer who might have wondered whether they were doing right by their Native American brethren.

In fact, years before the relocation program's introduction in 1952, federal officials had begun delineating the role non-Indian citizens should play in facilitating Indian people's plunge into "the stream of American life." In 1948, new Interior Department assistant secretary William Warne composed an article titled "The Public Share in Indian Assimilation" that pointedly urged non-Indian American citizens to get involved and welcome Indians with open arms. After first explaining that the "avowed objective" of the Indian service was to "work itself out of a job," Warne elaborated on the federal government's return to an unambiguous Indian assimilation policy, which depended on creating off-reservation job opportunities for Native people. Pointing to the increased number of Indians "drifting" from reservations in recent years, Warne suggested, "I am sure that this movement could be greatly accelerated if the public played its part in welcoming these graduates into economic and social equality." Doing so, he argued, would effectively solve "the age-old problem that our ancestors and we have created by occupancy of this great and beautiful land."

On the one hand, we can discern a postwar anti-racist call for cultural consensus and racial equality in Warne's article. As benevolent as Warne's agenda might have sounded at the time, however, it is important to acknowledge his primary goal—one of ultimately abolishing the Bureau of Indian Affairs and not, as the New Deal administration previously attempted (with mixed legacies), preserving tribal lands and Indigenous cultures. With his emphasis on the vital role non-Indian urban communities must play when receiving an influx of job-seeking Indians, Warne reflected a second important shift in the federal government's approach to its Indian problem. The non-Indian general public had always played a role in supporting Indian cultural assimilation—federal tax expenditures for Indian programs alone account for this. But in past decades federal initiatives to uplift the Indian race mostly transpired in relative isolation on remote reservations. Warne's solution, by contrast, was to pilot the "Indian problem" right into the urban headwaters of America's cultural mainstream, thereby making it a national project and, by extension, everyone's problem.[8]

Of course the general American public was not positioned to suddenly appreciate the complexities of Indian policy and history, but certainly it understood hunger and cold. That was worth something when, during World War II's aftermath, the Navajo and Hopi reservations vividly dramatized a growing reservation overpopulation crisis while providing an impetus for public pleas to help destitute Indians (the Hopi reservation is situated within the boundaries of the larger Navajo reservation). During the late 1940s, Navajo and Hopi people experienced a succession of especially catastrophic winters, marked by heavy snowfall and subzero temperatures, that exhausted tribal resources and left many struggling to find food and warmth. Exacerbating matters, the Navajo tribe counted roughly fifty-five thousand members, but reservation resources could only support about thirty-five thousand.[9] As a solution, President Truman and other politicians advocated a costly Navajo-Hopi rehabilitation program, which succeeded in arousing strong public support.[10] "To take full advantage of off-reservation employment opportunities, there must be a systematic training and placement program in order to overcome the handicaps of language, lack of special skills, and irregular work habits, which prevail among many Indians," President Truman suggested in an official statement. "Off-reservation employment must provide permanent security on a family basis, if the placement program is to be successful."[11]

In late winter 1948, the BIA began offering both a regional job services program and transportation to Los Angeles, Salt Lake City, and Denver for Navajo and Hopi people seeking food, warmth, and unemployment relief. Notwithstanding their efforts, Navajo-Hopi job placement officials struggled to get the program up and running. The reservation lacked efficient infrastructure and modern communication networks, rendering recruitment efforts difficult at best. For example, it could take several hours just to transport workers to a pickup point, and harsh weather could completely disrupt communication and transportation lines. "A seemingly mild breeze is sufficient to disrupt the use of a telephone," one BIA representative complained.[12]

Program representatives eventually found success by contracting with Arizona and New Mexico State Employment Services and the U.S. Railroad Retirement Board while intensifying their placement efforts in Denver, Los Angeles, and Salt Lake City. In April 1950, Congress authorized a ten-year Navajo-Hopi rehabilitation program, which, in addition to World War II Japanese American relocation, provided a second model for a national Indian relocation program. Impressed by the program's initial results, Congress approved a budget increase to $3.5 million, and in July 1951, the BIA, in anticipation of a national relocation program, began forming area recruitment offices in Oklahoma, Arizona, New Mexico, Colorado, Utah, and California.[13] During 1952, the program produced a total of twenty-two thousand jobs both on- and off-reservation, which brought Navajo and Hopi workers $14 million in combined earnings.[14] The Navajo tribal council officially supported the wider effort by forming the Tribal Enterprises Corporation to provide raw materials for work projects and training programs. Under the tribal council's directive, the corporation's official policy was to intentionally hire Navajo people who lacked English language skills and industrial training. Upon completion of the training and language program, they were expected to find off-reservation employment "so that another may be trained."[15]

During 1950, in his new capacity as commissioner of Indian affairs, Truman appointee Dillon S. Myer drew on both the Navajo-Hopi program and his leadership of the War Relocation Authority (WRA) for Indian policy models. He also brought in numerous colleagues from the WRA to fill out his BIA staff. When future Denver and Chicago relocation placement supervisor Stanley Lyman first accepted a position with the Indian bureau in 1952, he immediately realized that the former WRA people were "running everything."[16] For example, in 1951 Myer appointed former WRA agent Charles Miller as the first chief of the Branch of Relocation Services. Miller's experience with relocation was not limited to his service in the WRA; he had also led a program to bring impoverished Jamaican workers to the United States. All told, across nineteen years of federal government service, Miller—the "Great Mover of People"—proved responsible for the movement of over 400,000 Native Americans, Japanese Americans, and Jamaicans.[17]

Stanley Lyman also sensed that the WRA cohort was motivated more by its own need to integrate Indians into mainstream American society than by a deep understanding of Native people's needs as fellow human beings with their feet on the ground. "They approached this from strictly an intellectual viewpoint," he claimed. Still, Lyman was not entirely cynical about the program. "When you got down, then, to what we did from day to day, it was just a matter of talking to Indians . . . finding out whether or not they were interested in leaving the reservation, and frankly, urging them to do so," he explained. "In other words, to make it possible for the Indian people to move away and get a job where they could put beans on the table. They didn't have beans on the table at home, believe me."[18]

Reflecting on his experiences as commissioner of Indian affairs during the Kennedy and Johnson administrations, Philleo Nash, who boasted a PhD in anthropology from the University of Chicago, pulled no punches when criticizing Dillon Myer, whom he had initially recommended for the Indian affairs commissioner post. Nash reasoned that World War II resulted in the shrinking of the federal Indian bureaucracy at the same time that Indians were seeking opportunities away from reservations. "This then gave a push to those forces in American life which think that the solution to the Indian problem is to wipe out the reservations and scatter the Indians and then there won't be Indian tribes, Indian cultures, or Indian individuals," Nash asserted. "This is not the right solution; this is not a good solution; it is not one that is acceptable to a thinking person, but this is an area where we often reason by analogy, and if we think the melting pot was a good idea, then we think it would be good to melt off the Indians in the reservations."[19]

Voluntary Relocation Program advocacy was not solely the province of a coterie of BIA experts. Not unlike the termination policy, also gaining traction at the time, relocation found allies in junior politicians who implored President Truman to help impoverished Indians surrender tribalism in exchange for an individual role in competitive capitalism.[20] Toby Morris—U.S. representative (D-Oklahoma) and chairman of the House Subcommittee on Indian Affairs—supported this goal. In October 1951, he personally wrote President Truman to warn him that Congress's budget for the BIA's new relocation program was terribly insufficient. "I believe stepped up expenditures are absolutely necessary if we are ever going to make the Indians economically independent and have them take their proper place in our American society," Morris stated. He then pointed to a contradiction in the federal government's spending of vast sums of money on behalf of foreign peoples while "neglecting our first Americans." According to Morris, roughly 50 percent of all Indians were incapable of supporting themselves on reservations. Relocation, he ventured, would "integrate these people into the overall economy and would solve once and for all their special status problems." Tugging at Truman's heartstrings, Morris pleaded, "Knowing your great interest in all downtrodden peoples, I am sure that you want to do everything possible to help this group."[21]

Morris was likely influenced by influential Oklahoma historian Angie Debo's recently published *The Five Civilized Tribes of Oklahoma: Report on Social and Economic Conditions*, which Debo sent to the junior congressman in 1951. The book detailed the destitute living conditions with which Oklahoma's Native people wrestled daily. Chapter 2, titled "Poor Indian on Poor Land," might have made the strongest impression on Morris. The chapter illustrated Indian lives marked by dilapidated cabins, disappearing fruit orchards, and a diminishing land and water base. "I talked with scores of families living on undivided inherited land, paying no rent, squatting there as a natural right," Debo wrote. "Most of them seemed not to realize the precarious nature of their tenure, or to look ahead to the day when their refuge would crumble beneath their feet."[22]

Perhaps a letter that Dr. George B. Roop sent to Morris in June 1951 also made a strong impression on the congressman. Dr. Roop wrote to apprise Morris of conditions at Oklahoma's Anadarko Agency, where he practiced medicine and had been the only doctor for the past three years. The nearest hospital was an hour away in Clinton—a trip most of the local Cheyenne and Arapaho people could not easily make. When they did, they were frequently sent home without care if their problems were not deemed severe enough for hospital treatment. Roop explained that he tried to help as many Native people as he could, even though most could not afford to pay him. "They live in very poor, sordid surroundings, many of them in tents," he wrote. "They cannot possibly have anything simulating a normal diet. Hence, they are ill frequently, especially the children." Roop then concluded with a particularly grim story: "Recently, a week old baby died of lock jaw, due to infection from [a] contaminated umbilical cord. There was no doctor present at the birth."[23]

Limitations on the delivery of health care in fact posed serious problems on numerous reservations, especially in more remote areas that lacked sufficient infrastructure. For example, during the 1950s, South Dakota's Cheyenne River Reservation Indian Hospital provided only thirty beds. In most cases, it proved easier for Cheyenne River Indians to wait for the hospital's three doctors to come to them during "clinic days," when the doctors made rounds in remote communities. Because of the hospital's limited facilities, Native people who required emergency surgery had to race to the capital city, Pierre, 65 miles to the south. Those who needed ear, nose, or eye treatment required a referral to Aberdeen, 125 miles to the northeast. Tuberculosis patients had to trek even farther away, to Rapid City, 250 miles to the southwest. Finally, those in need of diagnostic procedures had to take referrals across the state border to Omaha's Creighton University, 350 miles to the southeast. Such inconveniences likely formed a push factor for Native people, who desired closer proximity to health-care outlets.[24]

Also in Toby Morris's possession was a copy of an essay titled "How Fare the Indians?" which Library of Congress sociologist William H. Gilbert drafted in 1950. In the essay, Gilbert refers to Native people as an "outdoor race" and "marginal people" who profoundly suffered from poor health conditions, a lack of steady employment, deficient reservation resources, and substandard housing. "The Indian, then, is partly in and partly out of our society," Gilbert stressed, before concluding, "There is an American Indian problem in this country which apparently will not settle itself." It is unclear whether Toby Morris's strong support for relocation as a solution to the Indian problem was the product of a deep personal conviction or a reflection of his responsibility to help the roughly fifty-five thousand Native people who lived in his state. It was most likely a product of both, and these documents in his possession provide some sense of the prevailing ideas and concerns that must have shaped his thinking when he wrote to President Truman.[25]

Federal officials like Representative Morris were not alone in their call for a new solution to the old Indian problem. For example, some members of New York City's Association on American Indian Affairs (AAIA) supported an intervention against what they perceived to be paternalistic overreach. In an editorial for the organization's magazine, Alexander Lesser roundly rejects the "Overprotected Indian": "Many of us who have seen the hopelessness and the attitudes of dependence that are widespread on the reservations today—the preoccupied helplessness with which many Indians become involved with the officialdom around them in so many incidents of their daily lives, their timidity to venture into the off-reservation stream of American life, the apathy and low level of aspiration that are all too frequent, and the easy turning back homeward to the reservation of thousands of younger Indians—must increasingly recognize these as symptoms of the overprotected environment of Indian life." Earlier in the piece, however, Lesser decries the prevailing stereotypes that cast Indians as "gullible and incompetent." Yet he quickly emphasizes the supposed "timidity" of reservation-based Indians, as though their failure to clear wide paths to mainstream America reflected some sort of innate fear of modernity. If Native people were so "preoccupied" with "helplessness," why then did Lesser want to expedite their plunge into the mainstream of American life? While attempting to dismantle one stereotype, he effectively constructed another. Such was the ignorant and contradictory nature of policy makers' and Indian rights advocates' proposed solution to the Indian problem during this period.[26]

These were not the first, and would not be the last, politicians and social experts to craft and critique Indian policy without a genuine understanding of who American Indian people had been, had become, and wanted to be. Native people had for years been quietly pursuing the very course of action whose relative merit policy makers and social theorists were busy debating. With few exceptions, Native people did not seem to fear that urbanization would result in culture loss. Those who chased new socioeconomic opportunities beyond their tribal homeland understood that they were exercising a choice and accepted the potential consequences. Moreover, they were determined to demonstrate Indian culture's resiliency. The era's concerned academics and social critics did not seem to understand this, as they worried more about Indian culture loss in an urban setting than Indians did. In hindsight, such doubts about the pliability and portability of Indian culture appear a subtle perpetuation of the old "vanishing Indian" trope. Indeed, midcentury federal policy makers' and social theorists' failure to reconcile Indian social, class, and spatial mobility with Indian cultural persistence echoed late nineteenth-century Indian rights advocates who became convinced that Indian progress could only ascend from the ashes of tribal culture.[27]

In an essay by a second AAIA leader and popular Indian rights advocate, Oliver LaFarge described the deteriorating economic conditions on the Navajo reservation and how a substantial population increase exacerbated them. Agricultural and railroad work, he insisted, was not the answer to the Diné people's problems. "If that is the best future we can offer a small nation which we have conquered, our whole civilization is a fraud and our boasted democracy nothing but a myth," he expounded. "The Navajos must be enabled to enter upon all levels of our economic life . . . as freely as do any of their fellow citizens." LaFarge's critique illuminates how non-Indians' solution to the Indian problem reflected concern not only for Native people but also for America's legitimacy as a right and responsible nation. Such arguments especially mattered in the context of the United States' efforts during the Cold War to portray republicanism and capitalism as the essential foundations for a just and prosperous society.[28]

In addition to concern for the United States' national reputation, some Indian rights advocates celebrated urban Indians for their potentially positive cultural influence on non-Indian people. In 1952, Alice Shoemaker— Los Angeles Indian Center director and former director of the University of Wisconsin's School for Workers—wrote an essay championing Native people's "tremendous vitality, humor, deep religious feeling, . . . appreciation and sense of oneness with nature, democratic procedures," and more. She contrasted her vision of uncorrupted Indian culture with the "gaudy merchandise" on display in the shop windows of Los Angeles's Wilshire Boulevard, and promised that Indians would "bring rich treasures to our frantic, fearful, jaded, over-mechanized civilization." Shoemaker's promotion of Native people as a potential panacea for vapid postwar materialism matched the sentiments of John Collier, Mabel Dodge, D. H. Lawrence, and their wider social reform cohort that promoted the Pueblo Indian communities they discovered in New Mexico from the early 1910s through the 1920s as a solution to all of America's problems. Departing from their logic, however,

Shoemaker wanted Native people to exercise their cultural purity not in their tribal homelands but in urban metropolises that appeared to be drowning in consumerism. On the one hand, then, the federal government during the 1950s ushered Native people's entry into the patriotic citizen consumer sphere that historian Lizabeth Cohen discusses, while anti-modern social reformers positioned Native people as props in anti-capitalist imaginations. If not all Indigenous people agreed on the potential benefits of urbanization and socioeconomic mainstreaming, then neither did many non-Indigenous people.[29]

Some social critics even demonstrated enough foresight to recognize the urgency in providing some sort of complementary program to encourage reservation development for Indian people who elected to remain in Indian Country. For example, anthropologist and Indian rights advocate Betty Clark Rosenthal wrote Indian Rights Association representative Theodore Hetzel to offer advice on an article he was developing on Indian migration to Chicago. Rosenthal suggested that Hetzel "emphasize the success of Indian men and women at work in the city and town situations—and then point up their adaptability." While she admitted that relocation had its "faults, and sins of omission or commission," she claimed that "picking on the relocation program" only emboldened local leaders who would rather criticize the initiative than help Indian families in need. She then made certain to stress the crucial import of bringing reservations into the discussion. Lack of economic development on reservations, she believed, was what social scientists really needed to "fix upon out of the relocation story."[30]

An informational pamphlet that the National Social Welfare Assembly (NSWA) created in 1953 identified four supposedly common Indian character traits that prospective urban social workers should consider before attempting to assist newly arriving Native people: their supposed distrust of "the white man and his motives," insecurity and lack of self-confidence, concern for personal privacy, and "lack of acquisitiveness and drive for personal achievement." The NSWA failed to consider that some Indians' main motivation for migrating to cities might have stemmed from personal ambition and a desire to compete both economically and intellectually within wider America. In fairness, the pamphlet's authors admitted, "One cannot generalize about 'the Indian' any more than one can generalize about the 'white man,' 'the Chinese,' or 'the Negro.'" That important insight notwithstanding, the authors stereotyped their potential Indian welfare recipients as provincial folks who lacked motivation and only thought of their immediate needs. Perhaps the authors also failed to realize that such sweeping assumptions about Indian indolence likely played a role in Native people's supposed "insecurity and lack of self-confidence, which may be expressed in timidity and diffidence." Indeed, these are the types of sociocultural assumptions that so often governed non-Indian bureaucrats, social workers, employers, and community neighbors' interactions with Indians.[31]

In addition to federal policy makers and public social theorists, Indian boarding school administrators continued playing an important role in both critiquing and encouraging Indian migration toward mainstream America as the most expedient path toward socioeconomic progress and equality. Whereas the former groups' intellectual musings mostly manifested within elite non-Indian circles, boarding school messages of uplift directly reached impressionable Indian students. In his commencement speech to South Dakota's Flandreau Indian School graduating class of 1956, school superintendent H. Bogard outlined three key strategies for success in the "dominant prevailing society." First, he encouraged graduates to recognize the centrality of time as a governing force in their lives. "The Indian, to get ahead, must recognize this and practice it so it will also be a part of his culture," Bogard lectured. Second, Indians must prove their facility for steady, reliable, and high-quality work. Finally, he assured Flandreau graduates that success in the "American way of life" depended on investing income to "let your wealth work for you as you are earning." On the one hand, this is basic boilerplate commencement speech fodder. Yet it also indicates how even those who worked most closely with young Indians seemingly failed to recognize that they could point to their people's long history of exercising such strategies. Indeed, Bogard did not even need to look to the distant past to locate useful examples. The thoughts of some students listening to Bogard's speech could have easily drifted to examples from their parents' lives. Even after World War II and several decades of Indians gradually transgressing spatial and cultural boundaries, politicians and social experts still seemed to imagine that ambition was foreign to Indian culture.[32]

In its final issue before May graduation in 1953, the Haskell Institute's school paper led with a piece that further illustrated the steady diet of uplift messages that boarding schools fed their students. "How Will You Face It?" the piece prodded beneath a cartoon portraying an apprehensive young boxer squaring off against an anthropomorphic Earth, with boxing gloves lifted beneath a menacing visage. "Yes," the article began, "how will you, as a graduate of Haskell Institute, face the future? Will you be a success? Will you use what you have learned here at Haskell, or will you sit back and wait for a 'handout'?" The message must have resonated as clear as a ringside bell. Imploring graduates to embrace the "real struggle" to come, and to think of future jobs and a metaphoric ocean lying before them, the article jabbed, "Are we going to attempt to cross the ocean? Or are we going to stand and look across it?" before concluding, "Let's cross the ocean . . . to success!"[33]

Such language—active versus passive, taking versus receiving—simultaneously reinforced negative stereotypes about Indians' labor and intellectual potential while challenging young Indians to overcome them. It also reflected how, despite their legitimate claims to a share of the socioeconomic fruits stemming from America's postwar ascendance, enterprising Indians often had to contend with low expectations and a fate tied to menial labor opportunities. For example, in a speech delivered to Indian boarding school superintendents toward the end of World War II, BIA education director Willard Beatty insisted that Indians' future in America lay in "service occupations," and that Indian girls "should be taught to bake pies and cakes for commercial purposes." Beatty suggested that boys from Haskell could work in the institute's Lawrence, Kansas, base as long as they made sure to "charge a full price and not work for a cheap wage." Finally, he implored superintendents to bend their respective school curriculums to trends in the marketplace and avoid teaching a particular subject "just because it is there."[34]

Beatty's emphasis on service occupations for Indians reflected not only the new assimilationist ideologies that took shape within the Indian bureau after World War II but also the old turn-of-the-century brand of racialized boarding school education that at best created the potential for Indian people to enter American society as second-class citizens. Vocational instruction, Beatty and other critics concluded, formed the most socioeconomically expedient strategy toward weaving America's Indian population onto the nation's postwar path. In this respect, non-Indian thinking about Indian people's potential had not developed all that much—it needed an update. This is ironic in that it was not actual Indian people, supposedly so insecure, who needed help navigating modernity. While thousands of Indian people were exploring new presents, it was non-Indian politicians and social critics whose ideas remained woefully wedded to distorted pasts.

Above all, federal policy makers and social critics privileged the most pragmatic and cost-effective solutions to their Indian problem. Their collective strategies left little room for Native people's, or even John Collier's, premium on cultural pluralism. Whereas boarding school progenitor Richard Henry Pratt once suggested that America needed to "kill the

Indian, and save the man," postwar policy makers seemed intent on killing the Indian but more to save money than to save the man. While the federal government continued spinning its wheels on a new postwar political and economic terrain, Indian people quietly continued traversing it, even as it trended uphill.[35]

. . . . . .

During the years approaching the BIA's formal introduction of its relocation program, thousands of Native people from across Indian Country continued to fan outward from reservations in search of reliable income and greater social opportunities in postwar America. But for many, the trajectory rarely resembled an expedited flight straight from rural reservation space to mammoth metropolises. Rather, as a nascent first step, migrating Indians often occupied spaces in between, just as they had during previous decades. As Native people achieved greater familiarity with mainstream American life, they increasingly strengthened their affinity for negotiating the migratory process according to their own terms, and for their own benefit. This would ultimately produce a tension in which the federal government increased efforts at directing Native American mobility precisely when the latter group had gained confidence in that process and had a clear precedent to draw on.[36]

Throughout the late 1940s and early 1950s, many northern Minnesota Indians were already pursuing work opportunities that demanded geographic separation of varying distances from tribal life. Adhering to a seasonal work cycle, thousands of Minnesota Indians worked beet and potato fields in the northwest, pulp mills in the north-central, and iron mines in the northeastern portions of the state. In 1951, the Consolidated Chippewa Agency relocation placement officer wrote his superiors to explain that he was struggling to manufacture any enthusiasm for the upcoming program launch because Indians in his district preferred seasonal work and did not want to migrate out permanently, as policy makers had hoped. Indian mine workers, in particular, signaled their determination to return to their respective reservations for wild-rice harvesting and duck hunting. Minnesota Indians' ability to exert influence over relocation by refusing to accept some elements of it caused the program to stumble out of the gate.[37]

For instance, a majority of Indians from Minnesota's Prairie Island Dakota community preferred working in the nearby town of Red Wing to distant permanent relocation. In late 1951, numerous Prairie Island people were busy manufacturing miniature drums and moccasin souvenirs, which they then sold to LeRoy Shane of Rochester and the Arrowhead Company of Minneapolis for statewide marketing. Others held construction positions for an outfit based in Hastings. Still others waited to see if they could get work at a new hospital development before entertaining the possibility of going on relocation. Interestingly, in what was by that point a rare example of New Deal thinking, BIA placement officer Kurt Fitzgerald offered his approval. "Our support of this enterprise may seem to run counter to the objectives of the placement program, but I doubt that it does seriously," he wrote his superiors. "I think it is incumbent upon us to help these people economically in any way that we can."[38]

In neighboring Wisconsin, BIA relocation officers struggled to convince Menominee Indians to apply for relocation. The tribe had recently been awarded an $8.5 million Indian Claims Commission settlement, and some feared they would not receive their share if they departed. Moreover, at Stockbridge and Oneida, practically all employment-eligible adults were already working at a tractor manufacturing plant in Clintonville and in shipyards at Manitowoc and Sturgeon Bay. However, Kurt Fitzgerald did not trust those opportunities as permanent solutions. He remembered how all the Indians from his district worked during the war. But then the shipyards closed, the mills slowed down, servicemen came home, and newspaper headlines alerted readers to "Starving Wisconsin Indian Communities." "Though the present good employment conditions at Stockbridge and Oneida may make us forget January 1950, we should not forget that no permanent industry is coming into these places and the population continues to grow," Fitzgerald warned. "This is no time to relax."[39]

Throughout 1951, BIA placement officers spent a substantial amount of time and energy trying to enlist people for relocation and prepare them to leave early the next year when the program would be in full operation. Still, Indian agents' overtures often failed to convince Native people of the program's merit. For example, in August 1951, Harold Gronroos—placement director for the new Juneau, Alaska, relocation office—arranged for Indigenous Alaskan people to work not at a distant urban center but at the U.S. Naval Station in Kodiak. The Alaskan Natives he approached, however, expressed no interest in the opportunity because they were looking forward to their fall fishing trip. Gradually, Gronroos's efforts gained traction as he continued cultivating a relationship with those assigned to his agency. For example, in November 1951, when a seasonal fishing trip failed to produce its typical bounty, Gronroos helped those in need of work secure positions at a salmon cannery on Kodiak Island.[40]

Meanwhile, Alaskan employers were warming to the idea of Indigenous employees after realizing the inherent benefits of a permanent local workforce, as opposed to the typically transient workforce that populated most area labor ranks. The American Federation of Labor's Anchorage office aggressively recruited Indigenous Alaskan workers when it negotiated temporary contracts that demanded an immediately available labor force. In June 1951, a construction company that landed a building contract two hundred miles north of Kotzebue on the Chukchi Sea hired 158 Alaskan Natives. By August, fifty among them held positions as carpenters, several more operated bulldozers and oiled machines, and seventeen of the company's eighteen truck drivers were Indigenous. In fact, with the exception of four white men, the entire crew was composed of Native Alaskans.[41]

Alaskan Native people must have been especially difficult to recruit for relocation as a result of their more extreme cultural isolation from mainstream America. At the same time, this should not be construed as evidence of their complete indifference toward work and cross-cultural explorations. Rather, it was indicative of Alaskan Natives' use of the Juneau relocation office according to their determined needs. In 1958, San Jose relocation field agent Marie Street wrote to the BIA's chief of relocation services, Charles F. Miller, to complain that some Native Alaskans who migrated through her office confessed that they had relocated only to "see what the states look like" and that they "just plan to stay until fishing season." At least for one year, a summer vacation in California became a feature, perhaps even the highlight, of some Alaskan Natives' seasonal migrations.[42]

While loyalty to fishing cycles came first, many Indigenous Alaskans proved willing to consider alternatives when that source of food and income failed. For example, in August 1953, an especially unsuccessful fishing trip sent "countless" Native people into Gronroos's office in search of relief. The overwhelmed travel agent did his best but had to confess that he simply could not meet all their needs. Perhaps this played a role in Gronroos's decision to vacate his position at the end of the year. Still, much of his tenure had been a success. During his leadership, the Juneau relocation office ranked third in total relocation departures, behind only the Anadarko, Oklahoma, and Gallup, New Mexico, offices. Considering the larger and more acculturated Indian populations in Oklahoma and New Mexico, that is a remarkable statistic.[43]

In 1951, the Baxco Company in The Dalles, Oregon, east from Portland along the Columbia River, hired forty Navajo to help make railroad ties for the Union Pacific. The Denver-based employment supervisor responsible for assembling the team of workers assured Baxco foremen that Navajo labor was reliable and "no different than other nationalities." Navajo worker Hugh Plummer emerged as his people's leader and interpreter, thus rendering him responsible for telling Portland area placement officer George La-Vatta that the Navajo men were unhappy with their meat rations and that they needed more because their work was so physically demanding. They also requested more bedding and better toilet and bathing facilities.

The disgruntled Navajo workers could have turned to the American Federation of Labor, with which they were in "good standing" according to their union representative, but they elected to manage their own negotiations. It worked. In addition to acceding to the Navajo workers' demands, Baxco promised them opportunities to rise within the labor ranks, with one caveat: they first needed to improve their English so that they could better understand orders. The Navajo men responded by enrolling in night classes in English and math. The Navajo men also expressed interest in bringing their families to Oregon and putting their children in the local public school if they could earn a higher salary to support them. To be sure, Baxco benefited from an asymmetrical power relation in their negotiations with the Navajo workers. They held a distinct advantage in that the Navajo they tried to discipline were far away from their own tribal power base. This likely explains why Baxco did not recruit Columbia River Indian workers from the nearby Umatilla Indian Reservation. Still, the labor dispute illustrates how some off-reservation Indigenous workers were gaining confidence in their capacity to manage their own affairs, however far from home. The inherent power differential favored the employer, but these Indian employees were not timid or rigid. They made sacrifices and embraced compromise but also stood firm on issues that mattered most: family, education, food, and warmth.[44]

Native people's determination to continue exercising agency over their own lives became especially clear when the BIA officially launched its Voluntary Relocation Program on January 1, 1952. Less than one month into the program's full operation, the Chicago relocation office sent representatives to wintry Wisconsin's Menominee, Oneida, and Stockbridge-Munsee reservations on a recruitment mission, but they found little interest among Indians who preferred to keep their steady jobs in nearby Green Bay and Manitowoc. If any field representatives were tempted to ignore mandated discretionary procedures in order to meet their recruitment goals, acting field placement officer Mary Nan Gamble proved quick to remind them that they were not to enroll Indians who demonstrated a history of bad work habits. "If he fails to measure up on the above-listed points he should be refused early consideration for placement as a disciplinary action," she stressed.[45] That same month, Peter Walz, placement officer for Minnesota's Red Lake Agency, reported similar disappointment in his attempts to recruit local Ojibwe people for relocation. Living conditions on the reservation had temporarily improved as a result of quarterly payments that came in from land sales, thereby resulting in scant enthusiasm for urban migration. More-over, Walz mentioned that Indians from his agency were already finding sufficient employment opportunities in northern Minnesota.[46]

Salt Lake City field placement officer Rudolph Russell expressed a simi-lar acute frustration with the Navajo people who filtered through his office during the summer of 1952. He found positions for them on area railroad gangs but complained, "These people come and go whenever they please. Their placement is not much of a problem; it's their failure to remain on jobs indefinitely that causes some difficulty." In his observation, a language barrier created a lack of understanding, which resulted in many of the Navajo workers becoming discouraged and leaving the job. Russell also com-plained that drinking had been a real problem and had resulted in the death of one Navajo worker—notorious for starting fights—from a blow to the head by a blunt instrument. This tragedy, needless to say, shook the placement office and the Navajo work community. "All sorts of leeches emerge and take advantage of the Indians by selling them intoxicants," Russell lamented. These disastrous events must have deeply affected Russell, who was him-self a Navajo man.[47]

While the relocation program initially faltered, various tribal councils emerged over subsequent years to critique the program and play an impor-tant role in improving its efficacy. During a July 1956 meeting with Indian commissioner Glenn Emmons, Standing Rock Sioux tribal chair Dan How-ard explained that his people were hesitant to leave on relocation because the tribe was awaiting the verdict on a land settlement that would po-tentially grant enrolled members a $5,000 rehabilitation loan, with one ca-veat: they had to reside within reservation limits. Therefore, not only were current residents wary of leaving, but many of the seventeen hundred tribal members living off-reservation could potentially return home to be eligible for their share of the tribal settlement. Assistant Indian affairs com-missioner Thomas Reid, also present, agreed with Howard: "Commissioner, we have had it hit us square between the eyes. . . . The minute they complete [vocational training courses] they go right back to the reservation; they won't go and get a job because under this act we have, they say 'Heck I am going to sit there until we find out how this is going to work out.'"[48]

One year after the relocation program's inauguration, the Portland, Oregon, placement office was still struggling to meet with any success. Because the Portland office did not station placement officers on reservations within its district, it depended on the formation of tribal employment committees to help raise interest in the program. This strategy initially proved ineffective because various tribal councils wanted to make sure they completely understood relocation's terms and goals before partnering with the Portland office. The Lummi Nation's employment committee, for example, insisted on a face-to-face meeting with BIA personnel to discuss the program's merit. Portland area placement officer George LaVatta answered their call and traveled north to meet with the tribe in Bellingham, Washington, near their reservation. Desperate to make a positive impression on the Lummi committee, LaVatta arrived with an entire team of representatives from the Washington State Employment Service, the State Vocational Department, the Plumbers and Steamfitters Union, and the Bellingham School District, among other groups, who worked together to convince Lummi leaders that they could trust the program. There is perhaps no more illustrative example of the degree to which relocation unfolded as a negotiated process rather than merely a plan to move Indian people against their will. Indeed, in this inversion of the relocation process, Native people forced a vulnerable BIA agent, hoping to succeed in mainstream America, to come to them.[49]

In December 1951, relocation placement officer Kurt Fitzgerald met with the Grand Portage Minnesota Chippewa Tribal Executive Committee to request their support for the new program. The tribal committee explained that while it was not entirely against the idea of permanent relocation, it did not feel compelled to voice its support, primarily out of fear that children born away from the reservation would lose tribal privileges. As a solution, the committee passed a resolution that guaranteed tribal enrollment for any children born off-reservation. With this action, the Grand Portage tribal committee reflected an important theme in Native people's evaluation of relocation as a valid remedy for some of their problems. They did not consider the potential benefits of urban life in isolation from what they knew about reservation life. They also did not consider urban migration a symbolic split with tribalism, nor did they predict a legal split. Regardless of the Indian bureau's use of the term "permanent relocation," Minnesota Chippewa people refused to allow the reservation to disappear in the hearts and minds of those ambitious enough to physically leave it behind. Like most Native people, they consistently thought about the city and the reservation as two points on a circular continuum.[50]

Prior to their roles as successive BIA commissioners during the Johnson and Nixon administrations, Robert L. Bennett (Oneida) and Louis R. Bruce (Mohawk) professed strong support for Indians who pursued success in mainstream American society. In 1955, Bennett argued that a dual goal of integration and Indian cultural persistence "is a monumental task." Likewise, Bruce penned a guest editorial in 1953 championing young Indians who rejected patronage from the "great white father" while "proving their right to have a voice in their future as modern Americans." In the process, they captured the full extent of an impulse within Indian Country to benefit from exposure to off-reservation society, an impulse that extended from individual tribal governments all the way to the federal Department of the Interior. Problematically, however, Bennett and Bruce advertised their integrative ideologies during the termination policy's most forceful attack on Indian Country. Yet that did not necessarily mean that Native urban migrants recognized off-reservation employment as an accomplice to termination. Bennett, who early in his career worked as a relocation placement officer in Aberdeen, South Dakota, insisted that economic development was essential for Native people's efforts to protect their culture, and that a sound economic base that allowed an Indian family to choose their own living patterns was imperative. In sum, Bennett did not see urbanization and Indian cultural persistence as mutually exclusive. Rather, he suggested the potential for one to benefit the other.[51]

These careful critiques and calculated maneuvers on the part of Native Americans should have mattered to the various politicians and social experts busily discussing the urban relocation program's value on the eve of its launch. To the program's eventual detriment, however, they clung to paternalism, convinced that they knew what was best for the Indians. Meanwhile, Native people quietly considered their options, continued pursuing established courses, and occasionally offered their own critiques—both positive and negative—of relocation as one possible solution to a range of problems in Indian Country. Their collective influence could take the form of everything from participating in a labor dispute to gaming the system for a free vacation. Otherwise diverse Indian people—ranging from manual laborers to future Indian affairs commissioners—were united in their pursuit of a better future for their families and people. Had program architects and critics accounted for all of this, they likely would have been less mystified when Indian subjects did not behave according to their plan. Alas, the complications program architects experienced during the product-rollout stage served less as warning signs than confirmation that Indian people, clinging to their seasonal work patterns and tethered to their homelands, really needed a push—really needed help. Subsequent to the program's unveiling, this trend would not only persist but also increase, as thousands of Native people sought to use relocation for their own purposes, frustrating many federal agents along the way.

· · · · · ·

In December 1952, closing the book on relocation's inaugural year and closing in on the end of his tenure as commissioner of Indian affairs, Dillon Myer went out to sell social and political power brokers on his burgeoning program's promise. During a speech he delivered in Phoenix to an audience of western state governors, he discussed an overpopulation and poverty crisis engulfing numerous Indian reservations. According to Myer, most Indian reservations had devolved into "broken homes, juvenile delinquency, bad health conditions, and general hopelessness." He then considered the larger nation's gradual shift away from agricultural work over the past decades as small family farms diminished. At present, he explained, only 17 percent of America's population resided on farms. Moreover, he claimed that even if all Indian lands were developed to their fullest capacity, there would still be a surplus of roughly half the Native population—around 200,000—that would need to depend on outside resources for survival. With that, Myer's concerns captured a fundamental transformation in the settler state's "Indian problem": First there was too much Indian land. Now there were too many Indians.[52]

Myer also appealed to governors' political power by confessing how much he needed their help. Convincing Indians to leave their reservations, he explained, was a monumental task because Indians, at least in his narrow imagination, lacked communication skills, rarely interacted with non-Indians, and feared the outside world. He also mentioned that Native people feared relocation because they associated the term with a legacy of pain rooted in nineteenth-century forced removals. While Myer certainly exaggerated the former points, he was perhaps on to something with the latter. For example, in 1960, Northern Cheyenne tribal president John Woodenlegs expressed reservations about relocation as a solution to his people's problems. The Cheyenne had already been "relocated" once before to Oklahoma, he reasoned, and it failed miserably. Presaging an argument that would become even more critical in subsequent years, when thousands of Indian people began relocating through the BIA's program or through continued self-relocation, Woodenlegs was instead determined to create jobs on his reservation, specifically mentioning that a sanitation development project could provide a major source of employment. "Our land is everything to us," he stressed. "It is where we talk Cheyenne."[53]

Commissioner Myer did not seem especially interested in such sentiments. Taken together, his points suggest that he was more concerned with relocation's potential for solving the federal government's Indian problem than he was with helping Native people identify and solve their own problems. Indeed, this statement by Myer is particularly revealing: "If we miss this opportunity to relocate and raise the standard of living of the surplus Indian population, it will mean a continued subsidy either by the Federal Government or the States indefinitely for the social and welfare services that will be necessary for these overpopulated and poverty-stricken areas." Mention of state subsidies must have perked up the ears of a room full of governors.[54]

Actually, the BIA's branding of Indians as a people who thought only of their immediate needs more accurately characterized its own administrative practices during this period. When Commissioner Myer contemplated Indians' response to relocation, he only imagined that they would exhibit a childlike fear of the entire enterprise. As this chapter has indicated, however, when Indian people proved difficult to recruit for relocation, it was more often because they had already fashioned their own employment networks and were trying to fit urban employment into their plans when it made sense. Why should they cede control of that system to a federal government so undeserving of Indian people's trust? As chapter 4 will confirm, this did not mean that they did not appreciate the opportunity extended to them or recognize that relocation *did* offer one strategy for survival in an ever-changing world. They wanted relocation to work on their terms, which meant making sure that tribal lands and tribal culture would be protected in the process. As former Denver and Chicago relocation field office director Stanley Lyman put it in a rare moment of non-Indian understanding of Indian motives, "Actually, an individual who was going on relocation did not think of it as national policy. He saw it as a means of satisfying his own needs."[55]

4 I Can Learn Any Kind of Work

Indian Initiative in Urban America

· ·

> So I grew up. You know, almost with the red, white, and blue
> draped around my shoulders. . . . I think the only thing I wanted
> to do was to get off the reservation as soon as possible.
>
> —Lester Chapoose (Ute)

On May 6, 1958, a tall, bespectacled Mohican man sat in rural Wisconsin's Stockbridge-Munsee Indian agency and filled out an application for the Bureau of Indian Affairs' Adult Vocational Training (AVT) program. In 1957, the BIA's initial Voluntary Relocation Program (VRP) reached its peak enrollment of 6,964 total Indians. Whereas the VRP provided only transportation, limited support for housing and food, and (hopefully) direct employment, the AVT program provided pre-relocation job training on the reservation or on-the-job training in various urban destinations for up to two years for American Indians between the ages of eighteen and thirty-five. These features made it a popular competitor of the VRP, whose enrollment began declining during the AVT program's first full year of operation in 1958. Although the program's name was not as glamorous as the cities to which it sent hopeful Indians, that proved no deterrent—at least not for the Mohican man who, reaching the end of his application, had but one clause to consider: "I further understand that the money is to be made available to me only on the express condition that I faithfully discharge my obligation to carry out to the best of my ability the vocational training for which I am accepted."[1]

Given his prior experiences, the man probably did not hesitate to sign his name on the line below: Myron E. Miller Jr. Initially hoping for an urban on-the-job training opportunity, Miller instead settled for an AVT program course in Wausau, Wisconsin, roughly forty-five miles west of the Stockbridge-Munsee community. Where his journey would take him from there was unknown, but however desperate he might have been, an array of previous off-reservation experiences must have engendered some confidence. Born in 1934, Miller grew up in Bowler, Wisconsin, where he lettered in basketball and baseball at the local high school. Upon graduation in May 1952, he joined the United States Air Force and served four years as staff sergeant in the Strategic Air Command, where he split time between various bases in the United States and England. Immediately upon his honorable discharge, he enrolled in a special electronics course at Keesler Air Force Base in Biloxi, Mississippi. Upon completion, rather than return home to his Stockbridge-Munsee community, he elected to join the UAW-CIO Local 348 in booming Milwaukee and landed a position with Allen-Bradley Company as a machine operator and maker of electronic resistors and control boxes.[2]

While Myron Jr. traveled far and wide developing his technician skills, his father remained an important fixture within his Stockbridge community, where he was born in 1898. Myron Miller Sr. worked as a state conservation department aide and enjoyed a local reputation as a master hunter and woodsman, who possessed a howl resembling that of a great horned owl. Indeed, one news reporter claimed that in addition to knowing the Stockbridge reservation "better than most men know their basements," Myron Sr. could "cover incredible distances in absolute darkness" and "read animal signs as other men read books." Thus, the senior Myron Miller pursued unparalleled local knowledge and a most intimate familiarity with his Indigenous community's place while his son looked ever outward, daring to breach potential new places of excitement and belonging—and being Indian. In this way, father and son in tandem reflected a generational trend typical not only of numerous Native American people but of thousands of rural people, regardless of race and ethnicity, dating back to the late nineteenth century.[3]

When the BIA accepted Myron Miller Jr.'s AVT program application and enrolled him in an electronics program, it amounted to less a rupture in his life trajectory than a continuation of a pattern he had established through autonomous efforts. The principal innovation came with the BIA's financial and programmatic support. At the Wausau Adult & Vocational Training School, Miller took courses in electronic drafting, math, psychology, economics, government, and AM radio. He earned all As and Bs, while his new bride excelled in her nursing courses. In support of Miller's training, the BIA awarded him hundreds of dollars for subsistence, tuition, and a stack of required textbooks, including *Math Essential to Electricity and Radio, American Politics, Political Science*, and a *Basic TV* lab manual. The program paid off. In May 1960, the Sperry Rand Corporation offered Miller a position paying $364 per month—in Philadelphia, Pennsylvania. Despite the distance, he did not balk at the opportunity. At 5:30 P.M. on June 9, 1960, Miller, along with his wife and newborn daughter, climbed into their 1956 Ford Tudor and set a course toward the birthplace of American independence.[4]

Myron E. Miller Jr. was one among thousands of young Natives who migrated to survive in America's new postwar landscape. When the Bureau of Indian Affairs offered a potential way out of the very socioeconomic predicament it proved instrumental in creating, thousands of Native Americans accepted the challenge. A total of 20,433 Indians migrated through the Voluntary Relocation Program during its first six years of operation, prior to the introduction of the Adult Vocational Training program in which Miller enrolled.[5] To be sure, not all participants were enthusiastic about relocating; many felt they had no other options for a better, or even stable, future. Others coveted new social, educational, and work opportunities. Of course, few sweeping generalizations apply to Native Americans from one period, place, or nation to the next. One that does, however, is that Native peoples, throughout their histories, did not tolerate or advocate isolationism or provincialism. Their collective histories demonstrate an enduring embrace of cosmopolitanism and a propensity for looking not only inward but outward. Across space and time, Indian nations included people in the world and also *of* the world.

This chapter deemphasizes statistical and program analyses in favor of more vibrant stories of Indian migrants' experiences "going on relocation," while stressing Indian initiative in real time. It focuses on Indian people in motion, going to work, breaching cultural boundaries, and seeking social mobility through spatial mobility. Indeed, a more nuanced understanding of Indian urban relocation can be achieved by focusing less on program mechanics and more on the human participants, whose lives deserve greater attention. Heretofore unused employment assistance applications and case files enable a more intimate understanding of what Native people found at stake in going on relocation. As well, handwritten letters that Native people sent to relocation officers in hopes that the program would lift them from dire socioeconomic conditions are especially revealing and, at times, rather heartbreaking. Just as the handwritten letters that inspired historian Brenda Child's study of boarding school students revealed a richer understanding of a comparably complicated and rightly maligned program to encourage Indian assimilation, the same is true of the relocation program. The picture that individual case files and handwritten letters produce is one of prevailing Indian initiative, fueled by Indians' own aspirations for their futures. This resulted in a program that took on a life of its own, notwithstanding its temporal relationship to the Indian bureau's disastrous attempt to terminate tribal sovereignty and erode Indian cultural distinctiveness against the backdrop of America's Cold War. Indeed, while federal policy makers linked termination and relocation, self-motivated Indians de-linked the programs. Some Native people even sought to strengthen reservation economies and thus totally contradict the termination policy's goals.[6]

· · · · · ·

In 1950, the BIA launched a pilot relocation placement program at its Aberdeen, South Dakota, and Muskogee, Oklahoma, agencies. On New Year's Day 1952, satisfied with the pilot program's results, the bureau officially inaugurated its national program by opening field relocation offices in Chicago, Salt Lake City, Denver, San Francisco, and San Jose. In 1957, the BIA expanded the program to include an AVT program counterpart that filtered Indian migrants through urban vocational training programs before releasing them into the general metropolitan workforce. That same year, the Branch of Relocation Services' total personnel increased from 90 to 240, while the number of reservation agency relocation offices increased from 14 to 41. Indicating the program's protean range of destinations, in 1958 six field relocation offices expanded to twelve, with new offices in Oakland, Dallas, Cincinnati, and Cleveland, as well as two experimental offices in smaller suburban locales: Joliet and Waukegan, Illinois. The Joliet, Waukegan, and Cincinnati offices failed to gain much traction, however, and all three closed within a few years.[7]

Indeed, the program often proved unpredictable, as it continually expanded and contracted area offices in alternating fashion, thus rendering what began as a negotiated process even more inconsistent. Not unlike individual Native people who went on relocation, however, this reflected the BIA's continuous effort to chase the best possible destinations based on local employment and housing prospects. For example, even after the Minneapolis area relocation office indefinitely suspended activities in July 1954, daily requests for relocation assistance continued pouring in from Indians who arrived in the Twin Cities without benefit of bureau support. The BIA simply referred them to the U.S. Employment Service, while the area relocation director pressured his superiors to reopen the Minneapolis office. Meanwhile, during May 1955, the pending arrival of warm weather resulted in many Indians withdrawing their applications altogether or asking that they be put on hold until fall. This reflected a decrease in unemployment rates typical of Minnesota during the summer. By that point, the BIA was considering reopening the Minneapolis office, but it now worried that it lacked a sufficient number of prospective migrants to make use of potential funds. At the end of the month, however, applications inexplicably began pouring in—more, in fact, than the BIA could process or fund. "From the backlog of inquiries, we may assume that Indians of this jurisdiction have developed a great interest in this program," the Leech Lake reservation superintendent concluded. Finally caught up and prepared to meet area Indians' needs, the BIA reopened the Minneapolis office in October 1955.[8]

Notwithstanding such inconsistencies, administrators worked hard to realize the program's avowed objective of assisting Native people's efforts "to become self-supporting on a standard of living conducive to economic security and to become a part of the economic and social life of the nation." The Gallup, New Mexico, area office provides a useful example of how the relocation process unfolded at the local level. Program officers in Gallup typically interviewed Navajo people interested in relocation and helped them choose a destination based on both their individual work experience and the currently available work opportunities in prospective cities. Once awarded relocation assistance, the Navajo individual or family in question would submit to a physical exam and produce supporting documents, such as birth certificates, social security cards, military service discharge papers, and marriage certificates. From there, a departure date would be established, and individuals or families would prepare to leave. On the Navajo and other reservations that lacked adequate infrastructure, office personnel typically collected a departing family right from their home and drove them to the bus or train station. Before leaving, the relocation officer also provided an individual or a family with a small amount of cash for food en route to the city, and then to rent a hotel room upon arrival.[9]

At the national level, BIA representatives began hosting informational sessions and hanging bright posters featuring homes furnished with radios, televisions, and refrigerators around various reservation offices. "They are available to families now! See your Relocation Officer," one poster enthused.[10] An Indian bureau presentation to the Navajo boasted that Indians in Chicago "live like kings and have apartments with sewerage."[11] More condescendingly, the cover illustration for a Billings area relocation services pamphlet depicted the arm of "DESPAIR" pushing down on an Indian man wrapped in a blanket emblazoned with the words "Hunger & Cold." "Stuck in Your Tepee?" the caption prodded, "A Way Out Through Relocation Services for Heap-a-lot of living."[12] Such promotional materials failed to mention that jobs were not guaranteed, housing was often substandard, BIA

"To Los Angeles." Box 1, folder 4: Great Lakes Agency, BIA Relocation Records, Edward E. Ayer Manuscript Collection, Newberry Library, Chicago.

services might not be available, and weekly stipends frequently proved insufficient.

It is difficult to overstate the particularly patronizing and paternalistic tone of a twenty-one page informational booklet that the BIA designed for Native people interested in the relocation program. Indeed, the booklet suggests that BIA personnel still thought of their Indian charges as children, even after a substantial number had fought and worked valiantly on behalf of America's successful World War II effort. The booklet's central protagonist appears as a rather odd composite of Warner Brothers' then popular Porky Pig cartoon character and a Mohawk brave, who leads readers through a series of replies to hypothetical questions about the program. "Maybe you have found that around here you can only work a few months each year, and that during the other months, there is no work," the booklet begins. "That is the reason why Field Relocation Offices were started in the larger cities—because there are jobs there all year round."[13]

After discussing the application process and the types of questions prospective relocatees should be prepared to answer, the booklet arrives at a page with the cartoon brave in a medical examination room having his

"Departing for relocation" (December 1956), unidentified family. Box 1, folder 15: Pierre, SD, Agency, BIA Relocation Records, Edward E. Ayer Manuscript Collection, Newberry Library, Chicago.

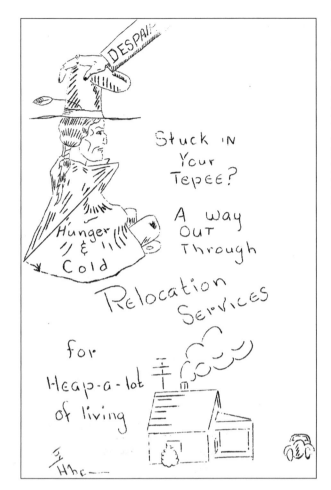

"Stuck in your tepee?" Box 17, folder, "Reports, 1951," "Vocational and Subject Case Files, 1951–1960," RG75, BIA Billings Area Office, National Archives, Rocky Mountain Region, Denver, Colorado.

blood pressure read: "This too is done only to protect you. When you get to your new location, you must be physically able to work." It further explains, "Your wife must be able to take care of the family, so she, too, must have a physical examination." The next page features the now clearly confused brave with dilated pupils and a series of question marks hovering above his head as he browses a rash of needed documents: social security card, marriage certificate, military discharge papers, and birth certificate.[14]

Having successfully passed the application and preparation stage, the cartoon brave, now donning pressed slacks and necktie, boards a train and waves goodbye to his people. Relocating families were allowed to ship up to a thousand pounds of personal belongings, which a relocation officer would be willing to help them select for the journey. Depending on arrival time, families were to go to a preselected hotel or straight to the destination's relocation office, where they would receive instructions on local bus routes and tips on how to hail a taxicab. Either way, the booklet promises, "There is one thing of which you can be sure—you will find a friendly welcome."

Settled into his new surroundings, the cartoon brave—now donning overalls and workboots, and inexplicably much more muscular than before but still with a feather darting upward from his Mohawk—heads to work, firmly gripping his lunchbox. The booklet promises a rewarding job but confesses that the market is competitive: "It may take several tries before you get a job. Remember, there are always several people after jobs, so you have to look your best and **really try** to get a job. If you are not hired, go back to the office and try again—and REMEMBER—NO ONE HAS YET FAILED TO GET A JOB—AND YOU WILL GET ONE."[15]

Of course the booklet warns prospective relocatees that they will need to be thrifty in order to survive in the city. In this section, the cartoon brave appears with his pants pockets turned inside-out, hands outstretched, shoulders shrugging, and a new thought bubble above his head containing the following symbols: "$$??!" His muscles have noticeably atrophied, and he cannot hide his distended belly. The message must have been clear: cling to your cash in the city!

Perhaps the final cartoon frame most succinctly captures the BIA's comprehensive vision of how relocation should unfold and what the entire process could amount to. The relocated brave now faces a stairway, with each step containing the following inscription from the bottom up: low income, seasonal jobs, desire for change, sincerity, careful planning, good work habits, educational opportunities, better jobs, better housing. Reaching the top step depended on the cartoon brave's own agency. He stares at the stairway, stroking his chin, contemplating that first step, with that ever-present thought bubble hovering above his head like a cloud of confusion: "??!!" Did he ever reach the top step? The booklet concludes with a disconcerting mixed message: "ONE FINAL WORD, RELOCATING IS NOT EASY. Relocation Services can help only those who help themselves! We wish you GOOD LUCK and we hope you like your NEW HOME." One can only imagine the thoughts of a Native individual who browsed this tediously didactic booklet. Did it appear patronizing? Promising? Both? Above all, the booklet suggested that successful relocations and Indian economic improvement depended on transformations writ large (character, race, and environment) and small (thrift and attitude). It certainly did not suggest that Indians could remain Indian within the urban experience.[16]

"It may take several tries before you get a job," *Information about Relocation Services*, box 27, folder 13, Sophie Aberle Papers, Center for Southwest Research, University Libraries, University of New Mexico.

In related fashion, the St. Louis relocation field office disseminated to prospective relocatees a panoramic brochure that boasted the myriad attractions waiting in the "Gateway to the West," through which famed explorers Lewis and Clark also once passed in search of a wider America. Included within the brochure were photos of massive suburban shopping centers, "pretty girls" dancing at the Muny Opera, sun bears swimming at the zoo, a chimpanzee jazz band performing at Forest Park, the colorful Missouri Botanical Garden, and Stan "the Man" Musial swinging for the fences at Busch Stadium. Taken together, the photos portrayed urban modernity and all its cultural curiosities.[17]

"Relocating is not easy," *Information about Relocation Services*, box 27, folder 13, Sophie Aberle Papers, Center for Southwest Research, University Libraries, University of New Mexico.

For some, the St. Louis brochure likely intimidated just as much as it attracted. As Coll Thrush discusses in his study of Indigenous people in Geor-
gian London, Western people's overt display of metropolitan splendor and
spectacle is an age-old colonization strategy intended to overwhelm supposedly "primitive rubes" into submission.[18] Yet although a significant number of Native people did experience profound culture shock upon arriving
in the city, which sometimes resulted in terrible tragedy (as chapter 5 will
discuss), the BIA exaggerated the amount of paternal hand-holding that

BETTER HOUSING

BETTER JOBS

EDUCATIONAL OPPORTUNITIES

GOOD WORK HABITS

CAREFUL PLANNING

SINCERITY

DESIRE FOR CHANGE

SEASONAL JOBS

LOW INCOME

??!!

"Relocation services can help only those who help themselves!" *Information about Relocation Services,* box 27, folder 13, Sophie Aberle Papers, Center for Southwest Research, University Libraries, University of New Mexico.

many migrating Indians needed when they solicited and accepted relocation assistance.

Relocation officers did not limit their recruitment venues to those of reservation agencies. Boarding schools continued functioning as a sort of rotary that spun Native graduates outward toward unpredictable but typically urban destinations. For example, in Utah, Brigham City's Intermountain Indian School—the largest BIA-operated off-reservation school of the 1950s—provides an illustrative example of this process. Between the school's first graduating class in 1953 and the winter of 1957, a total of 714 graduates had achieved placement in urban employment positions, with an estimated 200 more set to graduate at the end of spring semester 1958. The graduates mostly emerged from a special program designed for Navajo students, in which they typically learned one trade alongside the English language. In fact, the school provided its own relocation officer in Jack Womeldorf. As an example of his efforts on behalf of graduating students, Womeldorf once wrote to field agent Rudolph Russell at the BIA's new relocation office in faraway Joliet, Illinois, to see if Russell could find work in and around Chicagoland for fifty-seven Navajo boys. To support his inquiry, Womeldorf prepared a brief statistical overview and photo album for each of the boys in question. The album included snapshots of Navajo students working on cars, operating machinery in a metal shop, and studying an anatomical map of a milch cow, thereby implying their preparedness for vocational labor positions.[19]

As part of a newspaper story that interviewed Intermountain students on why they elected to attend a school so far away from their Navajo homes, John B. Helen claimed, "When I saw boys and girls come back from school in the spring they looked so nice." Chiming in, Joe R. Lee insisted, "No one told me to go, I decided myself to go this fall." Likewise, Ruth Denetclaw elaborated:

> I didn't know why I left the reservation until I came to Intermountain. Now I know why I left the reservation. It is because I wanted to have an education. I left the reservation so my kids will not have the same kind of life that I have had. Now our people are having a hard time and there are not many jobs on the reservation for all the Navajo people. They just don't have much food to feed their children, and there are not much water or grass for the animals. I want my life to be better than this.[20]

Relocation officials often directed their recruitment efforts and recommendations for urban adjustment at Indian mothers and wives. This reflects an extension of 1950s Cold War motherhood, in which American women were expected to create a tranquil home atmosphere where hardworking husbands could rest their feet after an exhausting shift battling communism.[21] For example, a counseling manual designed for relocation officers in Chicago suggested, "After decision has been made by the family to relocate, the wife should be discouraged from starting new allegiances or community ties such as acceptance of a job, membership on a committee or any other activities which would strengthen her desire to stay in the community." Relocation program architects expected women to serve as both household supervisors and as model representatives of the program's most ambitious goals. Relocation officers also advised Native women to manage the family budget, nurture friendships with neighbors, and stimulate their

"Mrs. Jose Ortiz walking her daughter alongside white woman," box 2, folder 24, BIA Relocation Records, Edward E. Ayer Manuscript Collection, Newberry Library, Chicago.

children's "interest in the adventure of new experiences." Moreover, they needed to aspire to an immaculate household. Finally, relocation officers emphasized the value of a tidy abode on grounds that it "relates to community recognition of the family and its influence in the family's acceptance in the new community."[22]

Program representatives not only expected Native women to facilitate good relations with fellow community members and with their children's school; they also expected Native women to safeguard the family against the big city's most unsavory characters. For example, the Chicago relocation manual encouraged field representatives to inculcate a certain degree of suspicion and vigilance within Native women: "DO watch for pickpockets"; "DO carry proper identification"; "Don't sign any papers without the advice of someone who is a reputable person in the community, such as ministers, employment advisors, etc."[23] At times, such warnings must have

"Billie family on sofa," box 2, folder 24, BIA Relocation Records, Edward E. Ayer Manuscript Collection, Newberry Library, Chicago.

made an impression. For example, Mrs. Atone, a Kiowa woman who worked for a Texas A&M program that dispatched home visitors to teach urban Indian women about nutrition, hygiene, and other housekeeping skills, recalled an experience with a Navajo housewife living in Dallas: "She told me that if I had not been an Indian she would not have let me in. . . . People feel that you will understand them if you are Indian."[24]

At the same time, while the BIA admitted that the big city could be a frightening place, it also tried to entice women with the promise that they would personally benefit from escaping what it perceived as the drudgery of reservation life. "The wife (homemaker) benefits from the added comforts and conveniences in the urban area where better housing with modern utilities is available," a BIA relocation manual from 1960 suggested. The same manual encouraged relocation officers to convince Indian women that modern appliances and hot running water available in cities would significantly reduce their daily workload.[25] To be sure, not all Native people needed to be persuaded on such matters. For example, Catherine Cloud (Assiniboine) told her area relocation officer that she wanted to leave her reservation because "she didn't care to haul water anymore or build fires in this cold weather." Furthermore, revealing some prior experience in an urban setting, Cloud claimed that she was "used to the facilities they have in the cities and likes that way of living."[26]

Because relocation officers often made unannounced visits to check up on migrated families, Native women had to constantly be on their toes— keeping their homes clean and their children behaved. When relocation officers dropped in on the Carson family's Cincinnati household, they found Mrs. Carson and her three children at home (Mr. Carson was downtown cashing his salary check). Mrs. Carson had no reason to worry (though she might have). Her house appeared clean, and the sparkling new furniture and television occupying the family room must have delighted the visiting team of agents. Indeed, Mr. Carson did not allow a disabled arm to prevent him from earning $125 on forty-four hours of work per week at the Heekin Can Company. The family managed its finances to the relocation office's satisfaction, putting away ten dollars each payday. Mrs. Carson had also managed to save $100 of her own money. The visiting BIA personnel were so impressed that they took six pictures of the Carsons with plans to promote the family as a model of success. It must, however, be noted that the family's "success" came at a cost that the visiting BIA agents might not have fully appreciated. One bureau representative noticed that the three children all spoke English. Indeed, Mrs. Carson explained, they could no longer speak their native Navajo.[27]

The Cincinnati relocation office's visit with the Whitehorse family failed to deliver a similar model of success. In fact, the Whitehorse family could barely make ends meet. Trying to do her part, Mrs. Whitehorse worked tenaciously to finish a nursing course by the end of the year so that she could supplement the family's income. This proved an especially vital concern because Mr. Whitehorse had recently been hospitalized. When healthy, Mr. Whitehorse worked as an X-ray technician at Christ Hospital. The Whitehorses occupied a nice home across from Xavier University, but they struggled to pay a high rent that slowly drained their finances. Still, Mrs. Whitehorse refused to move because "the less the rent, the poorer the neighborhood and environment, and she would not want to subject her children to a poor environment." Should it become necessary, she promised to "sacrifice other items" in order to remain. The next day, the Cincinnati relocation team visited Mr. Whitehorse in the hospital, at which point he mentioned that he was having trouble with a collection agency that was garnishing his wages for an unpaid furniture bill that he co-signed for a fellow relocatee who had split for the army. Needless to say, the White-horse family had by that point failed to achieve success comparable to that of the Carson family, but not for a lack of effort. Even as it descended into economic crisis, the Whitehorse family fought to hold its ground and make its situation tenable, not unlike its fellow Native relations who during decades prior refused to give up on rural Indian Country.[28]

· · · · · ·

BIA overtures about relocation's promise notwithstanding, Native people established their own motives for pursuing opportunities in cities. At times these motives overlapped with the relocation program's stated goals, while at other times they reflected the subjective desires of individual Indians, whose life experiences may or may not have prepared them for urban living. Some Indian urban migrants built on the earlier generation's premium on Indian racial uplift. Others responded to more immediate circumstances at home and sought to escape a potentially ruinous personal situation. In many cases, such push and pull factors could merge into one powerful rationale for seeking a better future far away from home.

Perhaps most indicative of Indian attitudes toward relocation and what Native people felt was at stake in seeking opportunities away from home are handwritten letters that several Indians sent directly to their respective relocation officers in request of assistance. "I have been unable to find any type of steady employment in Ponca City and must depend on odd jobs for a livlihood [sic]," wrote Arnold Conrad (Ponca). Admitting that he was blind in one eye, he claimed, "I am otherwise in good health and able to do most any type of manual labor." Conrad had been working as a day laborer unloading crate cars and furniture vans. "I am 29 years old, single, and can take work in any locality," he insisted.[29] Hannah Dodson's (Ponca) letter made sure to specify exactly where she wanted to go: "We are just willing to go to Los Angeles Calif. Where it is warmer we don't have enough clothes for Colorado [sic]. Please help us and get us out of Oklahoma. We both have nothing."[30] Fred Henderson (Pawnee) wrote, "We are wanting to go on relocation work but not at Colorado but to St. Louis Missouri if we can get the kind of work we want."[31] George Wolf hoped relocation would provide a path toward higher education upon his release from the army. He was specifically interested in a career as a mechanic or ranch manager. "Will you please send me all the information you have about the educational benefits for Indian students under the relocation program?" he wrote his area officer.[32] Finally, Edgar Hillman (Ponca), a disabled veteran with a child on the way, specifically wanted to go to Denver, Oklahoma City, or Omaha. "I can learn any kind of work," he insisted.[33]

In 1953, one single mother brought her three children with her on relocation from the Mesquakie settlement in Tama, Iowa, to Chicago's Hyde Park neighborhood. She specifically lobbied for relocation to Chicago because it was the nearest major relocation center to her tribal home and she had heard that it featured the best employment prospects. Sure enough, she found employment in a bakery and, in time, advanced to the position of supervisor. When asked to give advice to other Native people considering relocation, she offered, "They should make up their minds to stick to their jobs, be dependable, and give themselves a chance before giving up," and they should practice "the ability to get along with all kinds of people."[34]

Not only did Native people often play a proactive role in requesting relocation assistance, but many disappointed relocatees took every opportunity to criticize the program when it failed to meet their expectations. Charles Willing (Umpqua) moved from Oregon to Los Angeles, where a relocation officer promised him two years of schooling. When that promise fell through, Willing wrote the Indian bureau to complain that the devious relocation officer was "harder to hold than a greased pig."[35] A second Native man from Oregon insisted that his relocation office misled him about the amount of job training he would receive: "Now I am 'high and dry' in Denver with a sick youngster and my savings gone. It is a crime the way these people operate and always have operated."[36] In a final example, Indians from Oklahoma who struggled to find work in Dallas vociferously criticized their field office's lack of support. Taking matters into their own hands, roughly two hundred of them organized the Intertribal Club in a West Dallas housing project to help one another cope with unemployment and alcoholism.[37]

In a bold attempt to repair their lives, some applicants embraced relocation as a unique opportunity to escape problems that haunted them at home. For example, a disabled Kiowa military veteran expressed his desire to go on relocation in order to overcome alcoholism, earn a steady paycheck, and potentially remove his five children from foster care. Having already attempted relocation twice before, he confessed in writing, "Things did not work out for me so well at that time due to my own fault. The relocation office in Oakland did everything possible to help me. I realize now that I must be man enough to carry out and do the things that are right."[38]

Similarly, in 1959, Lewis Carter—an Assiniboine member of Montana's Fort Peck tribe—sent a handwritten letter to Chicago's relocation director, Mrs. King, that included a few questions about the program she administered. A Korean War veteran, Carter had pursued a series of temporary jobs that took him all the way to Indiana and back, but he struggled to land anything permanent due to a lack of required education and experience. He tried to enroll in the relocation program at his reservation office in Montana but, paradoxically, failed to meet a six-month steady residence requirement—he had no home there to speak of. Indeed, it appears that Mr. Carter carried with him a troubled past. "Mrs. King, I'm a veteran of the Korean War, however, I'm not proud of my record," he confessed in his letter. Following an "Undesirable Discharge," Carter took work in California and Idaho—"any type of Labor work I could find"—before arriving in the faraway Hoosier State. He begged Mrs. King to help him, while pleading that he is a "family man" who lacked a means of support on his home reservation.[39]

In another example, while applying for relocation in 1963, a Ponca man named Nathaniel Johnson wrote, "Although I and my wife went on it in 1956, which we eventually came home, but I realize now the mistake I done since then, which now, I want very much to better myself." Johnson then proceeded to confess that he had since served time in the Oklahoma State Penitentiary in McAlester. One can surmise that Johnson, knowing that his criminal past would weigh negatively in the minds of relocation officials charged with deciding his fate, had an incentive to own his mistakes and adopt a submissive tone. Read from a different perspective, there is perhaps no stronger evidence that relocation often amounted to so much more than a dead end that ground urban hopefuls down to a victimized pulp. For Nathaniel Johnson, a second chance at relocation could be his salvation, or so he believed when he penned his application's personal statement. Johnson's example, alongside the others in the foregoing section, runs counter to the often-mentioned fact that a substantial number of relocated Indians immediately returned home. It suggests that, for those who needed it, the adjustment process could be prolonged, that struggling relocatees at times blamed themselves just as much as the system, and that those who did return home were not necessarily so scarred from the experience that they felt too embarrassed or defeated to try again.[40]

· · · · · ·

Either unaware of potential program flaws, desperate enough to confront them head on, or confident enough in their ability to overcome them, thousands of Indians continued applying for relocation while countless others self-relocated without benefit of Indian bureau support. From 1945 to 1957, the year the BIA introduced its new AVT program component to its urban relocation program, roughly 100,000 Native people had migrated from reservations to cities. Roughly three-quarters among them migrated with no government assistance.[41] In 1960, almost a decade into the program, Oklahoma City featured the highest urban Indian population in the country. Yet Oklahoma City was not a federal relocation program destination; neither were Tulsa or New York City, which featured the fourth and fifth highest urban Indian populations.[42]

Within the federal program, numerous applicants exhibited enthusiasm for the new opportunity and some, such as Chicago migrant Ben Bearskin (Winnebago), revealed the influence of a generation gap: "They've kept the old folks as museum pieces, through ignorance and idleness, but we young Indians are going to free ourselves by education and work."[43] Tinker Air Force Base employee Fred Tsoodle (Kiowa) dismissed any notion of Native people sacrificing their culture in exchange for mainstream American citizenship. "We can be good Americans, making a decent living and still keep our Indian culture," he stressed. Tsoodle placed responsibility for success or failure directly in Indians' hands: "They'll have to do it themselves. They have to adjust . . . buckle down. It's within ourselves."[44] Likewise, Los Angeles–based Lockheed Company bookkeeper Patricia McGee (Yavapai) stated, "Whether we Indians make the grade in the city depends on the individual."[45] Finally, Korean War veteran Alfred Boneshirt (Lakota) and his wife, Mary Sue, regularly migrated back and forth between Colorado, Nebraska, and their home in South Dakota in pursuit of jobs during the 1950s and 1960s. When asked about their future plans, Mary Sue simply responded, "I think what we want to do is work."[46]

Rather than dismiss Indian cultural values as an impediment to success in mainstream America, some relocation advocates harnessed their cultural tradition as a source of strength. Former Indian Reorganization Act field agent and military police officer Benjamin Reifel (Sioux), who in 1956 became the first Native person to serve as superintendent of Pine Ridge Agency, encouraged his Indian constituents to be optimistic and resist defeatism that stemmed from prolonged dependence on the BIA. He advocated a "change of attitude for Indians to make the cultural adaptation necessary to function within the economic and social systems of the mainstream society." Further, he equated the Lakota people's tradition of bravery with the necessary qualities to succeed beyond the reservation's limits when he told his constituents to "be proud" and "think of Red Cloud and Crazy Horse."[47]

To be sure, enthusiasm for new surroundings and an appeal to stereotypes of Indian bravery could only carry a family so far once the realities of a capricious wage-labor market, urban congestion, language barriers, and geographic distance, among other hazards, manifested. Still, unemployment, alcoholism, and a retreat back to the reservation were not the only potential outcomes for hopeful Indian migrants. Indeed, many relocatees achieved varying degrees of success on relocation. If they struggled, it was not necessarily with the idea of working and living in the city. Their relative triumphs and tragedies reflected diverse socioeconomic strata among Indians before relocation as well as divergent goals upon arrival.

When a relocation counselor visited the Morrises one July afternoon in Los Angeles, she found the family's four children gathered around a new television to watch a children's program. Each morning Mr. Morris drove a 1950 Studebaker to the Chrysler Corporation, where he worked. The family occasionally attended the drive-in theater together, and Mrs. Morris expressed pride in her new sewing machine. The family's real dream, however, was to purchase their own home, toward which Mr. Morris contemplated putting his GI Bill loan.[48]

Similarly, a relocation officer who checked in on the Blake family in San Francisco concluded that they were well adjusted and happy. Earl Blake had landed a position with the State Harbor Commission after Buzell Electric Company laid him off. In their leisure time, he and his wife enjoyed serving on the San Francisco Indian Center Picnic Committee, and they also met every Monday night with a local square dance group. After each session, the square dance group would attend dinner together at a nice restaurant. Matching their parents' success, the three Blake boys were all excelling in their new community. The first served in the navy, the second attended electric welding school, and the third split time between ROTC and the high school debate team while landing on the high honor roll. The third son also washed cars on the weekend for extra spending money and helped his mother wash dishes at the Indian center. Mr. Blake admitted that the family was occasionally "homesick" for Montana, but noted that it didn't "take long for it to wear off."[49]

In a comparable example that the BIA likely embraced as a model of "success," Gary Lawrence wrote from his Bell Gardens, California, home to assure his relocation officer on the Sisseton Dakota reservation that he and his wife were "coming along just great" at their new place of residence. In fact, Lawrence confessed, "I only wish I would have come sooner." The family benefited from Lawrence's job working on cars at the Chrysler Corporation, a job that he had "always wanted." He also mentioned that he and his wife enjoyed the weather, and that he preferred walking to work. Lawrence was earning $2.08 an hour and predicted a pay bump to $2.17 an hour soon. "I know I couldn't beat that anywhere around there," he asserted. Lawrence did admit that his wife was scared to walk around downtown Los Angeles, before concluding, "I guess she will get used to it though."[50]

In a similar relocation experience that the BIA in fact *did* promote as an example of success, Mr. Charley (Apache) moved to Chicago precisely because it was the farthest relocation center from his reservation home in Arizona. Before migrating to Chicago, he had labored as a clerk in a tribal store and, briefly, as a farmer in Pomona, California. His reason for applying for relocation was less a matter of wanting to be in Chicago than a matter of wanting to leave his reservation, which he resented because the tribe repeatedly refused to provide him a loan, which he blamed on a perceived lack of personal "influence" with tribal leaders. That is not to suggest that he did not look forward to seeing the country, a practice he claimed Apache people historically embraced. "The Apaches are wizards in emulating one another in this aspect," he boasted.

In Chicago, Mr. Charley wrestled with two main problems. First, he struggled to master the English language at an adequate pace. Second, he and his family resided in a Chicago public housing project occupied predominantly by African Americans, with whom he failed to get along because they were "always looking for a fight." Although he did not mind his children playing outside with black children, he did impose a strict curfew; the fact that his neighbors did not, especially bothered him. Despite those obstacles, he experienced relative success in Chicago and attended evening college courses on a scholarship. Additionally, the Chicago relocation office handpicked him as a model for relocation success. The office featured Mr. Charley in a short promotional film on relocation to be shown to prospective migrants back on reservations, but it did so in deceptive fashion. Most of Mr. Charley's friends knew that he aspired to be a butcher. So Indian bureau personnel photographed him cutting meat at a local butcher shop. However, Mr. Charley did not actually work at the butcher shop. In fact, he was not a butcher at all. The promotional broadcast also betrayed his struggle to master English (and perhaps a Freudian slip) when Mr. Charley proudly declared, "The relocation program is the ultimatum." Notwithstanding his relative success in the city, Mr. Charley ultimately desired to one day return to his reservation and tell his people that education is "good for anybody"—but not too soon, he explained, lest he be branded a "failure" for returning too quickly.[51]

Even as the relocation program matured, Native people continued influencing its terms and potential for success. For example, via the "moccasin telegraph," Indians who had migrated to California from Montana's Fort Belknap and Rocky Boys Reservation encouraged their tribespeople back home to cancel plans to join them in California during December 1953 because the North American Aviation plant where they labored was in the midst of a heated strike and labor dispute. "Reports from the workers in California continue to be blue and discouraging," Fort Belknap superintendent J. Wellington noted. Adding to Wellington's frustration, Indians from the Fort Belknap reservation tended to migrate according to weather patterns. "The mild winter weather has contributed to a lack of interest for relocation away from the reservation," he reported in February 1954, before explaining that the heavy snows and extreme cold weather during the previous month had only temporarily stimulated his subjects' interest in relocation. During the following month of March, in yet another sudden shift in enthusiasm on the part of prospective relocatees, Wellington became inundated with more relocation applications than available funding could possibly support.[52]

Indeed, no matter the degree to which program officials tried to guide participants with a paternalistic hand, many Indian migrants proved determined to shape relocation according to their own desires. Earl Sargent's experience vividly illustrates this assertion. On September 25, 1959, he and his wife drove their 1952 Ford sedan to the Red Lake Indian Agency to interview for the AVT program. Earl did most of the talking, but his wife made certain to voice her support for their decision to apply. In response to the interviewer's question about what he hoped to gain by enrolling in the program, Earl did not hesitate: "A lifetime career, a skill, something to look forward to so that the family would be able to live off the reservation."[53]

For Earl Sargent, the AVT program represented a way forward, even if the off-reservation world was not exactly uncharted territory. Indeed, he could point to an abundance of experiences in Indian Country, mainstream America, and beyond. Born on Minnesota's Red Lake Chippewa Reservation in 1932, Sargent first underwent vocational training at the age of fourteen when he took one-year courses in carpentry, auto mechanics, masonry, and drafting at South Dakota's Flandreau Indian School, where he competed with the traveling boxing and football teams. At age eighteen, he enlisted for service in the U.S. Army and received an honorable discharge after returning from Korea in 1952. During his service, he took a ten-week training course in engineering at Fort Belvoir, Virginia, and also trained in heavy military equipment. Upon his discharge, Sargent labored as a sawyer for the Marvin Cedar and Lumber door factory in Warroad, Minnesota, but was fired for attempting to unionize the plant. He then returned to Red Lake and worked seasonally with the U.S. Public Health Service. In 1959, he landed a job as a truck driver with a construction outfit based in Brainerd, Minnesota. But after his hours and income declined, he recognized in the AVT program a new opportunity.[54]

In January 1960, the BIA accepted Sargent's application and enrolled him in an auto mechanic training course in Minneapolis. Having lost interest in the program, however, Sargent suddenly quit in May, taking a job with a Minneapolis construction crew that he found through his own efforts. All told, the scorned BIA spent $1609.19 on Sargent's relocation and vocational training and, in return, received a stark reminder that some program participants were intent on guiding their own relocation process to reach their own ends, regardless of BIA intervention.[55]

Despite many Indian urban relocatees' prior off-reservation experiences, tenacious efforts at making it in the city, and strong individual motives for having left in the first place, BIA field relocation officers found it necessary to maintain a high degree of paternalistic oversight. At the local level, however, some BIA officials proved quite sympathetic toward Native people who took a chance on relocation and needed support. This came in the form of food, shelter, clothing, and useful tips for the job market. During the early 1970s, for example, Lee Cook, director of Minnesota Indian Resource Development in the Twin Cities, kept in his desk drawer pairs of black socks, which he would distribute to Native American people who came in seeking job assistance. "[Employers] expect certain kinds of people to come through the door," he explained, "and if you are noticeably Indian, you wear white socks, you don't shake hands, you are dead before you say 'hello.'"[56]

Similarly, a twenty-three-year-old Chippewa man from Stone Lake, Wisconsin, landed a job at Chicago's Republic Steel before leaving Wisconsin. Upon his arrival, the company learned that its new Chippewa employee was "industrially blind" in one eye and subsequently dismissed him. Stepping in, the BIA helped the man purchase new eyeglasses and land a job in the insulating department at Lindberg Engineering. Before long, he had saved enough money to bring his father to Chicago. In time, the father also found steady work, not through the relocation program but through his son's personal connections.[57]

In some instances, Indian relocatees exhausted their supporting funds, thereby threatening their potential for a successful adjustment, before they even arrived at their first scheduled job shift. Relocation field agents would then scramble to conduct triage in hopes of saving the mutual investment. For example, in April 1952, two Indian friends in their late twenties relocated together to Chicago, where they hoped to work at the same company because they "felt strange in Chicago." They successfully landed jobs as mechanics in a photography firm for $50 a week. But the night they arrived in the city, they met with a friend from their reservation, had "a good time," and spent all their money. The next day, one of the men had enough change to make it to his first day of work, while the other called the Chicago relocation office asking for money. Making matters worse, neither had made a down payment on their hotel room. After the men pleaded for another chance, the Chicago office called their employer and talked him into keeping the two men. To help the men get established, the employer agreed to let them draw daily pay, as opposed to weekly pay, and "offered to take a personal interest in the two young men." After three weeks, both men were still employed with zero counts of absenteeism. "At the end of the second week, one of the men proudly showed us his bank book with an initial deposit of $5.00," relocation officer Kurt Dreifuss stated.[58]

Among the Chicago-based institutions with which the Indian bureau contracted to administer technical training for AVT enrollees was the Metropolitan Business College, founded in 1873. Here, relocated Indians could take courses in bookkeeping, clerical work, stenography, and accounting. According to figures for the 1963 school year, eighty Indians were currently enrolled, while thirty-five had completed training that year. Among those thirty-five graduates, thirty-one had found permanent employment in Chicago, twenty-one in their specific field of training. Course lengths ranged from eight months to two years. Regarding course length, a school brochure urged its students to "Be more concerned with what you will get rather than how long it will take!" "Remember," it concludes, "the average American works many years. Preparation is the key which will make your years happy and productive."[59]

More revealing were the school's efforts at teaching Native students exactly how to succeed in "mainstream society," as it encouraged the performance of acceptable gender stereotypes via instructions in proper professional etiquette and attire. Relocated Indians who read the school's welcoming brochure would learn that "the natural, well-bred look is the METROPOLITAN LOOK" and that "Your first impression is a lasting one." Female students were required to wear one-inch minimum heels to class. Excessively long fingernails and "extreme hairstyles" were against the rules, as was excessive makeup. For their part, male students needed to arrive clean-shaven, with shined shoes, pressed trousers, and a shirt and tie. Levi's jeans were absolutely forbidden. Finally, both sexes were expected to demonstrate well-mannered and courteous etiquette because "business demands it."[60]

Notwithstanding such examples of altruistic assistance or heavy-handed paternalism, relocation's lofty promises frequently broke down, and when they did, the help a confounded program official could offer often amounted to a mere vote of confidence or an inspirational platitude. During an interview in 1972, former Denver and Chicago relocation field officer Stanley L. Lyman recalled the measured role he often played in convincing struggling Indians not to surrender hope: "Then much of it was in the form of a pep talk, you know, kind of like sending a replacement into a football game." This suggests that, despite its paternalistic overreach, the BIA to some degree understood that potential success in the city ultimately boiled down to Indian initiative and fortitude. Indeed, Lyman confessed that his relocation offices made a habit of intentionally ignoring newly arrived migrants because that "was the time when this shock of looking at that damn city had to be felt."[61]

Lyman's heuristic approach did not, however, mean that relocation officers were not trained to be especially aggressive when trying to help families navigate the adjustment process. The *Denver Field Relocation Office Operating Manual*, for example, instructed field agents to closely monitor their subjects' job activity and financial planning. Moreover, they were encouraged to conduct several follow-up reports and interviews while pressuring relocated Indians to confide in them, even at the expense of manipulation. "His telling of his experience will make him feel at ease," the manual suggested. "An effort must be made to get his opinion. If the counselor does all the talking, a one-way conversation may ensue in which the relocatee gains nothing from the interview. *Take plenty of time*," it cautioned. "Try to pitch the level of the discussion to the relocatee's background and apparent experience."[62]

The BIA's occasionally forceful method for directing relocatees' adjustment period is perhaps best illustrated by the experiences of Randolph Lussier. During 1958, the BIA awarded Lussier $91 to support his relocation from Minnesota to Los Angeles, where he had been accepted into a dental laboratory technician training program. Shortly before departing, however, he switched to a drafting program at Long Beach City College. On May 5, 1959, Lussier's field relocation officer, George Felshaw, visited Lussier's home on East Fifteenth Street in Long Beach to make a follow-up report. To Felshaw's dismay, he learned that Lussier had mysteriously returned home just four days prior. Piecing together information, Felshaw gathered that his missing subject had been excelling in his training course before becoming upset over his failure to find part-time employment to supplement his school stipend. During Easter vacation, Lussier landed work as a ride operator at Disneyland, but it was not enough to prevent him from returning home. In Lussier's official relocation subject file, Felshaw noted that Lussier was a "chronically dissatisfied person."[63]

Within less than a month, Lussier attempted an about-face when he wrote Felshaw asking for a second chance in Los Angeles. After admonishing Lussier for the manner in which he "simply disappeared," Felshaw arranged to have Long Beach City College take the mercurial man back. Felshaw also demanded that Lussier return with a "positive attitude" and that he provide his own funds for transportation to Long Beach. On June 30, accepting these terms, Lussier arrived in Long Beach, where he resided in a hotel for two weeks before moving into a communal house occupied by fellow vocational training students. Lussier's trajectory provides an important example of how "going on relocation" often encompassed much more than a linear shot from reservation to city. Numerous relocatees counted years of prior off-reservation experience and engaged in multiple migratory attempts before landing in a place that felt right.[64]

Lussier's close relationship with his program supervisor also reflects how relocation officers often acted as personal friends and confidants to Indian people in their care. In fact, official BIA relocation manuals encouraged field agents to behave in such a manner. "If an individual loses his job, the Relocation Officer (Employment) will listen to the relocatee's story in considerable detail," the Denver area operating manual instructed. Not only did relocation officers need to provide a sympathetic ear, but their superiors also expected them to boost migrant Indians' morale if it waned. "The family needs to be proud of themselves in their new environment," the manual suggested. "Help in the proper selection of clothes can insure this pride." Similar to the practices of Carlisle Indian Industrial School administrators from the not-too-distant past, relocation officers were also supposed to document migrated families' or individuals' adjustment through a series of before-and-after pictures, first taken upon arrival and then again three to six months later, when the family or individual would theoretically be settled in and ready to smile for the camera.[65]

Above all, relocation field agents were supposed to assume Indians' lack of facility for city living while nurturing their adjustment, often by soliciting supplemental support from local mutual aid societies and religious groups. For example, between October 1956, when the BIA officially designated St. Louis a relocation center, and February 1958, a total of 375 Indians had migrated to the symbolic Gateway to the West. To assist them, a group of various civic, social, and religious groups formed a base of operations at the Kingdom House, with financial support from the United Fund Agency. To help Native people overcome loneliness in St. Louis, the group sponsored the All-American Indian Club several Saturdays each month at the Kingdom House. St. Louis staff director Charles Coffee admitted that the office's initial policy of keeping relocated families separated in order to expedite assimilation had been shortsighted at best. The office eventually backed away from that policy and allowed the development of Indian communities within larger housing projects. Indeed, Kingdom House director Ralph Koeppe confided, "The most horrible thing that could happen would be if the Indian were swallowed up and didn't retain his heritage. . . . We hope we're never guilty of trying to over-Americanize the original American."[66]

Despite the profound life consequences at stake, relocation officers' daily objectives could border on the mundane, such as taking an Indian family on their first trip to the grocery store. What likely amounted to an exciting experience for Native families that had long been at the mercy of government commodity food and limited options on remote reservations, however, could itself devolve into a frustrating exercise in Indian bureau paternalism. For example, Chicago field relocation officer Joe La Salle escorted a newly arrived family to a grocery store and apparently upset the family's mother when he reached into her cart, removed the chicken she had selected, and instead replaced it with beef. La Salle then lectured the Native mother on how she was not allowed to purchase chicken because it was too expensive—she must only purchase beef. Not stopping there, he then removed a package of cookies from her cart. Cookies were, after all, a luxury. "This is all too fast," the rebuffed mother remarked. As historians Philip Deloria and Alexandra Harmon have noted, destructive and restrictive stereotypes about Native people's propensity for "squandering" money ran rampant throughout the twentieth century. Certainly BIA officials were not immune from allowing such stereotypes to structure their relationships with relocated Indian families.[67]

For Indigenous people from Alaska, urban mainstream America was geographically, and perhaps socially, much farther away. At times the Juneau relocation office ranked as one of the busiest in the nation. Indigenous Alaskans typically filtered through the Seattle Orientation Center, which a newspaper reporter described as a "motel unit near the University of Washington campus." In pursuit of better jobs and social opportunities, Alaskan Natives could be seen walking across campus in heavy parkas, wool pants, and mukluks. Reflecting a condescending attitude toward exotic Yupik and Inuit people, the BIA referred to the Seattle Orientation Center as a "halfway house"; a shopping center near the motel as a "school"; and supermarkets, banks, dime stores, the post office, and drugstore as "textbooks."[68]

Relocation offices across the country were typically understaffed and underfunded. Moreover, because relocation officials often lacked a deep understanding of the unique challenges Native people faced, many Indian urban migrants were truly on their own.[69] Marlene Strouse recalled how her family of Pima people migrated through the relocation program from their tribal home in Arizona to Chicago during 1952. In order to establish residence and employment and thereby make the transition process easier, her father and his best friend left in advance of the larger family. At home on their Pima reservation, Marlene's father could not earn enough money through his position as a farmhand to support his six family members. "And so when they heard about the relocation program, they jumped at it," Marlene explained.[70]

Growing up, Marlene was used to her father being gone as long as six months per year when he harvested wheat in Kansas and Nebraska. This time, however, Marlene would go away with him. After successfully establishing himself in Chicago, her father sent for the whole family. According to Marlene, relocation was "practically a life saver you might say." And to be sure, all credit for the Strouse family's success went to their own hard efforts. When Marlene's family first arrived, they were "practically on [their] own. You were just pushed out there right away, you know . . . sink or swim," Marlene explained. Indeed, her mother initially struggled in Chicago, losing weight and refusing to leave the family's apartment. In time, however, the family made a successful adjustment. Later, Marlene met her husband when he came in for a haircut from Marlene's father, who filled the role of community barber for Indian men in Chicago.[71]

Often overlooked, such examples of individual and family resolve regarding relocation proliferate across space, time, and tribal lines. In 1969, a Cheyenne veteran police officer in Dallas told sociologist James Goodner, "I came from a town of about three hundred, and that was when you counted all the dogs and cows. Here you just do like the Romans and you'll make it."[72] Likewise, according to a Native woman who migrated from Oklahoma to Dallas, "At home we were isolated by tribes and we get along fine. But here we search for each other. My husband drives a bread truck and if he sees an Indian he will go around the block and search him out."[73]

Roughly half of the 1,487 relocated Navajo surveyed for a 1957 report sponsored by the Navajo tribal council mentioned that they struggled to adjust in their new places of residence, and many felt compelled to return after only a short period. Yet their reasons for returning proved as diverse as their reasons for leaving. In fact, no single reason for return accounted for more than 5 percent of all survey responses. Reasons given can mostly be categorized as subjective and complicated. For example, one Navajo man insisted on walking to work each day. But after developing a terrible case of blisters, he hopped into a car with a friend headed home to the Navajo reservation, rested his feet for a brief period, and then returned to the city ready to try again. In a second, possibly apocryphal and at the very least exaggerated example, a Navajo man encountered a crisis after being asked to work the graveyard shift at his job. A Navajo cultural fear of the dead supposedly resulted in him telling his employer that he "wanted no part of any graveyard." In a final, more plausible example, a Navajo man became terribly sick in Chicago and, as a result of being bedridden for a protracted period, began running out of money. Afraid he would become stuck in Chicago with no lifeline, he returned to Gallup, but not before expressing an ambition to return to the Windy City when healthy. In fact, he personally wrote the Chicago relocation office staff to assure them of his resolve: "I really did like my job and I like the town of Chicago. I like to go back there again some time. I would have stayed if I have gotten over my illness in less time that I did. I am sorry it happen that way [sic]."

Indeed, supposed "failure" in the city did not necessarily result in failure upon returning home. For example, the same Navajo Tribal Council report mentions a Navajo man who spoke very little English and had virtually no work experience but, through his "determination," somehow gained programmatic support for relocation to Chicago. Within six months, he was back home on the Navajo reservation but not defeated. Rather, the report praised him as a "considerably more knowledgeable person," who immediately secured work at a reservation uranium mill—a position that the report's author insists he could not have gained without off-reservation work experience. "For a goodly number of those who have returned," the report suggested, "relocation, although temporary, has been the equivalent of a short course in modern living."[74]

Of course, not every relocated individual or family necessarily intended to stay permanently in the city. Some Native people had already orchestrated their eventual return *prior* to leaving home. For example, in 1963, Carl Larson (Aleut), his wife Dorothy (Yupik), and their three children migrated all the way to Chicago from Anchorage, Alaska. An army veteran who worked in Alaska as an angler, bus driver, and mail carrier, Carl began taking electronic technician courses upon his arrival in the Second City. Rather than remain in Chicago permanently, however, he planned to migrate back to Alaska and open a television repair shop. Thirty-six hundred miles from their Alaskan home, the Larsons from the outset understood their journey as a transient opportunity to improve their education and economic standing not for a life in Chicago but for one back home, among their people in Alaska.[75]

Similarly, when St. Louis relocation officers went to check up on the Millers, they found a seemingly content Meskwaki family occupying a four-bedroom apartment. Mr. Miller was holding down a steady job at McDonnell Aircraft, earning $2.43 an hour. Still, Mrs. Miller claimed that relocation was "only a temporary thing as home will always be Tama, Iowa." She explained that the family would return to Iowa as soon as their two daughters graduated high school. Her daughters objected, however, and told the relocation officers that they wanted to stay in St. Louis. But Mrs. Miller insisted that the "city is too crowded," thus suggesting an emerging generational divide.[76]

Native people who persisted in the city and remained determined to succeed often faced more than just a competitive job market and the occasionally condescending attitudes of BIA representatives. In many instances, they were met with frustrating, even painful, stereotypes about their character and expectations for their behavior.[77] "Group discipline" marked one strategy that some urban Indians deployed in an effort to rehabilitate non-Indians' negative assumptions. For example, in an effort to overturn stereotypes, a Native dance group in Dallas did not allow its members to drink alcohol at events. "We don't want people thinking that we are just a bunch of drunken Indians," their leader stressed.[78]

Still, despite Native people's better efforts, a system of negative stereotypes about Indians manifested in mainstream America long before Indians arrived in cities on a mission to overturn them. An article titled "A Brave Move" in the newsletter of the Fox Valley Manufacturers' Association, based in Joliet, Illinois, provides a useful window into not only the stereotypes and assumptions that saddled relocated Indians as they trekked into the industrial labor force but also the patronizing contempt that some non-Indians shared with one another about their communities' newcomers. "It is a very worthwhile idea to try to take these red-blooded Americans off the dole-like existence of the reservation and make useful taxpayers and citizens of them," the article suggested. "Our observation has been that they are usually very hard workers . . . not often skilled or well educated but very useful in the proper job and naturally dexterous craftsmen."

At the time of the article's publication in May 1958, Joliet was mired in the adverse consequences of a nationwide recession. The article therefore put added pressure on Fox Valley businesspeople to quickly repair the local economy in order to play a productive role in relocation's success. Indeed, the author stressed that "we can foresee a time when Navahoes, Choctaws, Winnebagoes, Cherokees and Apaches will once more be hunting the buck in the Valley." Mention of distant tribes such as the Navajo and Apache "once more" hunting in Fox Valley, Illinois, as well as the mention of "taxpayers" betrays middle America's profound ignorance about Native people. Indians relocating from reservations to cities largely concerned themselves with breaking down stereotypes, while non-Indians, at least in this case, treated relocation as an opportunity to deploy every Indian stereotype and joke in the community book. "As we described this program to Bill Gramley, personnel 'chief' at All-Steel," the article concluded, "he observed that this would be welcomed since we frequently had too many Chiefs and not enough Indians—Ugh! (They have squaws, too!)"[79]

. . . . . .

Although the process of going on relocation demanded a potentially dangerous degree of separation from tribal communities and loss of tribal support, tribal governments did not wholly forget or resent their citizens who felt compelled to seek better opportunities in cities. Indeed, several tribal governments worked to ensure that their people were being cared for in distant metropolises. Many tribal councils kept open files on their relocated citizens, conducted surveys, and met with BIA representatives to make program recommendations. Some tribes even formed committees to go visit their people in distant locales and gather a firsthand impression of relocation that they could posit as evidence should program officials behave misleadingly or downright dishonestly. In the process, some tribal councils offered sincere support for the program, while others spurned it. In either case, they kept an eye on it.

For example, the San Ildefonso Pueblo Tribal Council complained that the BIA should try harder to locate jobs for Indians closer to their tribal homes, while claiming that program publicity "is not honest, it breaks up the Indian family."[80] In related fashion, the Cahuilla complained that the BIA "is using destitution as a club to achieve unwanted assimilation."[81] Finally, the Goshute tribe officially stated, "We here disapprove the relocation program because we do not know how we will manage without a reservation."[82] Regardless of some Indian people's attempt to de-link the programs, Goshute leadership saw relocation as something designed to mitigate or even expedite the fallout from termination.

By contrast, the Sac and Fox Tribe of Oklahoma claimed that its members liked relocation and that the program had been adequately explained during the interview process. All that mattered, they insisted, was that their people had steady work.[83] The Standing Rock Sioux Tribe also claimed to be "in complete agreement with the relocation program. The rapid shrinkage of Indian owned land on the reservation makes it impossible for most of this next generation to make a living on the reservation."[84] Echoing the sentiment of both Sac and Fox and Standing Rock Sioux tribal leaders, Cherokee principal chief W. W. Keeler wrote to executive director of the AAIA Sophie Aberle and her husband, former commissioner of Indian affairs William Brophy, to share his opinion on relocation: "My hope has been that when Indians want to work and there is none in the area, that government will help them find opportunities to do so." While he admitted that the program had been "far from perfect," he generally approved of the basic concept.[85]

In June 1956, eight tribal presidents personally met with Indian commissioner Glenn Emmons in Washington to request a full evaluation of the program. They demanded improvements in program administration and greater involvement by tribal officials. Seemingly neither for nor against what they termed "integration," they insisted that the socioeconomic merging of Indians and non-Indians was inevitable and that "Indian people know this is the direction in which they are going." "Integration," they reasoned, "has already taken place with half the American Indian people, and with relatively little difficulty as compared with other minority groups in this country." The tribal delegation's use of the term *integration* rather than *assimilation* is a subtle but perhaps important indication that they believed Indian people could live in cities and work among white people and still remain Indian.[86]

Six months later, twelve tribes from Oklahoma, alongside the Mississippi Choctaw, met with Commissioner Emmons for similar purposes. Under the leadership of chair Napoleon Johnson, the intertribal committee officially stated: "We favor the expansion of the present relocation program in all areas wherever practical and feasible." Yet the committee did not want to see relocation's expansion result in a wider gulf between tribal homelands and individual Indians. The committee would rather see those Native people work closer to home, where their talents could more easily benefit their tribe. "It is recommended that employment be obtained as near the Indian population as possible," the committee added, while recommending that the BIA open vocational training program branches within the Anadarko and Muskogee areas.[87]

During a meeting in Omaha between the Winnebago tribal council and Indian affairs commissioner Glenn Emmons in 1956, Winnebago vice chair Charles LaMere expressed sincere support for the relocation program, especially its ability to help Indian people get into good homes. Yet he wanted to know if some of his young people who went out on their own, such as a Winnebago mother and her three children who went to Omaha, were eligible for relocation benefits. Emmons informed LaMere that the answer was no because relocation was "all sort of a trial basis" and Omaha was not technically a relocation center. BIA area superintendent Alan Adams then explained to commissioner Emmons that numerous Winnebago and Omaha Indians had self-relocated to nearby urban communities, with the Omaha mostly going to Omaha, and the Winnebago typically going to Sioux City. At that time, for example, twenty-four Winnebago families consisting of 58 total people were living in Omaha, and fifteen Winnebago families consisting of 55 total people had taken up residence in Sioux City. According to official reports, the families were doing well and benefiting from "the finest relationship and cooperation" with the state employment offices, a relationship the Winnebago nurtured without BIA assistance. Winnebago tribal chair Frank Beaver then added that several members of his tribe had been living in Los Angeles and Detroit, having migrated of their own accord. Clearly, Beaver argued, the Winnebago were enthusiastic about working and pursuing opportunities. So why not establish Omaha as a relocation center?[88]

Assistant Indian affairs commissioner Thomas Reid pushed back. He explained that the BIA was hesitant to open relocation centers in too close a proximity to reservations because "there is a great tendency to go back home and not be back to work on time and that is the first reason of falling down on the job." Reid championed the strong relationship the Winnebago and Omaha had with their state employment agencies and encouraged Beaver to have his tribespeople apply for training at a new Western Electric factory that was preparing to hire three thousand people at a new plant in Omaha. But he made it clear that the BIA would not establish Omaha as an actual relocation program destination.[89]

In October 1956, sixty-eight-year-old Chippewa tribal representative W. D. Savage ventured from his Fond du Lac reservation outside Duluth, Minnesota, to a meeting with Indian affairs commissioner Glenn Emmons and a handful of other Minneapolis area tribal leaders and Washington bureaucrats. The three-day conference's central agenda included forums on the BIA's relocation program and plans for reservation economic and education development. Savage certainly felt up to the task of conferencing with the commissioner. Despite only possessing a fourth-grade education, he claimed to have "learned a lot in travel . . . among Indians of different tribes in the United States and Canada."

Indeed, Savage did not hesitate to expose his avidity from the meeting's outset. Commissioner Emmons had not yet completed his opening remarks when Savage interrupted him to explain that he was on special orders from his tribe "not to accept absolutely nothing." Emmons immediately went on the defensive while attempting to explain the potential benefits of the programs his administration was busy fashioning. Unconvinced, Savage pointed to unfair blood quantum requirements for Indian scholarships before expressing general distrust toward Emmons's economic rehabilitation overtures. "Your economics, all these other things and social standing, we have that on the Fond du Lac Reservation," Savage asserted. "We can stand among the white people just the same as I am now."

The eager Chippewa leader then proceeded with details. "I can show you letters of recommendation from the Weyerhauser Lumber Company," he submitted, "and my name is pretty good there, and you can take the whole tribe there, and anybody that isn't working, it is his own fault. We have one of the biggest paper mills in the world. We have the Diamond Match Company." When Emmons asked if most of the Fond du Lac Chippewa were steadily employed, Savage assured him, "Yes, at one time we had 1400 on the reservation; we only got 300 now. 99% work and own their homes, and we own tribal property." Savage eventually revealed his own personal incredulity over the notion that Indians needed the federal government to arrange jobs for them. "I was only 14 years old when I went out to work at $2.50 a day, and I have practically been working ever since. . . . What is to prevent other Minnesota Indians from doing the same?" he urged. With that, momentum suddenly shifted in Emmons's favor. If initially troubled by Savage's rousing intervention, Emmons now saw in the Fond du Lac ambassador's message something he could exploit. After all, Savage's appeal fit the BIA's then overarching tribal termination policy like a glove. "I want to hand it to you people," Emmons praised. "You have what it takes."[90]

However insensitive Savage's remarks were toward tribes that lacked such a vibrant reservation economy, the Fond du Lac tribe's general position on Emmons's relocation and reservation economic rehabilitation programs pointed to an important quandary where relocation was concerned: not all tribes needed it. In no uncertain terms, various tribes' divergent positions on relocation and the invasive, unpredictable nature of the BIA's cyclic initiatives were directly proportional to their degree of economic desperation. On the pressing matter of whether or not to embrace urban work opportunities, tribal governments proved no more passive than the thousands of Indian individuals who enthusiastically accepted or rejected relocation services.

Indeed, official tribal involvement in the relocation program at times meant more than simply offering praise, criticism, or useful recommendations. Some tribes fashioned their own supplemental programs to facilitate off-reservation employment for their citizens. In 1956, Colorado River Indian tribal chair Pete Homer introduced a program to place his tribe's female high school graduates in Los Angeles homes, where they could labor as domestic workers. An announcement in support of the program stated, "We think it is high time that our old custom of caring for our youth is changed to one that encourages our youth to go out and seek new avenues of self help, and not to be dependent on the old folks, parents, the tribe or the government for help." At the time of the announcement's printing, nineteen girls had been successfully placed in jobs in and around Los Angeles. In fact, domestic work—the quintessential subaltern job—proved common among female relocatees in all urban destinations. Working from a position of hindsight, scholars have often dismissed such work as regressive and telling of Native people's subordinate position within American society during the 1950s. This comment by the Colorado River Indian Tribes, however, suggests a different way of thinking about the value of admittedly menial work to Native people at that time.[91]

The following year, the official newsletter of the Colorado River Indian Tribes ran a series of articles in support of the Indian bureau's relocation program. One particularly illustrative piece offered behavioral tips to prospective relocatees: "You don't have to be a fashion plate, but—a bath is important"; "Fellows—a tip—get that hat off as soon as you enter a room"; "No matter how tired you are, a slouch isn't fashionable"; "Girls—a tip— not too much makeup. You aren't a movie star yet"; "When the interview is over, don't jump up like a scared rabbit. Few interviewers hire on the spot." Such bits of advice suggest that paternalistic attempts at controlling Indian behavior were not the province of BIA agents alone.[92]

As the national relocation program continued gaining traction during the 1950s, some tribal leaders also made certain to advocate for a similar brand of economic rehabilitation and vocational training for those who rejected urban living. If the Indian bureau had any intentions of abandoning reservation-based Indians, some tribal leaders worked to keep the Indian bureau honest in its obligations. For example, during October 1955, Commissioner of Indian Affairs Glenn Emmons announced that the bureau was preparing to introduce a new education program for adult Indians who chose to continue residing on reservations. The Indian bureau selected five tribes—Florida Seminoles, Tohono O'odham, Rosebud Sioux, Turtle Mountain Chippewa, and Shoshone-Bannock—for participation in a pilot version of the program. Credit for the program's genesis, however, went not to Commissioner Emmons but to Seminole tribal leadership, whom Emmons had met with the previous year in Florida. While Seminole tribal leaders expressed satisfaction with efforts to educate their children in Westernized curricula, most adult members of the tribe lacked the language and writing skills necessary to compete in the capitalist American economy. According to Emmons, "These people, like those on many other reservations, are at a definite disadvantage because they are separated by a language barrier from the modern world in which they find themselves."[93]

Perhaps no tribal council paid closer attention to relocation than that of the Navajo, which officially supported the program and arrived at that conclusion through its own extensive research of the program's merit. During fall 1956, the Navajo council formed its own four-man program investigation committee that visited its tribal citizens in their new urban homes. Offering firm support for the program, one committee member wrote:

> I pictured before them the Relocation Program, because of necessity we cannot and will not attempt to say this is a bad program. . . . We have taken advantage of it and many reports have reached me from those who have benefitted and [are] holding a permanent job in some town, in some city quite a ways from home. They tell me "This is the first time I have had steady income for so long and my family has benefitted greatly." . . . We feel that it is not right to deny to any of our people the right to seek a job somewhere to better their condition, since we cannot offer these individuals anything in the way of a steady income on the reservation. . . . We are not forcing anyone to go off and seek a job. It is up to them.

The report took care to explain that Navajo people had pursued distant work opportunities "as far back as recorded history goes," and that therefore the relocation program's assistance marked the only real innovation.[94]

The report also mentioned that nearly all of the relocated Navajo people could at the very least point to seasonal off-reservation work experience, and that most had worked off-reservation or enlisted for military service during World War II. Still, the report was also careful to note that prior off-reservation experience did not guarantee success. Relocation "pioneers," the report chided, were anxious to try something new "without thinking through all the possible results." By the end of the program's first year of operation, roughly half of all Navajo relocatees had returned home. Yet some Navajo became convinced that they could improve on those unsuccessful attempts and embraced relocation as a competitive gauntlet. "As time went on," the report suggests, "a number made substantial adjustments, and this report also came back to the reservation." During 1952, only twenty-two Navajo migrated out with program support. That number steadily increased over subsequent years, however. In 1953, a total of 140 Navajo went on relocation. By 1956, that number had risen to 877.[95] Additionally, thousands of Navajo must have practiced self-relocation, without BIA support, during this period. According to Indian Rights Association representative Theodore Hetzel, who toured numerous reservations during the 1950s to gather data on the relocation program, among the roughly 75,000 total Navajo people counted in 1955, approximately 15,000 were working away from the reservation—roughly 20 percent. According to Hetzel's report,

"People undertake this step for a definite reason, invariably economic. They are not led to expect an easy time, and they go with the knowledge that they are taking a hard path."[96]

In a survey conducted in 1957, the Navajo Relocation Committee, commissioned by the Navajo tribal council to evaluate the relocation program, gave the AVT program high praise. In particular, the committee pointed to a solid record of job placement for Navajo graduates. At the same time, a few observations failed to meet the committee's approval. The committee did not, for example, like the fact that area offices competed with one another by placing Native vocational training students in fields where job opportunities were scarce. Additionally, the committee learned that those students who failed in their coursework might not have been properly screened at the reservation level. In a final criticism of the program, the committee called for increased school-sponsored recreational opportunities for Native students. Among the 189 students interviewed, church attendance was the most popular non-school-related activity, with participation at Indian centers a close second. Although it is not clear why the committee was dissatisfied with the recreational opportunities available, they did mention that they would like the training school's extracurricular activities to more closely mirror those found at regular colleges.[97]

In 1962, the Navajo Tribal Council formed another relocation committee that made a two-week visit to California's Bay Area and Los Angeles. With assistance from area offices in San Francisco, Oakland, San Jose, and Los Angeles, the committee visited relocated Navajo people and documented their experiences as part of the AVT program. A total of 1,028 Navajo persons and 619 family units migrated through these offices from 1960 through 1961. Among them, 353 total persons and 217 total family units returned to the Navajo reservation—roughly one-third. According to the committee's observations, however, most of those who returned were single people who only left temporarily due to job layoffs and planned to return if and when rehiring occurred. In addition to those who returned home, 286 total Navajo men and women left their respective jobs to attend trade schools.[98]

In sum, despite some criticisms of housing, the committee had a generally favorable impression of Navajo relocation to California. They found especially impressive a Navajo family who had relocated to Newark, California, where the father worked as a cable splicer for General Electric. A second relocated Navajo family in Gardena, California, earned mention for their "lovely home comparable to those of the non-Indian neighborhood in which they reside." At the end of each visit in Oakland and Los Angeles, the committee met with over two hundred relocated Navajos to hear of their experiences in their respective cities. The meetings, which were conducted in the Navajo language, further convinced the committee that relocation was a relative success for their people. Additionally, the committee visited several factories that employed Navajo people where they gained the impression that "in every instance the Navajo employees were well liked." Moreover, they found that local church influence had helped abate the destructive effects of alcohol among transplanted Navajos. In conclusion, committee chair Haska Cronemeyer exclaimed that "seeing is believing; hearing is misinformation." He invited fellow tribal council members to accompany him on any future visits to relocation centers and "see for themselves." Whereas the BIA can easily be accused of bias in promoting its own program, the Navajo Tribal Relocation Committee's assessment of the relocation program may provides a more honest rendering of an initiative that hardly proved disastrous for all concerned parties.[99]

· · · · · ·

On July 11, 1968, an inmate at El Reno Federal Reformatory in Oklahoma wrote employment assistance officer Jim Huff at the Shiprock, New Mexico, BIA office to request information about the relocation program. "I'm an inmate of this federal reformatory, voluntarily would like to correspond through you," he noted. "Concerning my plans for a parole plan in the near future, want to take this relocation program. While on parole if possible," he elaborated. The letter's author, who had been working in the prison hospital as a nurse's aid, was in fact referring to a special parolee release program that the BIA had added to its relocation program during the late 1960s. Ostensibly, he envisioned relocation as an opportunity to take a practical male nursing course and then "work my way up as an x-ray tech." It hardly bears explication that relocation must have meant much more to him than that.[100]

The El Reno prisoner's letter perhaps delivers the most striking and convincing example of how Native people were often so much more than victims of the Voluntary Relocation Program. In many respects, hopeful Indian relocatees sought to exploit cities less as terminal geographic destinations than as rotaries through which they could exit in any number of directions.[101] Ultimately, in accepting relocation's challenge, Native people demonstrated significant agency. This should be emphasized not to render them culpable for the program's failures but to appreciate the difficult and demanding decisions they made on behalf of themselves and their families.

Native people contended with rigorous promotion on the part of the BIA, but this did not necessarily result in an entire generation of Indians being duped by the white man. To suggest otherwise is to portray Indians as being incapable of reading between the lines or seeing value in off-reservation employment. Maneuvering through critical conditions, thousands of Native people refused to further subject themselves to the limited potential of reservation economies and social opportunities without entertaining the promise of something more. When offered the opportunity to transcend physical and cultural boundaries of the reservation and a resolutely second-class citizenship, Native people weighed the potential consequences and made bold decisions about their futures.

Relocation Has Degraded Indian People
Urbanization's Catastrophic Potential

· ·

On a reservation, you know everyone. Here, no one.
—William Redcloud (Ojibwe)

Had he not made it by 6 A.M. sharp, his entire day would have been wasted. Arriving even one minute late could have meant missing the bus that collected pools of hopeful workers each morning. Alongside a Norwegian immigrant also out learning the ropes, he kept close to their official chaperone, so as not to get separated in the throngs of desperate individuals. Upon reaching the final destination, he stepped off the bus and descended into the pits of Chicago's frenzied day-labor office. Once inside, he first encountered a man barking out want-ad capsules between puffs on his cigar, whose pungent fumes must have been an eye-opener for anyone needing a second alarm. Surveying the room, he observed men in motion, donning everything from threadbare work clothes to pressed gray-flannel suits. The clothing hierarchy notwithstanding, the men stood equal in that they could at best anticipate eight hours of work for a mere eight bucks—if they emerged with any opportunity at all.[1]

In the "female section," Anglo, Latina, and American Indian women with "poor clothes and unkempt" features listened for their name's attachment to a daily assignment, while an overflow crowd huddled outside in the January cold. The lucky ones dashed to the "L" station and hopped a train, now anxious to arrive on time at a random job site—always the pressure of the clock. The unlucky ones emerged crestfallen, left in the cold in more ways than one. Some scanned the sidewalk for cigarette butts worth a drag or two. They faced the clock, too, but theirs was negative time. The ticks that day would measure not in dollars but in elevated stress. Chicago area relocation supervisor Stanley Lyman called these offices "slave markets." For the Native American man breathing in the experience for the first time, they were his salvation. The next morning, he was on his own.[2]

Preceding chapters have framed Indian urbanization not only as an effect of unchecked machinations of the postcolonial settler state but also as an Indian initiative, in which Indigenous men and women—both through and apart from the Indian bureau's relocation program—sought to improve their lives, even if that meant moving into, and not around or away from, the cultural, economic, and political nexus of the settler state.[3] Yet urbanization, especially under the auspices of the federal program, proved disastrous for thousands of Native people. Among the numerous individual subject case files employed for this book, many include examples of Indian urban relocatees who quit work, failed to show up for interviews, suffered from alcoholism or other ailments, returned to their reservations, or some combination thereof.[4]

For many Native American people who went on relocation, their experiences revealed the relative limits on their potential for belonging in urban— and, by extension, "mainstream"—America. With few exceptions, this was not a problem of Native people being incapable of coping with modern life and technology or holding steady blue-collar jobs. Rather, this reflected problematic national trends that stemmed from the nation's gradual shift from a manufacturing industrial economy to a service economy. While Native people relocated to American metropolises in search of the latest version of the "American dream"—homeownership, steady employment, education, upward mobility—the dream was busy relocating over the next seemingly insurmountable horizon, somewhere removed from the old urban industrial centers. Upon arriving in various cities, many Native American people discovered a cruel consolation prize: an opportunity to integrate into a growing racialized mass of disenfranchised people who had become trapped in declining inner cities. At times urban Indian people were subjected to frightening racism. Caught in the maelstrom of urban racial hierarchies, some Native people even internalized racial ideas and spoke the appalling language of racism as they found themselves competing with other minority groups for low-wage jobs and low-income housing.

· · · · · ·

While Indian people typically confronted a significant range of problems upon their arrival in various cities, numerous Indians were determined to escape the problems that had begun at home. The potential for feeling a sense of "failure," either personally or as a socioeconomic critique, was not unique to urban destinations. Tribal leaders often suggested as much. For example, in 1956, Colorado River Indian Tribes chair Pete Homer (Mohave) wrote an article for his tribal newspaper that conveyed his people's enthusiasm for expanded relocation services through the Adult Vocational

Training program, set to formally begin the following year. "While we regret very much the conditions which necessitated your voluntary decision to leave the reservation," he explained, "we also would like to commend you and your families on the wise move you are making under the circumstances." After expressing disappointment over the lack of tribal land development, he blamed himself and his administration: "It seems that we have failed miserable [*sic*] in our obligation to you and for the welfare of the others who are taking the same initial step."[5]

Unlike Pete Homer, Northern Cheyenne tribal president John Woodenlegs offered no praise for relocation. In fact, he admonished six of his people who went on relocation from their Montana home to California, immediately returned, and ultimately wasted $600 of programmatic support each. Yet his repudiation of relocation notwithstanding, he also decried the BIA's paltry support for reservation-based economic initiatives. Woodenlegs insisted that the "BIA blocks everything" and that they "laughed at us for building in winter." Problematically, the BIA encouraged the Northern Cheyenne tribe to develop its "endless" coal resources before shipping in its own coal from Wyoming to use as a reservation fuel source, thus undermining the tribe's opportunity to capitalize on its own mineral resources.[6]

Because of the BIA's flagging support for reservation development, some area relocation officers split time as local job agents who sought employment for tribal citizens on and around their respective reservations. For example, relocation officers in Montana established connections with local contractors, farmers, ranchers, and railroad lines to find employment for area Indians. "We have canvassed the hotels, motels, and larger stores for jobs," one relocation officer enthused. While local employment opportunities were especially important when relocation assistance funds ran out, as they frequently did throughout the year, relocation officers' efforts at securing them often went in vain as reservation economies proved limited in their ability to provide stable employment. Moreover, local employment often amounted to seasonal work only. "It does seem to me though that due to lack of relocation funds we are putting too much emphasis on seasonal employment," relocation officer William Ames wrote. "This type of employment has been a curse to the Indian people for many many years in the past. . . . It is so bad in this area that many of the Indian workers have accepted the fact that they are only seasonal workers and will not accept employment for any great length of time."[7]

In referring to seasonal employment as a "curse," Ames must have been unaware that some Indigenous peoples had worked tirelessly across decades to nurture seasonal employment networks. For Ojibwe rice harvesters around Lake Superior, or Round Valley Indian ranch workers and hop pickers in Northern California, migratory labor amounted not to a "curse" but to an annual cultural practice central to their Indigeneity and capacity for self-sufficiency, a practice "fundamental" to the way people "formed their communities and survived as indigenous people" in the nineteenth and twentieth centuries, as historian William Bauer tells us.[8] In a second example, historian Paige Raibmon discusses how Tlingit hop pickers practiced seasonal work migrations around Washington's Puget Sound, which wove an "economic safety net" through participation in a "burgeoning capitalist economy." The hop pickers were part of a diverse Tlingit labor profile that also included fishing, canning, sealing, and farming.[9]

Federal officials in Washington also struggled to see past cynical appraisals of rural Indian Country's economic potential. They perhaps failed to consider the staggering amount of land that everyone from presidents and members of Congress to homesteaders and squatters had for centuries illegally wrested away from tribal nations. After decades of federal corruption and mismanagement, and after World War II ultimately foiled the New Deal administration's controversial plans for comprehensive economic development of reservations, conditions in postwar Indian Country did not appear markedly better than they had been nearly a hundred years prior. For example, in 1867, the Sisseton Dakota people's newly established Lake Traverse reservation in the Dakota Territory consisted of 918,779 acres of land, which provided home to 1,350 people. Tragically, by 1956 the Sisseton land base had diminished to 113,802 acres of land shared by 1,890 Indian residents. Among the Sisseton people who resided on the reservation that year, 24.5 percent survived on what the BIA considered "irregular wages," with only 17.1 percent earning regular wages. Additionally, 13.1 percent of the people depended on aid to dependent children, with 11.1 percent more dependent on full public assistance. Hoping to rescue the situation, a new postwar crop of Indian affairs bureaucrats began introducing bold innovations to federal Indian policy. Meanwhile, raised socioeconomic expectations stemming from wartime work opportunities and military service encouraged thousands of Indians to continue seeking off-reservation employment, even as the war industry contracted. By 1956, for example, 1,478 Sisseton people—almost half their total population—were living off-reservation.[10] Nationally, between 1953 and 1957, the Department of the Interior opened 1,790,650 acres of Indian land to individual tract ownership and fee-simple titles, thus making it susceptible to taxation and vulnerable to further dispossession.[11]

Taken together, these examples suggest that it is important to acknowledge that cities and reservations did not produce or reinforce Indians' socioeconomic immobility in isolation from each other. Native people consistently put both spaces in dialogue with each other when evaluating challenges that lay ahead. Weak reservation economies mattered not only as possible push factors that drove Indians into the arms of relocation agents but also as subjects for comparative socioeconomic evaluations. While it is tempting to position a bustling city as the antithesis of an Indian reservation, Native people who sought to overcome poverty and social marginalization understood that they were facing a systemic problem that linked reservations with cities. Problems in one venue brought into focus the relative value of the other. Of course, spatial mobility alone was not necessarily capable of mitigating economic problems for Indian people or political problems for federal policy makers. But neither was repetition of the same fruitless strategies that at best only preserved Native people's position as impoverished tribal citizens or second-class U.S. citizens.

Problems with the relocation program itself often began at home, prior to departure. Anyone determined to expose the program's potentially false promises typically needed to look no further than the posters and advertisements displayed on reservation agencies' windows and bulletin boards. For example, a Native man named Mr. Able recalled how, before moving his family to Chicago, relocation officers prodded him with pictures of a "successfully relocated" family from his own reservation. One step ahead, Mr. Able informed them that the family in question had in fact recently returned to the reservation. Unfortunately, the relocation officers' no doubt embarrassing blunder proved something of a portent of things to come for the Able family, which ultimately professed acute disappointment in their relocation experience and, like the family in the picture, returned home. Back home on the reservation, Mr. Able explained, his family might go hungry, but his people would never allow them to outright starve. "I can stand poorness, I have been poor all my life," he reasoned. "It is my children, I want something for them."[12]

Such misleading program advertising could indicate simple clerical mistakes. Yet it is quite apparent that program boosters faced profound pressure from above to make relocation succeed at any cost. After all, alongside the federal government's concurrent policy to altogether terminate tribal sovereignty, relocation promised to finally deliver federal policy makers from their centuries-old "Indian problem." Failure was not an option. Relocation officials were therefore compelled to twist arms and practice subtle coercion—even when that approach was unnecessary, as was often the case. "There were quotas to be filled and I have this on the information of one of the relocation officers himself," recalled Father Peter Powell, director of Chicago's St. Augustine's Center for Indians. "The Indian bureau was giving the relocation staff here a quota of people to bring into [Chicago]—the initial follow-up was made, and then they were dropped."[13]

During a speech delivered to the Indian Rights Association in 1959, Roger Ernst—assistant secretary of the Department of the Interior—boldly broke with his colleagues by pointedly criticizing the relocation program. In particular, he took umbrage with the same false advertising the Able family experienced and the same pressure relocation officials faced to meet the quotas that Father Powell decried. "I have been on reservations where I've seen beautiful views of beaches in Southern California posted on bulletin boards," Ernst revealed. "Also pictures of homes with swimming pools . . . certainly things [an Indian individual] is not going to be in a financial position to have right away." But for Ernst, the program itself was not the problem so much as the dishonesty surrounding it. Pointing to misleading relocation advertisements, he concluded, "This seems to smack a little bit of meeting a quota." Here we can appreciate Ernst as one of the few federal officials who seemed to understand that honesty was important when dealing with Native American peoples who throughout their histories had lost so much to dishonest state officials. One important irony here is that, as has been previously indicated, plenty of Native American people became interested in relocation not as a result of persuasive propaganda but as a calculated response to their own experiences. Federal officials did not need to lie when selling their program. But when they did, they contributed much to the program's bitter legacy.[14]

Meanwhile, some BIA officials were quick to suggest that they too wrestled with their own problem of misinformation and sensationalized assertions about the relocation program. "It sure burns me up when I read an article written by some person that says the purpose of the relocation program is to get Indians off the land so that white men can steal it," Commissioner of Indian Affairs Glenn Emmons grumbled during a meeting with Winnebago people in 1956. "That makes me pretty mad when I read things like that and a lot of people when they read that, a lot of them believe it and it makes it sort of discouraging sometimes."[15]

Problems with misinformation or lack of information often persisted within relocatees' new urban destinations. Indeed, if relocated Indians were bringing the "Indian problem" with them to the city, then in whose realm did jurisdiction over the "Indian problem" reside upon its arrival? Numerous Native people complained that the BIA was evasive when asked about exactly how much financial support was available, and for how long. When weekly stipends ran out, relocated Indians often expressed confusion over where to turn for help. Some turned to fellow relocated family members, religious organizations such as St. Augustine's Center for Indians in Chicago, or urban Indian centers, which often doubled as cultural meeting places and outlets for jobs and housing tips.[16] Others seemed unclear on whether BIA services remained an option. Some relocated Indians learned this the hard way when they went to urban social services agencies only to be turned away by social workers who insisted that Indians were supposed to get help from either their respective tribes or the federal government. Relocated Ute Jim Olquin considered the program a failure because the BIA offered so little in the way of meaningful or substantive support. Olquin certainly would have benefited from a wider safety net. In and out of jail repeatedly, he noted that when he wanted to reach out for help, he had no idea where to go.[17]

In his July 1970 "Special Message to the Congress on Indian Affairs," President Richard Nixon acknowledged this problem when he included urban Indians in his list of recommendations for improving Indigenous people's socioeconomic status as citizens of the United States. "Lost in the anonymity of the city, often cut off from family and friends, many urban Indians are slow to establish new community ties," he explained. "Many drift from neighborhood to neighborhood; many shuttle back and forth between reservations and urban areas." In the city, Nixon pointed out, roughly 75 percent of Indians lived in poverty, but BIA services were no longer available to them after their initial adjustment period. Making matters worse, Native people who struggled with language and cultural differences often failed to locate urban social welfare services available to them in the absence of BIA support—that is, if they even knew such outlets existed. "As a result, Federal, State and local programs which are designed to help such persons often miss this most deprived and least understood segment of the urban poverty population," Nixon concluded.[18]

· · · · · ·

One primary goal of the Voluntary Relocation Program was to achieve the "melting down" of politically and culturally distinct Indian nations into the consensus American body politic. In previous decades, especially during the introduction of the Indian boarding school system, federal policy makers and social reformers alike suggested that Indians could figuratively, almost *literally*, become white through a coordinated process of assimilation. Given this, Indians' wider acceptance into mainstream America should have come more easily than it did for other disenfranchised groups that resided further outside the matrices of white privilege. Yet that often was not the case, as Indian families frequently pointed to racial discrimination as a major reason for their failure to gain firmer footing in urban America. Consider an Indian family of four from an unspecified tribe who relocated together to Chicago after the family's mother refused to let her husband go alone to establish residence and employment. Things seemed to be going well when they located an "unusually desirable" two-room kitchenette apartment and made a $5.00 deposit. But when they arrived with their belongings, they learned that the building owner had ordered the apartment manager to deny them entry and to return their deposit because they were Indian. To its credit, the BIA fought on the family's behalf and threatened to enlist the Better Business Bureau, at which point the apartment owner finally relented and allowed the family to assume residence.[19]

In 1960, Chicago Indian community leader Benjamin Bearskin (Winnebago) experienced a similar, albeit more hostile, situation. After relocating his family to Chicago from South Dakota in 1948, Bearskin had worked for twelve years as a welder and construction laborer by day and board chair of the Chicago American Indian Center by night and on weekends. His hard work seemed to be paying off when he moved his family of seven into a new apartment in Humboldt Park—a 99 percent white neighborhood at that time.[20] "We spent all day May 14 moving into our flat after we had worked hard to clean and decorate it," Bearskin's wife, Fredeline (Winnebago), recalled. "That night we went to a party at the Indian Center. When we reached home, we found the windows had been smashed by stones." A menacing blend of stones and shards of broken glass covered the floor of the front room. Vandals had broken every window in the building. Attached to one stone was a note: "You mex, get out of here. This is only the beginning. No kidding. [Signed] The Whites." Bearskin refused to let the incident compromise his resolve or his sense of humor: "I feel it's an honor to be taken for Mexican."[21] Ten days later, the Bearskins' frightened landlord evicted the family from their new apartment. "They fear the neighborhood will be overrun by Negroes, Puerto Ricans and Mexicans, I guess," Benjamin reasoned. Undeterred, he imagined a harmonious future devoid of the racial and ethnic hierarchies his family was suffering: "[My] ideal neighborhood is one where you might find 10 or 12 nationalities all getting along together." After describing a situation in which a stranger had threatened to beat one of the Bearskin children for dropping a gum wrapper, Fredeline Bearskin concluded, "It's tough to have to take such treatment—we belong to this country."[22]

While the Bearskins had self-relocated years in advance of the BIA's program, they represented the program's most benevolent aspirations: sociocultural integration, class mobility, and economic self-sufficiency. Yet the BIA often made such goals difficult to achieve by channeling a majority of relocated Indians straight into substandard housing immediately upon their arrival. During the program's initial phase, substandard housing proved the main obstruction against successful relocations to Denver. "True enough, there is some cheap rental housing but such housing very definitely is undesirable as quite often the so-called cheap housing may be converted sheds, garages, barns; yes, and even chicken coops," Denver field placement officer Leigh Hubbard confessed in 1952. "We do not feel that it is advisable to ask people to move into Denver when we can offer them no better than this latter type mentioned."[23]

Discrimination against urban Indians was not limited to housing markets. Relocated Indians could also face prejudice at their new places of employment. For example, during the 1960s, most Minneapolis industries resisted hiring Indians. According to one published study, only the Honeywell Corporation had made serious efforts to recruit Native workers. Although there were some available jobs in surrounding suburbs, Indians mostly failed to apply—often because they lacked reliable transportation. Moreover, local Twin Cities employment agencies that attempted to assist prospective Native workers' job searches faced additional obstacles in the form of shifting skill requirements, lack of tools, lack of educational credentials, and, at times, Indians' "disillusionment" with the employment process. According to employment services agents, suburban corporations were amenable to filling their affirmative action quotas with Indians, but their uncertainty about Indians' ability to adequately adjust to contemporary working and living patterns often precluded further interest.[24]

Indian people who did not suffer housing and employment discrimination might have been struggling just to be noticed at all. In some instances, the comparatively small number of urban Indians resulted in their presence and needs being obscured by larger minority groups that commanded greater attention. In 1956, for example, an official from the Mayor's Commission on Human Rights in Chicago explained why three to four thousand Indians residing in the Windy City were not the focus of urban welfare initiatives. "Look," he pleaded, "We have almost that many colored people moving into the city every two weeks from the South. We simply don't have the resources to give time or attention to so small a minority." "This is profoundly regrettable," Indian Rights Association representative Harold E. Fey countered, "not only because of the long delay in justice to the Indian but also because it is wrong to apply a numerical standard to a problem of human relations as old and as important as this one."[25]

Native people residing in Gallup, New Mexico, decried a different brand of invisibility when they disseminated controversial pamphlets titled *When Our Grandfathers Carried Guns* during the city's Tribute to the American Indian public ceremonial. The fiery polemic argued that the City of Gallup presented Indians as two-dimensional stereotypes from the past and failed to draw needed attention to contemporary Indians with contemporary problems. Simply put, the pamphlet insisted that Gallup officials exploited the Indian image for public entertainment but offered no substantive, reciprocal service in the ceremony's aftermath: "The Ceremonial does not give a true picture of the Indian. Just because Indians sing and dance for you, that does not mean that they are happy. . . . Do not believe it. At the night performances, you will hear what a proud and happy people we are. Do not believe that either. Do not think that the City of Gallup respects the Indian because it gives them a free barbecue." The pamphlet then highlighted Native people's high unemployment and low income rates, alongside high suicide and infant mortality rates. While 72 percent of all commercial businesses in Gallup conducted commerce with Native people, the city in general devoted little to no attention to its Native population's socioeconomic health. According to the pamphlet's authors, the "Indian Capital of the World" was a social cesspool where visitors could witness local police "savagely beating helpless drunk Indians." Finally, the authors railed against the fact that municipal leaders had recently been designing a Gallup city flag that included Indian imagery, despite the designers' failure to invite any creative input from the city's Native community.[26] The racism and discrimination Native people experienced in Gallup was likely more acute than that which Indians experienced in more cosmopolitan communities such as San Francisco. After all, Gallup remains a reservation border town where, according to anthropologist Thomas Biolsi, Indians' "deadliest enemies" reside.[27]

Indians who did not take to the streets to protest racist stereotypes might simply have been too busy trying to keep their job or too busy trying to find steady work. Father Peter Powell, who founded and administered St. Augustine's Center for Indians in Chicago and assisted thousands of relocated Indians across several decades, explained how Native people in his city who lacked secondary education and skilled labor credentials fell victim each year to typically high layoff rates between November and March. Those unfortunate Indian workers fell under the banner of "last hired, first fired." "After they have lost their jobs, in most cases they are ineligible to receive Welfare assistance, as they do not meet the year's residency requirement," Powell elaborated, before adding, "Most of them do not desire Welfare assistance anyway."[28]

Given the turbulent nature of most unskilled labor markets, numerous urban Indians became dependent on day-labor offices. Betty Jack, an Ojibwe woman who in 1951 relocated to Chicago's Uptown neighborhood in search of better employment opportunities, is perhaps illustrative of the daily grind Indians experienced in Chicago's day-labor system. In an interview with the *Chicago Tribune* in 1971, she elaborated on how she and several members of her Chicago Indian community became trapped within the day-labor system:

> I'd get up at 4:30 A.M. to go over and get in line to try for day labor. We'd get on the bus at 6:30 A.M. and be at work by 8. It was mostly packing plants. The guy in charge speeds up the conveyor belts to get more work from us, since we're not union and can't scream. Then at 5, we get on the bus and come back. They take 50 cents for the bus, and you get low pay. You've spent all that time, and you get maybe $12 for the day. They don't want you to get ahead. You never get far enough ahead to take time to look for a regular job. At the end of the day, every place is closed but the bars; so that is where you go to cash your check. Working day labor is like a drug addict. You can't get out of it. That's one reason all of us live together in one apartment. There's no choice.[29]

Day laborers in Chicago often settled for positions through Manpower or Ready-Men, two employment offices notorious for exploiting desperate workers. "If you're lucky, you may wind up with 8 dollars before you take out car fare, lunch, and taxes," one worker protested. "The tops I ever got was $1.25 an hour. A family man can't make it on that."[30]

While day labor offered the lowest rewards for the highest risks, even those fortunate enough to land more reliable work often had to compete with other members of the lowest socioeconomic class. In 1965, Charles Munson held a job making $53 a week as a maintenance supervisor for Los Angeles's Jewish Home for the Aged. According to Munson, the home hired him as a painter but had only reserved room in its budget for two painters, and two Mexican American men ahead of him boasted both seniority and families to support. Therefore, when the home needed to make budget cuts, it dismissed Munson first. He subsequently struggled to make a weekly $5 rent payment on a room he did not like. "Just a sleeping room is never any good wherever your [sic] at," he expressed. "Just four walls if you know what I mean." During a relocation progress evaluation, he requested assistance with locating an Indian club or Episcopal church where he could meet other Indians. "There's none around here," he explained, "just Mexicans and Japanese mostly." Interestingly, despite his struggles to maintain steady employment and afford adequate housing, his chief complaint concerned smog: "I couldn't take another summer of this smog. I don't see how anyone can stand it in summer, burns your eyes and lungs." Moreover, he expressed deep frustration over his inability to purchase a television or even just a coffee maker—two pieces of technology often featured in BIA relocation promotional materials.[31]

· · · · · ·

Among those who worked tirelessly to make ends meet, it must have been frustrating to learn that the Bureau of Indian Affairs typically counted any relocated Indians who simply remained in the city for at least one year a "success." That dubious conclusion notwithstanding, many Native people struggled to adjust to their new surroundings, and not for lack of effort. Father Peter Powell, who worked closely with relocated Indian families in Chicago, could only characterize the early years of the relocation program as "indescribable." "Families were brought in here on a one-way ticket," he recalled. "After a month, it was assumed the Indian family had adjusted and all aid was dropped."[32] During relocation's peak period of activity, he admonished the program as "the most immoral one in over half a century."[33]

During an academic conference held at Chicago's Newberry Library in 1980 on the topic of urban Indians, eminent University of Chicago anthropologist Sol Tax offered a negative appraisal of relocation. He recalled how during the 1950s, the Chicago Field Relocation Office refused to tell those who desired to help relocated Indians—including local social services agencies, churches, private citizens, and the Chicago Indian center—which trains relocatees were arriving on, because the BIA sought to avoid outside interference with its program. Moreover, Tax claimed that the field offices would only support one change of employment for relocated Indians who did not like their jobs. Beyond that, the BIA would tell them to "get lost."[34]

Tax suggested that the fundamental flaw with the relocation program was that it amounted to a one-way bus ticket when it should have been round trip. Guaranteeing Indians the opportunity to return, he argued, would have rendered the program far less disastrous in that it would have allowed Indians greater flexibility in deciding whether or not the potentially demanding process of adjusting to urban life was indeed right for them and their families. Moreover, Tax argued, relocated Indians could have returned home and shared the knowledge they gained about mainstream America. In sum, he regretted that the relocation program was not more of an extended urban education program, wherein Indians could have gained valuable experiences that would have allowed them to help their people back home. In the absence of such possibilities, he asserted, relocation was but a "scandal."[35]

Dakota tribal council member Paul Harrison pursued similar reasoning for his objection to relocation. "Sure, if he at least maybe had a high school education he can do it," he conceded. "But why send a person out there who has only an eighth grade education or a fifth grade and then assist him for about a year . . . and then drop him all of a sudden," he questioned. Moreover, Harrison pointed out that some tribes, including his own Crow Creek tribe, disenrolled their relocated citizens and denied them tribal services. A better strategy, he suggested, would have been to have tribal people work in towns closer to reservations so that they would not become stranded in a bad situation. He mentioned that many of his people had found steady employment in nearby Pierre and Rapid City, South Dakota. Such a strategy held the potential for Native people to benefit from outside employment opportunities without separating from the tribe.[36]

At times, even the boarding schools that for decades had embraced cities as venues for Indian uplift began souring on the program. For example, in 1962, the Haskell Institute recruited Minnesota Labor Committee director Louis Lerman to help secure jobs for five recent graduates. Lerman succeeded in finding work for the students in the Twin Cities, but in a letter to influential Minnesota senator Hubert Humphrey, he expressed frustration with the system. "The BIA has not done a thing outside of educating these Indian youth," he railed. "We have to look for subsistence to other sources until they get their first pay check. . . . The local BIA office is helpless." He also pointed to ideological gridlock within the Indian bureau that stemmed from a lack of personnel turnover. "The bureaucrats who are between [Indian commissioner Philleo] Nash and the field staff run things," he insisted. "They are there for 40 years under all administrations and run things as they see fit."[37]

When relocation's promise broke down, some Indian bureau officials did their best to try to salvage the situation and convince their charges not to give up. In a letter to a Native man who was struggling to adjust after relocating from Montana to California, Fort Belknap Agency superintendent J. W. Wellington exemplified the persuasive nature of BIA agents' overtures to Indians on relocation. He repeatedly implored his letter recipient to stay in California and resist any temptation to return home. According to Wellington, many people were out of work on the reservation as a result of bad winter weather: "It is much better to live where you can earn a living the year round than to be unemployed and unable to have the necessities of life six months out of every year." After challenging his subject to resist the power of homesickness, he added, "You are aware of conditions on the reservation and know the hardships that many of the people face, particularly during the winter months. After giving careful thought and weighing the opportunities and conveniences which you now enjoy I feel confident that your judgment will advise you to stay and to exert further effort to make a success and permanent home in the community where you now reside." In so many words, Wellington was suggesting that however bad things were in California, it was worse back in Montana. Whether or not that was true, it was not exactly a ringing endorsement of the program.[38]

Still, for some Indian urban migrants, no amount of individual fortitude or Indian bureau advocacy could prevent a descent into socioeconomic despair. While exact figures do not exist, a substantial number of Indians succumbed to alcoholism, homelessness, and unemployment. Such tragic outcomes go far in explaining relocation's maligned legacy. Richard Elm (Oneida) shared his impression of directing St. Augustine's Drop-In Center for Chicago Indians who struggled with alcohol and substance abuse: "They just can't handle the city. They come here from the reservations to get jobs. But there were none. That's why they turned to drink. All I can do is keep them alive a little longer." Contextualizing relocation within a historical legacy of colonialism and military conquest, Elm concluded, "They used to just blow you away. Now they do it in other ways."[39] Similarly, a relocated Ojibwe man's candid statement to a news reporter perhaps reflects the sense of defeat some members of Chicago's Indian community felt when they accepted social welfare: "I ain't no Chicago Indian. I'm from the Bad River reservation in Wisconsin. There was nothing up on the reservation. I wanted to come down to see the big city. All my friends came too. I show up here [the Ready-Men day-labor office] every day. When they don't send me out, I go get drunk. I can't hold a steady job. You know how Indians are. Once we start on the bottle, we're stuck. I'd like to go back to the reservation now. Give me the money to live on and I'd go back tomorrow."[40]

When Korean War veteran Darrell Gardner (Ute) and his wife went on relocation to Denver during the 1950s, things initially seemed promising. Gardner recalled that he liked his job, and his wife was happy to attend beauty school. Before long, however, he concluded that relocation had been a mistake. Recalling his experience in the program, he claimed, "They tried to push them out too fast. You can't change a people. What's in their heart and their souls, you know. You can't change it over night." Gardner expressed particular frustration over how relocation precipitated many Indians' descent into alcoholism. No amount of cosmetic veneer could mask alcoholism's pernicious effects, he reasoned. "Maybe the outside appearance: they put a suit on them," he expressed. "But they're not the same inside." Moreover, he claimed that many relocatees' pride had been hurt when they realized that white workers earned higher wages for working the same positions as Indians. He also felt that the city was bad for Indian children in that it rendered parents' responsibility for looking after their children more difficult. He did, however, confess that he appreciated the opportunity to "see a little bit different point of view," and that the only thing he initially missed from the reservation was the smell of sagebrush.[41]

For Taos Pueblo leader Telesfor Romero, relocation was not even worth an opportunity to see a different view of life. He shared his conviction that relocation did "a great deal of damage in breaking down the old ways and religion" among young people from his tribe. Those who left, he asserted, essentially forgot that Taos existed. "Their property goes to pieces, they lose their water rights on the reservation," he elaborated. Romero mostly saw cities as consumerist traps designed not to safeguard or provide access but to separate Indian people from the fruits of their labor. He claimed that in the city, Indians became vulnerable to unscrupulous salespeople who "have sugar talk and they get [Indians] to buy more than they can pay for."[42]

On some occasions, city officials became the targets of distressed Indians' anger over the most traumatic features of urban living. In 1956, Minneapolis mayor Eric Hoyer confessed that there were a disproportionate number of Native people residing in the city's welfare workhouse. In 1955, for example, Indians made up 12 percent of the Minneapolis workhouse population, despite making up less than 0.5 percent of the city's total population. In 1956, a group of urban Indians were so distraught that they marched into Mayor Hoyer's office and confronted him in person: "Why do you let us come into Minneapolis and make drunkards out of ourselves and prostitutes out of our women and daughters?"[43]

· · · · · ·

Given such potentially catastrophic conditions, it is understandable that thousands of relocated Indians returned to their tribal homes in order to regroup and try urban life again at a later date, or to remain home on the reservation permanently. Interestingly, when surveying the explanations Native people provided for returning home, many appear just as contingent and subjective as their reasons for initially departing for the city. In response to a survey on relocation conducted by anthropologist Sophie B. Aberle, Domingo Tenorio (Pueblo) shared his experiences going on relocation to Inglewood, California. In his leisure time, he drove his car around town, visited the Indian center daily, caught a movie once a month, occasionally bowled and shot pool, and enjoyed reading sports magazines and newspapers. He only went to the bar "once in a while." A visitor lived with him briefly but failed to help with the rent. Ultimately, Tenorio did not see much benefit in relocation and eventually returned home. He did, however, express pride in the three cars he purchased while he was away and brought one home with him as a souvenir. Happy to be back home, he shared a somewhat vague impression of why he had been so eager to return to the reservation: "It's benefits living are reservation supporting mother. And work on farm and jewelry work [sic]." Asked to specify what he considered to be the disadvantages of urban life, Tenorio responded, "Traffic violations—strict laws on streets and strict rules on paying room and board." Before relocation, Tenorio had served in the military and worked for two years on railroad gangs in Texas. He had had off-reservation experiences and demonstrated no mentionable character flaws. Urban life, it appears, simply did not appeal to his personal sensibilities.[44]

As part of the same survey, World War II veteran and fellow Pueblo relocatee Joe D. Chavez expressed a negative appraisal of relocation similar to that of Tenorio. In California, Chavez socialized only with other Indians he knew from New Mexico, especially his Jemez Pueblo neighbors. He initially liked relocation because of the steady work and ability to purchase clothing for his children. He also loved reading popular magazines that were unavailable back home and enjoyed going to the movies. But he was bothered by a particular brand of urban confinement. Whereas numerous Native people pursued urban life as an escape from reservation confinement, Chavez's experience marked an inversion of that motive. "In Reservation it our own living home. No taxable and can do any other things when on the reservation," he wrote on his relocation questionnaire. "In city can not do as we please when have three or four children they don't allowed our children to be on the street," he elaborated. When the questionnaire asked if he was happy, he responded, "Yes, right where I am again going back and forth into city of Albuquerque N. Mex. and back to Pueblo of Santo Domingo Pueblo." Upon returning home, Chavez first landed a job with Chrysler, earning $320 a month. After being laid off, he shuttled back and forth between his Santo Domingo reservation and Albuquerque, where he worked on bridges for a local contracting firm, before self-relocating permanently to Albuquerque for a warehouse stockman position. Relocation to California clearly did not prove suitable for Chavez. At the same time, his return did not render him a victim of the program. California merely amounted to another stop on a life trajectory marked by mobility.[45]

In 1951, during the program's pilot stage, the Doubleheads from Stillwell, Oklahoma, became the first Cherokee family to relocate to Chicago. During a newspaper interview in 1976, patriarch Hiner Doublehead recalled how his family immediately struggled to adjust to their new home. Most problematically, his two eldest children spoke only Cherokee and could not communicate with their new urban peers. Moreover, Hiner pointed to Chicago's overwhelmingly labyrinthine arrangement as a particular source of frustration: "I know people who used to get lost in Stillwell. By God, they're up in Chicago now. No wonder they turn into alcoholics." After twelve years, the Doubleheads returned to Stillwell, where they owned over ten acres of property. Hiner called their return "the best decision I ever made," mentioning that the only thing he missed was Chicago's famous Polish sausages.[46]

In 1956, during a meeting in Omaha with various tribal council members and BIA commissioner Glenn Emmons, Aberdeen area BIA director and future U.S. congressman Ben Reifel (Lakota) delivered a brief synopsis of how quickly relocation's promise could unravel: "Here's what happens—a family leaves the reservation and goes to Omaha, Chicago, or Denver. He gets a job which may pay him around $250 a month. A salesman comes along and sells him a television set, or a car on the installment plan and before long he will have more payments than he can pay and he does not have anything with which to pay the grocery bill. He gets discouraged and comes home." So efficient was Reifel's summary one can imagine he had recounted or heard it numerous times. The overarching problem he identified was one of budgeting and income. On the one hand, federal officials attempted to sell Indians on the promise of owning televisions, automobiles, and even new homes. But in reality, those same federal officials reduced relocated Indians to a victimized talking point while emphasizing their inability to manage finances.[47]

A 1959 study of returnees who initially relocated through the Billings area office in Montana gathers numerous subjective and unpredictable reasons why many Native people waved goodbye to various urban locales in pursuit of a happier future back in rural Indian Country. John M. Old Coyote's motive for returning to his Crow reservation largely stemmed from insufficient wages in Dallas. (Interestingly, he did not receive a warm welcome home from his family members, who told a BIA representative that Old Coyote returned because he "was always spoiled.") Harvey Driftwood mentioned that his family simply could not get along with each other in the city and felt that a change of scenery would help. Benjamin Cloud explained that because his family was lonely in the city, they made a visit home during Christmas but consequently exhausted their finances and therefore could not get back to Los Angeles; their break with urban living happened by accident. Joseph Longjaw mentioned that he was getting along fine in Dallas before a "reservation buddy" with a drinking problem showed up and exhausted his patience and finances. Finally, Gerald La Franier departed Los Angeles after he was almost hit by a car and simply could not shake the frightening experience. The unifying link between these examples is their circumstantial nature. These were not uniquely "Indian" problems, and they did not result from individual failure.[48]

In some cases, however, tribal cultural traditions did introduce a real obstacle to Native people's achievement of the BIA's ideal version of success. Most notably, commitments to reciprocal generosity burdened numerous families that struggled to make ends meet and therefore had little to offer. Moreover, some urban Indian migrants upheld a tradition of extended kinship support in which hosts were obligated to accommodate any visiting member of their respective tribe for as long as the guest desired to stay. For example, sociologist James Goodner, who conducted extensive research on the Dallas urban Indian community during the late 1960s, claimed that several Indian people he interviewed suffered at the hands of imposing family and friends who sojourned to Dallas and drained their finances. Still, these examples suggest no personal failings stemming from indolence or failure to cope with new surroundings. Rather, they reflect some Native people's determination to practice tribal cultural values in a new setting.[49]

While relocated Native people attempted to guide their own fate and navigate their own problems, some BIA personnel, whom critics of the relocation program frequently accused of being useless and insensitive, went to great lengths to help families adjust to their new surroundings. On occasion, however, relocatees arrived in their care with personal problems that steady employment and a change of scenery alone could not cure. In 1959, the Wilson family relocated from Montana to Chicago, where Mr. Wilson landed work as a grinder and polisher at Consolidated Railway Equipment. He quickly lost the job, however, as a result of his struggles with alcohol. Mr. Wilson earned some money shoveling snow before the relocation office found him a second job at Corn Products Refining Company. But Wilson was fired from that job too. Chicago field relocation officer Stanley Lyman paid the struggling Native man a visit, at which point he "reviewed our services again and stressed his obligation in this relocation which meant he must work every day." According to Lyman, Mr. Wilson had decided that because his employer had been calling his home looking for him, he would "get even with them by not going to work." Lyman attempted damage control by moving the family into a new home and making amends with Mr. Wilson's employer. Alas, within a few weeks Wilson again quit going to work and appeared to be descending deeper into alcoholism. With both food and hope running out, alongside the persistent nature of Mr. Wilson's "inability to hold a job, drinking patterns, and immature attitude regarding family responsibilities," Lyman finally decided to send the family back to the reservation.[50]

Tragically, this resulted in the partial breakup of the family, as two children stayed in Chicago to live with Mr. Wilson's sister. The point here is not to dwell on alcoholism and perpetuate a negative stereotype about urban Indians; Mr. Wilson struggled with alcoholism before he arrived in Chicago. Still, his case suggests that the BIA at times failed to conduct adequate screening of program applicants. Either way, his example suggests that the burden for making a successful transition to urban life and new work environments ultimately weighed on the shoulders of the relocated Indian people, for better or worse. It also suggests that some relocatees not only wrestled with new problems unique to urban life but also struggled to overcome old problems that chased them from the reservation and continued to haunt them no matter how far they traveled.[51]

Returning home was not necessarily an easy solution. Some Native people encountered resentment on the part of fellow tribal citizens who had remained on the reservation, held the community together, and had no wild tales of urban adventure to share. This occasionally caused a painful and lingering estrangement between certain tribal members that would not have been unfamiliar to numerous boarding school graduates who, during previous decades, had returned home to a sense of alienation. Department of the Interior information specialist Pauline Bates Brown, who had previously worked in the War Relocation Authority, hosted a relocation informational session in Phoenix in 1956 that acknowledged this problem. She warned Native people interested in the program that they would officially represent the U.S. federal government and would therefore attract suspicion from those who avoided the program. "Our Bureau is often the whipping boy for the sins of others," she goaded.[52] Relatedly, in December 1959, future Taos Pueblo council secretary and interpreter Telesfor Romero wrote anthropologist Sophie B. Aberle to share information he had gathered while visiting relocated Pueblo people in an unspecified city. He somewhat cryptically described his findings as "not so satisfactory." Moreover, alluding to a pervasive sense of shame among those who had supposedly failed in the city, Romero concluded from his discussion with Pueblo returnees that they "do not seem to want to tell out right on account they do not want to be embarrass [sic]."[53]

· · · · · ·

Despite many relocated Indians' struggle to adjust, the Bureau of Indian Affairs worked hard to promote the benefits of its pet program and, in the process, diluted its criteria for determining "success." In 1960, Commissioner of Indian Affairs Glenn L. Emmons claimed that 70 percent of all relocated Indians had "become self-supporting in their new homes." Problematically, however, Emmons equated "success" with any Indian individual or family that remained in their urban destination for at least one year. He touted these figures as evidence of what Indian people could achieve "if they are only given a reasonable opportunity." Emmons also pointed to vociferous support from a four-man Navajo committee that formed in the fall of 1956 and visited numerous relocated Navajo families in their new urban homes. In the group's final report, committee chair Haska Cronemyer, who also served on the general Navajo tribal council, admonished those who emphasized the difficulties relocated families experienced while exploiting such difficulties in order to "fight the Indian affairs bureau and the whole relocation program for their own purposes or publicity." "We think the relocation program is one of the best plans the Federal Government has ever had," Cronemyer elaborated. "Had it been in effect 50 years ago, the Indian would be much better off today."[54]

Some Native people refused to corroborate such triumphant claims, however. In 1959, *Dallas Morning News* correspondent Richard Freeman (Osage) wrote influential Oklahoma senator Robert S. Kerr to rail against suggestions that Indians who relocated to Dallas were living comfortably. Assistant Secretary of the Interior Roger Ernst, for example, had claimed that only 20 percent of Dallas relocatees had returned to their reservations, and that only one in 130 Indian families living in the Dallas Housing Authority project experienced housing eviction. Freeman countered that wage earners were not necessarily better equipped to provide for their families in Dallas, as compared to their reservations. Even if that were true, Freeman argued, the federal government should not boast about it because its treaty obligations were to help Indians on their reservations, not in the cities. Freeman pointed to an unspecified study conducted the previous fall that found that 25–33 percent of relocated Indians in Dallas were unemployed or only working part time. Moreover, he insisted that too many relocated Indians ended up in "slums of the city" or "hobo jungles." "Apparently, only the success cases are important to the Bureau, with the unsuccessful ones being immaterial," Freeman scorned.[55]

Father Peter Powell, founder of St. Augustine's Indian community church and social welfare agency in Chicago, recalled how his impression of Indians' experiences in Chicago hardly squared with BIA claims of high success rates. Powell argued that the BIA's assertion that 75 percent of the roughly 35,000 Indians who had relocated between 1953 and 1960 had successfully adjusted was "an absolute lie. Our people were in the midst of the most terrible turmoil one could imagine." Powell claimed that education and employment promises frequently failed, and that most relocated Indians could not take advantage of city welfare programs because they lacked a one-year residency requirement.[56]

While both Freeman and Powell can be considered authorities on relocation's relative "success" in their respective cities of Dallas and Chicago, they also serve as a reminder that the potential for success typically depended on the subjective socioeconomic conditions of a particular destination.

Regardless of Commissioner Emmons's "success" rates, faceless statistics tell us little about relocation's relative efficacy across space and time. Indeed, no one city can adequately represent the relocation program's relative value. For example, in an annual report from 1958, the Joliet, Illinois, relocation office confessed that it was failing to meet its objectives, which it blamed on a national recession that resulted in a dearth of low-rent public housing and job openings. Relocation to Joliet in general, alongside that of Waukegan, reflected the BIA's short-lived attempt to filter Native people not into a major urban area but into a major suburban area. Such communities, however, proved even more vulnerable to adverse market shifts. It did not help that the Joliet office—managed by Rudolph Russell, a Navajo man who had previously headed the Salt Lake City relocation office—operated on a shoestring budget: "one dirty room about 9×12 feet in size, with one borrowed desk and a telephone."[57]

By contrast, when asked why Los Angeles and Chicago typically registered as the two cities where relocatees had the most success, former relocation field officer Stanley Lyman noted that it was not so much a matter of those cities benefiting from better personnel or better program enrollees. Rather, Los Angeles and Chicago consistently featured an adequate number of job openings, even during economic recessions. "At a time when there were 250,000 unemployed in the Chicago area, we were still able to find jobs for Indians," he recalled. This mostly reflected those particular offices' strategy of matching an Indian to a job, rather than a job to an Indian. Simply put, the Los Angeles and Chicago offices produced better results by finding work that made sense for Indians' individual skill sets rather than trying to shoehorn Indians into industries that would never entirely accept them. This point perhaps demands that we think more critically about the BIA's apparent practice of intentionally routing relocated Indians toward low-wage jobs. To be sure, such low-wage jobs were not a feature of relocation recruitment propaganda. Yet such propaganda mattered little when relocation officials needed to make pragmatic decisions to keep the program solvent. According to Lyman, even the Los Angeles office failed at first because it worried too much about securing jobs well in advance of Indians' reservation departure. Chicago, in contrast, was more successful from the outset because the office there brought a set number of Indians in first and then found them a job; this worked because it allowed relocation agents to spontaneously jump on openings and then quickly fill them. Los Angeles eventually found greater success when it adopted the Chicago strategy.[58]

When You . . .

NEED WORKERS

- SKILLED   • UNSKILLED
- FULL TIME   • PART TIME
- PERMANENT   • TEMPORARY

Men   -   Women

Call

BUREAU OF INDIAN AFFAIRS

433 W. VAN BUREN STREET, ROOM 929   PHONE: 828-4480

BIA Chicago Office job appointment card (front), box 2, folder 24, Chicago Field Office—Employment, Families, Photographs, 1956, BIA Relocation Records, Newberry Library, Chicago.

Despite the BIA's public assertions that relocation had so far been a smashing success, behind closed doors numerous federal officials confessed that the program needed improvement. In December 1957, during a conference with tribal officials in Rapid City, South Dakota, BIA officials gathered information on relocatees' reasons for returning to their original homes. Additionally, both parties collectively brainstormed strategies for improving the program. Taken together, their findings are quite revealing about some of the struggles urban Indians faced. Chief among the meeting resolutions for improving program mechanics and morale was to announce home follow-up visits in advance, so that families could clean up and be prepared. "If you drop in they close up on you and won't talk," one meeting participant stated. A second solution mandated greater honesty about the potential for a "colored family" living next door, thus implying that some relocated families found such prospects disconcerting. "We must all be very frank with them in explaining possible conditions," the minutes stipulated. Finally, meeting attendees resolved to improve housing conditions after acknowledging that too many relocatees were subjected to apartments that were dirty and infested with cockroaches.[59]

Notwithstanding these important concerns about the program, leading officials who attended the Rapid City meeting also suggested that everyone involved simply needed to relax. Not only did Charles F. Miller, the chief of

BUREAU OF INDIAN AFFAIRS
BRANCH OF EMPLOYMENT ASSISTANCE

TO _____

_____

_____

This will introduce:

_____

Whom we discussed. Your cooperation is greatly appreciated.

_____

GPO 801-251   Phone No. _____ Ext. _____

BIA Chicago Office job appointment card (back), box 2, folder 24, Chicago Field Office—Employment, Families, Photographs, 1956, BIA Relocation Records, Newberry Library, Chicago.

relocation services, insist that all concerned parties were devoting far too much attention to return rates, he also—quite paradoxically and with a hint of Orwellian doublespeak—insisted that the program was failing because it was working: "If you are helping the people you should be helping, and not those who didn't need help to begin with, then naturally you will have returnees, they are struggling because they need help integrating." Relocation placement officer Mary Nan Gamble agreed: "They are only going to overcome it if they make themselves available by recognizing that the guy next door may not have been there any longer than he has, go do the normal things that come, speak to people." Gamble suggested that some relocatees never had any intention of establishing permanence in the city, and that they were only pursuing "a nice vacation at government expense."[60] Finally, during a newspaper interview in 1971, Chicago office acting director Virginia Roberts expressed a similar attitude toward Indians who might have been simply taking a vacation on the government's dime. After mentioning the example of a Native Alaskan family that regretted its move to Chicago, Roberts complained, "They want to be sent back home. But that will cost $694 and they want this office to pay it all. I don't have that kind of money for pleasure."[61]

If Billings area relocation specialist Jacob Ahtone (Kiowa) had been in attendance at the Rapid City conference, he likely would have agreed with

Charles F. Miller that all involved parties needed to take a deep breath and remember that no one promised that relocation would be an easy affair. During a round of correspondence the following year, Ahtone expressed acute frustration over Indians so quickly being tagged as failures if they moved or changed jobs subsequent to their initial relocation. Such an assessment lacked fairness, Ahtone asserted, because roughly 20 percent of the national population, regardless of race, relocated each year in response to changes in economic markets. "Too many of our critics expect Indian people to maintain their initial employment and remain forever at their original destination," Ahtone stated, before concluding that mobility is a natural and often necessary condition of American employment.[62]

Such pleas for greater patience and understanding were nothing new. As early as relocation's inaugural year of 1952, Chicago relocation field placement officer Kurt Dreifuss expressed a similar conviction that relocation would work if only granted more time and wider support. He requested greater community involvement in Indians' social adjustments and insisted that most Indian people who returned to reservations did so because "confusion and loneliness in a strange environment" too often rendered alcohol a tempting "alternative to constructive preoccupation."[63] Indeed, Dreifuss implored his BIA superiors not to give up on Indians who went on "benders" after arriving in the city. To Charles Rovin, assistant chief of relocation placement, he forwarded several examples of relocatees who eventually achieved stability after persevering through an inauspicious start. He requested that the BIA make stronger attempts at individual counseling while trying harder to understand that such benders did not indicate that relocated Indians were naturally bibulous or prone to alcoholism.[64]

Kurt Dreifuss's concern for alcohol's undermining potential was legitimate. Indeed, he was likely drawing on a recent example from his Chicago locale. After risking his life during the Battle of Iwo Jima in February 1945, and subsequently helping hoist the American flag as part of a Pulitzer Prize–winning photograph, Private First Class Ira Hayes (Pima) returned to the United States as a decorated veteran—the most famous Indian war hero from America's "good war." Capitalizing on an opportunity to exploit the charismatic soldier's celebrity, the Bureau of Indian Affairs recruited him as a poster boy for its Voluntary Relocation Program. In 1952, Hayes made headlines when he relocated to Chicago and took a position at International Harvester as a tool grinder. In the shadows of the media's spotlight, however, he further descended into a drinking problem that had first gripped him during the war and worsened when he began touring U.S. cities as a featured participant in postwar victory parades. It was common for admirers to buy him a drink in tribute to his battlefield courage, and Hayes repeatedly felt obliged to accept the kind gestures. Friends in Chicago noted that this resulted in a bad case of "heroitis."

Despite Hayes's enthusiastic attempt at carving out a new life as an industrial laborer in Chicago, he repeatedly landed in prison for public intoxication. On one occasion, the *Chicago Sun-Times* raised bail on the beleaguered veteran's behalf, orchestrated his release, and sponsored his brief stay in an area sanitarium. In a somewhat bizarre turn of events, Hayes subsequently attempted a new life in Beverly Hills, working as a chauffeur for Rat Pack entertainer Dean Martin's estranged wife Elizabeth. In Beverly Hills, Hayes again landed in prison for public intoxication. The judge offered him a choice between incarceration and a return to his Pima reservation in Arizona. Hayes chose the latter, but the return home did not restore his health. In late 1954, he was arrested in Phoenix, at which point Indian bureau officials brokered a deal with Hayes: if he agreed to stay out of the city, the BIA would guarantee him steady work on the reservation. This marked a last chance to get his life together.[65]

Alas, in January 1955, Ira Hayes's dead body was discovered in a ditch outside a reservation village where his parents resided. While it obviously did not help, it would be irresponsible to suggest that Hayes's alcoholism was solely a product of urbanization. Not only would that be an oversimplification, but it would deny the strong possibility that post-traumatic stress disorder was a factor. Either way, Hayes's fate provides a reminder that relocation's relative success depended on numerous subjective and contingent factors. Even in his darkest times, Hayes advocated urban relocation as a solution to, and not an explanation for, his pain. Just before his death, he told friends and family that he dreamed of one day returning to Chicago and resuming his training as a tool grinder. "I still like Chicago," Hayes wrote in a letter to Commissioner of Indian Affairs Glenn Emmons. "To make out a guy has to watch his drinking and not drink the way I was. International [Harvester] was pretty nice to me. Who knows I might go back whenever I know for sure that I have my two feet on the ground."[66]

· · · · · ·

Taken together, this chapter indicates that federal officials lacked both a coherent understanding of the underlying causes of Indians' problems in the city and a viable set of solutions for those problems. It often seems that program administrators were making it up as they went along. Meanwhile, relocation's promise could diminish just as rapidly and unpredictably as it once emerged. At best, relocation amounted to a lofty experiment. It seems the only reliable given was that Native people would play a subjective and impactful role in determining the outcome of a process that inherently featured a wide margin for error.

Ultimately, competing and fleeting critiques of "success" and "failure" mattered little to Indian individuals on the front lines of the urban relocation experiment. They were busy fighting to advance their careers, protect their children, help family members back home, and navigate life in vast and unforgiving industrial metropolises or, on a smaller scale, hostile neighborhoods and workplaces. They were tasked with doing most of the heavy lifting to make the program work (when it did). Moreover, there were few, if any, reliable predictors of whether or not a particular individual possessed the necessary mettle to make it in the city.

But if relocation's potential was entirely subjective, then why do examples of urban Indian pathology, maladjustment, and life on skid row persist so forcefully, and often at the expense of empowering counternarratives? Why did they become the story? By attempting control of a process that thousands of Native Americans had already set in motion, Congress corrupted, if not wholly undermined, Native urban employment and social networks that had developed organically across previous decades. Congress's offer to subsidize urban relocation at first appeared a boon to many among the roughly sixty-five thousand Native people who had recently fought overseas or filled war-industry positions in urban centers such as Seattle, Los Angeles, and San Francisco. But soon the realities of an underfunded and dishonest program became apparent. Thousands of relocated Indians confronted a capricious labor market that resigned them to the ranks of last hired–first fired. Moreover, just when thousands of Native people began arriving in cities, the most coveted contemporary version of the American dream relocated to the suburbs—Lewis Mumford's critique notwithstanding.[67]

The urban America advertised in colorful posters tacked to bulletin boards on various reservation agency walls was gradually slipping away, and in some places was already gone, if it ever really existed. The federal government had pulled a bait and switch. According to historian Steven Conn, "For a century and a half, the growth in the American economy had been inextricably bound to the growth of the American cities. By 1960, that was no longer true."[68] In Chicago, for example, the total number of manufacturing jobs declined from 688,000 in 1947 to 277,000 in 1982, a 59 percent drop. Moreover, the Western and Sunbelt urban metropolises that exploded in size and cultural stature during the postwar period mostly conformed with a decentralization impulse, fueled by lingering racial segregation, which resulted in many middle- and upper-class white Americans conducting a "white flight" to new suburban communities. During that same period of 1947–82, suburban Chicago manufacturing jobs around Cook County increased from 121,000 to 279,000, a 131 percent increase.[69]

Thus, while cities held some potential for cosmopolitan experiences and raised incomes, metropolitan sprawl and a resolute determination on the part of numerous (sub)urbanites to avoid racialized minorities compromised urbanization's potential for facilitating new forms of Indian belonging. Access to cross-class and racially integrated social opportunities, if there ever really were such opportunities, depended on automobility, leisure time, and disposable income—luxuries a substantial portion of the relocated urban Indian population both desired and lacked. While they qualified as "urban" according to census data and other objective criterion, many Native people who relocated to cities ended up relatively isolated within impoverished ghettos, rendering "urban" more of a place than an idea. As Anishinabe writer Gerald Vizenor puts it, "[The] meaning of life in the city for many *oshki anishinabe* families is little more than an inside toilet."[70] Realizing that the version of the American dream that once resided in cities could not wholly be theirs, urban Indian people—most visibly urban Red Power groups that emerged in the Twin Cities, Chicago, Los Angeles, San Francisco, and other Indigenous metropolises—more forcefully articulated the centrality of sovereignty and land to their identity as Indigenous peoples. They did so even as they remained in cities and exercised not only dual citizenship between the United States and their Indigenous nations but also dual cultural identities as urban Indians—"Dallas Indian," "Chicago Indian"—and separated but inseparable members of Indigenous cultures: Lakota, Cheyenne, Mohawk, Navajo, and so on.

One tragedy of Indian urban relocation is that regardless of numerous people's success with it, for many Indian and non-Indian people, the failures confirmed expectations for Indian failure in cosmopolitan urban space. As with previous failed colonial initiatives, the federal government blamed the Indian people. And some Indians internalized that blame. This contributed to a zero-sum outcome in which people either failed at city living or succeeded at city living but then, by virtue of that very success, still failed in their commitments to their people, nation, and land.

With that, many urban Indians became both subjects of and participants in America's postwar anti-urban critique. This experience became a contributing factor to what it meant to be an *American* Indian during the postwar period.[71] "Relocation has degraded Indian people," Dakota Episcopal priest Father Vine Deloria Sr. charged during a meeting with Commissioner of Indian Affairs Philleo Nash in 1961.[72] There is perhaps an important, but subtle, insight in Deloria's statement. It was not mobility, or even urbanization, that he indicted for crimes against Indian people. After all, he had himself traveled all over during his life as an athlete, an activist, and a clergyman. It was the program itself and the federal government's attempt to supervise Indian mobility that did the damage. And when relocation's promise collapsed, many disenchanted urban Indians began looking back to their tribal homes as places of opportunity, purpose, and strength.

6   They Always Come Back

Urban Indians' Return to and Influence on a
Changing Indian Country

• •

We are nomads of old on wheels. You see, we can always
go home again and have a home to go to.

—Vine Deloria Jr. (Dakota, 1968)

This summer I shall
Return to our Longhouse
Hide behind a feathered hat,
And become an Old Man.
"Ambition"

—Phil George (Nez Perce, born in Seattle)[1]

One important and enduring criticism of the Bureau of Indian Affairs' mid-twentieth-century urban relocation program is that it drained reservations of an entire generation of promising young Native Americans. As influential former Oglala Lakota tribal president Gerald One Feather recalled, "Many people who could have provided tribal leadership were lost because they had the motivation to go off the reservation to find employment or obtain an education." The emigration of numerous bright young Indian minds hurt deeply in the context of Indian Country's fight against the termination policy and persistent land and resource dispossession.[2] For some, however, urbanization was merely a by-product of an alternate path toward supporting tribal sovereignty and self-determination. Urban spaces and experiences became valuable resources—places where people could either fight for Indian people from a distant cultural, capital, and political crossroads or gain new socioeconomic skills that could be carried back home. Many urban Indians returned home and became leaders in tribal government, and some were even recruited by their people to serve as tribal chiefs. At a conference in 1970, Herb Blatchford (Navajo), a cofounder of the National Indian Youth Council and director of the Indian community center in Gallup, New Mexico, discussed how urban Indians were gaining important technical knowledge. Having recently toured several reservations, he found that the leaders and administrators were all coming from the cities: "They are much more capable of analyzing the Reservation scene than they would have been if they had remained there. A competitiveness is building up on some Reservations, where traditionally trained leaders and urban cycle leaders are forming a new type of brain trust."[3] These emerging brain trusts countered the negative consequences of the brain drain.

With that, it is important to consider the historical implications of *reverse relocation* from reimagined urban Indian Country to ancestral and rural Indian Country. Many people returned not because they failed in the city but because they saw a more promising future back home on tribal lands. Many members of an emerging generation of urban Indians began reimagining rural Indian Country as a new place of opportunity.[4] And why not? Reflecting on the subject of urban Indians in 1970, Dakota scholar Vine Deloria Jr. claimed, "[The urban Indian scene] has relevance to development on the reservation, too, because I don't see that much difference in life between the two. When you go from one to another, there is really very little outward difference, and even little difference in economic problems."[5] Many urban Indians decided that if they were going to work hard and still struggle to make ends meet, they might as well do so at home, among and on behalf of their people.

Stories of Indian urbanization typically conclude with a perceived crisis that produces the Red Power movement. In the denouement, urban Indians, awakened to the realities of yet another federal government sham, realize they are better off being Indian and form activist groups to voice their anger and disenchantment.[6] This chapter brings the story of urban relocation to a different conclusion, one that does not necessarily end in crisis or catharsis, and one that does not end in the city. Urban Indians maintained fluid relationships with their tribal homelands. Moreover, both urban and rural Indians constantly put cities and reservations in dialogue with each other while considering how and where they wanted to live and belong as Indigenous peoples. In most historical accounts of twentieth-century Indian urbanization, reservations tend to disappear once our Indian subjects arrive in the city. But in reality, reservations and ancestral lands remained ever visible in the rearview mirror.

· · · · · ·

Representing the Red Lake Band of Chippewa during a conference with Indian affairs commissioner Glenn Emmons in 1956, Joseph Graves projected mixed feelings about the urban relocation program. "If you want relocation you will have to destroy the Reservation first. They always return. There seems to be an instinct similar to the fish," he suggested. Graves spoke from a position of extensive off-reservation experience. After attending school in Philadelphia and working in a steel mill for several years, Graves, on Hall of Famer and fellow Chippewa Indian Charles "Chief" Bender's recommendation, played professional baseball for the Philadelphia Athletics during the early 1920s. Moreover, he was but one member of a prominent Red Lake Chippewa family that included his father, Peter, who served as chief of the original Red Lake General Council, and his daughter Verna, who regularly traversed the nation as an educator, political activist, and Episcopal minister. If the Graves family did indeed resemble fish, then they had certainly swum far and wide.[7]

It is not surprising that Graves did not position himself against the relocation program in principle. He bristled at the notion that Indians had been "chained down on the Reservation," only to be freed by relocation. At the same time, he felt a strong "instinct of returning to the Reservation," an impulse he also witnessed among young people from Red Lake. He therefore advocated healthy maintenance of the reservation, especially as a refuge during times of illness. Still, citing examples of Red Lake boys who failed to return to work after a reservation respite, he did not want Indians to get too comfortable in any one place. Ultimately, he promoted movement, because movement promoted growth. Satisfied with his own life, he only regretted that it had not been easier. "I wish I was living in their age where I would be relocated," he reflected. "That would be real valuable."[8]

Among tribal leaders, Graves was not alone in his trust that young Indians would only benefit from time spent away from Indian Country. During a Taos Pueblo tribal council meeting in 1959, Severino Martinez expressed no concerns about young Indians leaving the pueblo. He felt confident that Pueblo youth had been sufficiently trained in the Indian ways and religion and therefore "would someday come back to the pueblo and follow the old customs." Regardless of geographic distance, Martinez seemed to suggest, Taos Pueblo people would always be tethered to the tribe through spiritual faith.[9] In 1968, Navajo tribal councilman Howard Gorman gathered a similar impression about young Navajo men and women who mingled with mainstream America. "There is probably a certain amount of custom and tradition that they hang on to which causes them to come back," he speculated. "Every now and then when vacations roll around instead of going down to Mexico or down to Florida or someplace back east, they come right straight home."[10]

Among the generation of ambitious young Indians whom tribal leaders trusted would someday return to help their people, Matthew Pilcher provides a most illustrative example. In the early 1950s, Pilcher left his Winnebago reservation for a brief stint in the army. Once discharged, he migrated from Los Angeles to Chicago, where he found steady work as a construction company foreman. "When I first got to Chicago there were older people who had been there for years," he recalled. By 1970, he had assumed the assistant directorship of St. Augustine's Center for Indians, a busy social services agency and community church in Chicago's Uptown Indian neighborhood. His successful trajectory from military serviceman to construction foreman to social services agency administrator informed his conviction that Indians needed to strive for something more satisfying and profitable than vocational training projects, which only "served to stymie and to negate the intellectual growth of our young people." Better opportunities, he argued, waited within the walls of academic institutions, such as the University of Illinois Circle Campus, where he helped establish a Native American studies program. "It is heartening to see [Indians] studying in areas of academic endeavor that were unattainable to [them] only a few short years ago, simply because Indians were shackled to the myth that we are incapable of intelligent thought," he reflected.[11]

Still, Pilcher saw the city as more of a resource than a permanent destination. "I always think the relocation program backfired on the American government," he reasoned. "It made a lot of Indian people in the city realize the importance of education." He wanted to see a generation of young college-trained Indians "carry this education back to the reservation areas" while providing "models for other Indian youngsters." He appreciated rural Indian Country as a sort of sanctuary, where educated Indians could escape "the throes of economic deprivation in urban areas." In the clearest sense, he embraced the city more as a socioeconomic means than as a geographic end. Indeed, he began remaking his home in Winnebago, Nebraska, during the early 1980s, at which point the tribal government quickly recruited him into its fold. Across subsequent years, the skills Pilcher had developed in Chicago played an essential role in his successful tenures as tribal councilman, treasurer, and finally president. Drawing on administrative experience gained in Chicago, he successfully secured numerous private and government grants, supervised audits, and balanced the tribal budget. Pilcher's story represents a larger process that noticeably shifted in

Matthew Pilcher (Winnebago): "Winnebago, Nebraska, is home. I was only *living* in Chicago." Photo in author's possession.

reverse. Whereas Native people from earlier decades fanned outward toward cities to escape the limited potential of reservation economies, by the early 1970s urban Indians had begun reimagining tribal lands as places of opportunity and respite.[12]

Lack of gainful employment opportunities and growing disenchantment with the city played a significant role in this reversal. But underneath that cynical surface persisted a trend of Native people mostly pursuing opportunities wherever they could find them. As painful as relocation may have been, numerous Native people emerged wiser for the experience and with newfound strength. The enduring goal had always been to return to the reservation and make it "something better than what we left it with," Herb Blatchford suggested. "This seems to be an Indian philosophy that doesn't die out, as bad as things get. . . . That spirit doesn't seem to die and it doesn't die in the urban scene either."[13]

By the early 1970s, anti-urban sentiments had crystallized among numerous Native people who had attempted city living but concluded that it was detrimental to their health. Lac Court Oreilles tribal councilwoman Violet Hayes mentioned that during the early 1970s, her reservation instituted a land-assignment waiting list for people who wanted to come home—a complete reversal of the early years of the relocation program, when many reservations featured a waiting list to leave. Likewise, National Congress of American Indians acting executive director Leo Vocu claimed, "I know very few urban Indians who intend to die in the urban areas in which they live. . . . All of them want to go home." Vocu's theory was that Indian people had begun realizing that without a land base, they would cease to exist as a distinct people within the United States. "Can you understand that?" he asked. "They would look like Indians, or act like Indians, but they would have no home." One Native man from Chicago's Uptown Indian neighborhood summarized numerous Indians' dismay with the relocation program when he quipped, "We want the Indian to get off his reservation and get a welding job in Detroit so he can afford to buy a steak which he won't be able to eat because he has gotten ulcers, or, in other words, 'Why don't you get a mortgage like us?'" Finally, William Wildcat, who had operated a gas station in Chicago for fifteen years, appreciated his Lac du Flambeau reservation as a sort of paradisiacal sanctuary. "White people work all year so they can have a couple weeks to vacation here," he boasted. "Well, we live here year 'round—with 126 lakes."[14]

In 1971, Tim Wapato, a member of the Confederated Tribes of the Colville Reservation, noted how the BIA misled Indians into believing that simple vocational skills prepared them to compete in the city. Wapato knew something about competing in the city. He was born in one: Chicago. Raised among his Colville people in Washington State, he migrated to Los Angeles upon reaching adulthood and earned the rank of lieutenant in the LAPD. "I bet I have talked to a thousand Indian welders in the city of Los Angeles," he reasoned. "I don't think there are jobs for a fifth of that number, and yet we seem to keep training Indian welders." At age forty-four, Wapato moved back home to Washington, where he took a position with the Columbia River Inter-Tribal Fish Commission. From there, he went to work in Washington, D.C., for numerous federal departments and commissions. He later entered the private sector and founded the National Indian Gaming Association and played an active role in the National Congress of American Indians.[15]

Wapato's observation reflected a larger unemployment epidemic among the nation's urban Indian population. In 1971, the national Indian jobless rate registered at 39 percent, with an additional 19 percent who could only claim seasonal work. Given these figures, it is not surprising that a cohort of educated urban Indians began looking outward from the city and across distant prairies for new socioeconomic opportunities. Yet those who remained home did not sit idly by, waiting for a generation of college-educated Indians to swoop in and save their reservation. Rather, they actively worked to facilitate their own opportunities and, in the process, engaged in their own "reimagining" of Indian Country.[16]

· · · · · ·

Urban Indians did not necessarily find immediate refuge upon returning home to the reservation. They often encountered a situation in which BIA representatives and tribal leaders alike scrambled—often at odds with each other—to rehabilitate neglected reservation economies.[17] Indian affairs commissioner Glenn Emmons recognized that there was a deficiency of reservation development projects capable of challenging the appeal of urban work opportunities. In a round of personal correspondence with Indian Rights Association representative Theodore Hetzel, Emmons claimed, "I do not believe and never have believed that relocation is the only way of providing Indians with broader and better opportunities for making a decent living." Acknowledging that some Indians would always prefer to remain at home, Emmons continued, "So it is now definitely a part of our program to encourage the establishment of industrial plants in the vicinity of important reservation areas."[18]

In 1956, under Emmons's direction, the Bureau of Indian Affairs announced a series of new industrial development projects for the reservation. Out east, Cherokee Leathercraft in North Carolina hired 40 Eastern Cherokee to produce moccasins. Up north, 100 Northern Cheyenne labored at a fishing-tackle plant in Lame Deer, Montana, and 100 Sioux workers helped construct trailer homes in Rapid City, South Dakota. To the southwest, 125 Pima and Tohono O'odham sewed garments at Casa Grande Mills in Arizona. Sanctioned by a unanimous tribal council vote of 56–0, the Navajo tribe directed $344,000 from its own tribal fund toward an effort to attract two California-based corporations to the Navajo reservation. The plan succeeded. Lear Navajo, affiliated with Lear Electronics from Santa Monica, and Navajo Furniture, a subsidiary of Baby Line Furniture from Los Angeles, moved in and hired one hundred Navajo workers each. Interestingly, Baby Line Furniture's decision to contract with the Navajo was in part influenced by the corporation's positive experience employing Indian workers at its Los Angeles plant, thereby forming a uniquely important link between urban Indian Country and rural Indian Country.[19]

One year earlier, in 1955, BIA commissioner Glenn Emmons had installed Carl Beck to the new position of assistant to the commissioner, a position created in part to help oversee these important tribal business operations. Beck had worked in the Indian service for twenty-one years, interrupted only by a brief foray into Arizona's private business sector. His duties were not limited to the supervision of reservation economic development, however. Emmons also appointed Beck to the post of relocation program supervisor, which proved a fateful decision. By 1957, the entire operation was in disarray. Lear Electronics in Flagstaff had closed; Casa Grande garment factory had gone bankrupt and closed; Baby Line Furniture, supported by the $344,000 Navajo investment, faced trouble for violating minimum wage laws; and Beck had been unceremoniously dismissed. According to Neal Jensen, relocation officer at the United Pueblos Agency, Beck fell victim to jealous, competitive conflicts between the relocation and reservation development branches of the BIA's operation in the Southwest. Meanwhile, Jensen faced his own obstacles in trying to find jobs for Pueblo Indians in nearby Albuquerque and Alamogordo, which were experiencing something of an economic boom. As Jensen explained it, this had everything to do with New Mexico senator Dennis Chavez warning him against interfering with the New Mexico Employment Security Service.[20]

This debacle notwithstanding, Pueblo and Navajo business leaders persisted in their efforts to bring factory jobs to their reservations. In 1964, for example, several Laguna Pueblo Indians gained employment at a new electronic components factory that the tribe had built for $450,000 from its own mineral resource funds and subsequently leased to New York–based Burnell & Company. Excited about the new potential for steady income, tribal chief Irvin Santiago declared, "This could mean a new life for the Indian." Raymond Nakai, chair of the nearby Navajo tribe, expressed similar optimism: "With a situation like this, our only direction can be forward and upward." Santiago and Nakai had good reason to voice their enthusiasm. At that time, roughly 50 percent of all reservation-based Indians counted themselves as unemployed.[21]

From 1958 through 1963, only four industrial plants opened around the Navajo and Pueblo reservations in New Mexico. By contrast, in just the first half of 1964 alone, seven corporations had arrived in pursuit of profits and cheap labor. But credit for corporate investments often went to the tribes. In the previous ten years, for example, the Laguna Pueblo had invested $12 million in corporate securities. Outside corporations, then, could enjoy the benefits of accessible workers and resources without fear of a losing business venture. Still, while the situation clearly proved advantageous to corporations such as Burnell & Company, the Laguna Pueblo persisted.

Recognizing the inherent limitations of the mining industry, Chief Santiago continued to actively solicit the BIA's help with attracting outside industries.[22]

To be sure, the Laguna Pueblo were not the sole practitioners of this economic strategy. In the early 1960s, the Jicarilla Apache, Navajo, and North Carolina Cherokee had in similar fashion attached their hopes to high-risk capitalist endeavors. Moreover, both the tribes and the businesses they attracted believed in the potential for a righteous outcome. For example, in 1966, B.V.D. underwear corporate executive Harry Isaacs claimed that his company's plan to open a manufacturing plant near the Hopi reservation would result in a "high social good" for prospective Hopi workers. Tribal leaders must have agreed. To get the project started, they invested $1.5 million from their own tribal funds, which at that time counted as the single largest tribal commercial investment ever. To demonstrate their enthusiasm for the burgeoning factory, several of the two hundred Hopi new hires donned buttons that read "Ask Me about B.V.D."[23]

Pursuing every feasible strategy toward economic rehabilitation, numerous tribes embraced America's expanding family road trip trend and the growing popularity of western tourism. A Red Lake Indian Reservation informational brochure from 1963 invited tourists to visit the "scenic, historical" reservation in Minnesota's northern paradise. Instructing prospective tourists to "Bring Your Camera," the brochure paradoxically proclaimed that Red Lake was a venue within which visitors could "see the Past at the Present." Indeed, on the same south shore of Lower Red Lake, tourists could visit both the "Site of the Last Battle in 1765 between Sioux and Chippewa Indians where the Sioux were annihilated" and the tribe's pristine automated sawmill, which had recently replaced their obsolete steam-driven sawmill. Included among the brochure's myriad photos and colored-pencil drawings were black-and-white snapshots of the Red Lake Tribal Council studiously poring over a mess of documents in their office; two young Red Lake girls outfitted head-to-toe in beaded buckskin as they staffed an arts and crafts table at the tribal office; Senator Hubert Humphrey posing alongside tribal chair Roger Jourdain and a troop of Indian Girl Guides; and a photo of beloved Indian affairs commissioner Philleo Nash, dressed in a contemporary suit and black tie that clashed with an oversized feathered headdress that partially swallowed his furrowed brow. The brochure's overarching message seems fairly explicit: Red Lake offered tourists a vibrant cultural experience that allowed them to intimately mingle with a romantic American past—without fear of getting lost, hurt, or even dirty.[24]

Calculated promotion of Indian cultural traditions also played a feature role in some tribes' efforts to lure outside business interests across reservation lines. In September 1963, as part of an effort to attract the A&E Tool and Gage Company of Rockford, Illinois, to the communities of Wolf Creek and Poplar on Montana's Fort Peck reservation, the Sioux and Assiniboine tribes prepared a book of facts that juxtaposed the tribes' exotic past with a capacity for present-day ingenuity. For example, the book opened with a dazzling photo of Williamette Belle Youpee—winner of the tenth annual Miss Indian America pageant—outfitted in beaded buckskin and wrapped braids that framed her gleaming face. Across subsequent pages, the book boasted of the reservation's excellent schools, churches, hospitals, and civic organizations before emphasizing its valuable agricultural and oil resources. Demonstrating Fort Peck tribal leaders' business acumen, the promotional book provided an outline of typical utility rates before concluding with a detailed breakdown of Montana's state tax system.[25]

In similar fashion, a brochure that the Oneida tribe of Wisconsin disseminated in the late 1960s to attract industry highlighted its reservation's numerous selling points. First, the brochure emphasized that the Oneida tribe "is a sophisticated and progressive tribe, which employs approximately 400 people and provides governmental services to 3,000 tribal members." The brochure then specifically cited a "progressive effort" that was currently underway to construct a $10.5 million hotel. Pointing to the reservation's close proximity to Green Bay, the brochure writers made sure to list the bustling nearby industries: papermaking, food processing, metal work, textiles, cheese, and meatpacking. The tribe's central selling point, however, was its thirty-two-acre industrial park, "located on prime land within the Green Bay metropolitan area" and zoned for light manufacturing. In closing, the brochure assured prospective industrial partners that "the Oneida tribe stands ready to assist private industry in the areas of venture capital, and to construct buildings that suit the needs of a company." In one final stipulation, the brochure mentioned that companies that hired Oneida workers "will be provided with lease payment reductions and a job training subsidy package." Perhaps more interestingly, a second brochure apologized for the Oneida's past course of "passive aggression" before claiming, "Now that we are actively seeking ways of becoming more involved with industry and the 'world of work' we have established and developed The Oneida Industrial Park," which, as the informational brochure stressed, came with a readily available labor pool of Indian people. Emphasizing a promising intersection of the romanticized Indian of the past and the modern Indian of the present, the tribe artfully manipulated its own stereotype by promising prospective employers that "Indians have inherent manual dexterity and eye/hand coordination."[26]

Some tribes attempted economic rehabilitation not by inviting businesses to indulge in tribal traditions within reservations' vicinity but through the exportation of factory-produced ephemera posing as "traditional" cultural artifacts. In 1966, as part of its on-the-job training program, the Aberdeen area office contracted with Golden Eagle Arts and Crafts to establish a manufacturing plant in Macy, Nebraska, on the Omaha Indian Reservation. The contract amounted to $5,050.00 and employed twelve Omaha Indians who crafted khaki-colored tepees that sold for $14.49 at Brandeis Department Store in Omaha. According to one business executive, the Indian workers produced "top quality" work. In this case, the marketing of supposedly traditional Indian culture from a bygone era provided the Omaha workers an opportunity to engage in industrial labor within their reservation limits. Simply put, Omaha workers merged past and present as a survival strategy. The Plains Indian tepees that filled urban department store shelves contradictorily contributed to the endurance of a romantic Indian past, while reservation-based producers practiced a modern Indian present—the fruits of urban relocation inverted.[27]

At times, the same penchant for domestic paternalism that the BIA practiced in its relocation program overlapped with reservation development projects. For example, in 1963, the BIA advertised "A Living Dream for Pine Ridge Indians," which took the form of a new housing project supported by the federal government's Housing and Home Finance Agency. For some Lakota residents, life in the new addition meant first exposure to a confined neighborhood, community codes, and monthly rent. Indeed, some residents were quick to complain about "losing their freedoms." Similar to the experiences of thousands of urban relocatees, Lakota residents of Pine Ridge's "Living Dream" had to navigate a team of pesky BIA domestic experts who descended on them with tutorials in meal preparation, house cleaning, and furniture arrangement. Also similar to relocation program paternalism, BIA agents monitored family budgeting and finances, and made unannounced visits to grade Lakota women on their performance of housekeeping duties— even disseminating booklets on how to conduct chores and how to use an electric stove. To encourage enthusiasm for the new housing, the BIA distributed posters that resembled relocation flyers in their emphasis on new appliances and living-room leisure. One might have concluded that Indians who dismissed the relocation program were going to have it brought to their doorstep anyway.[28]

At times, urban Red Power activists and reservation business leaders clashed over competing visions on how to improve reservation economies. Outside activists wanted to defend a vulnerable workforce, while tribal business leaders wanted to prove that Indian Country was safe for capitalistic development. On February 24, 1975, the American Indian Movement staged an armed takeover of the Navajo reservation's Fairchild electronics plant, which had recently released 140 Indian employees. AIM answered with a seven-and-a-half-day occupation, which backfired. As a countermove to AIM's occupation, Fairchild elected to close its Shiprock, New Mexico, location, which, needless to say, held inestimable negative consequences for the community. To fill the tribe's now vacant manufacturing plant, tribal leaders scrambled to court competing electronics corporations, including Texas Instruments and Motorola.[29]

Meanwhile, AIM maintained that Fairchild was going to terminate operations in Shiprock anyway, and that the corporation had for too long been exploiting Indians as a cheap labor source. Lisa Nakamura's study on this topic agrees. She argues that corporate capitalists saw the Navajo people as an ideal workforce because, in contrast to striking workers in other parts of the country, they could not relocate. Therefore, the immobility and vulnerability of Navajo workers was rhetorically spun into an act of purposeful and care-driven cultural preservation on the part of the corporation. The corporation also presented the appeal of circuit board work in gendered and racialized terms that also manipulatively appealed to tradition: Navajo women supposedly had "nimble fingers," and making a circuit board was supposedly similar to weaving a Navajo rug.[30] Among the company's 473 employees, most were Navajo women. In fact, the company at that point ranked as the largest non-federal, non-tribal employer of Indians in the country. In the debacle's aftermath, tribal employment director Jack Silango avowed, "All we want is to be recognized as a people equal to our counterparts bordering the reservation."[31]

Despite many Indians' desire for wider socioeconomic equality, industrial employment near reservations did not necessarily produce satisfaction among the local Indian population. In July 1962, the Omaha tribe and the Bureau of Indian Affairs entered into a partnership with the Chairs Unlimited Corporation to provide industrial training and employment for Omaha Indians as part of the BIA's vocational training program, enacted through

Public Law 959 in 1956. Chairs Unlimited initially installed its factory in Omaha with the promise of relocating to Macy, Nebraska, on the Omaha reservation, within six months. This would theoretically allow the company to conduct requisite training sessions while gaining a viable foothold in the area. Under that agreement, Omaha workers began carpooling and commuting seventy-five miles from their reservation to the new worksite. Unfortunately, relations between Chairs Unlimited and the Omaha tribe deteriorated as quickly as they had come together.

By December 1962, the Omaha Tribal Council was expressing deep discontent over Chairs Unlimited's policy against hiring female workers. By that point, the Omaha tribe had also begun doubting the sincerity of the corporation's promise to relocate to Macy. In April 1963, the tribe attempted to force the company's hand by discontinuing its biweekly supplementation of trainees' salaries. Chairs Unlimited fired back, claiming that it was incapable of relocating because there was so much absenteeism on the part of Omaha trainees that it could not get production up to a level necessary to support the move. The BIA tried to arbitrate and convince Chairs Unlimited that if it moved to Macy, attendance would stabilize. The BIA's plea initially fell on deaf ears, but by August there was a break in the impasse and Chairs Unlimited announced that it was ready, albeit eight months late, to begin planning a move to Macy. In a surprising turn of events, however, the Omaha Tribal Council officially voted against the move, noting that the corporation had "let them down." On the one hand, the Omaha tribe sacrificed an opportunity to lure industrial work within the reservation limits. On the other hand, the Omaha people boldly asserted that they would not be exploited by outside interests, and that the ultimate fate of economic rehabilitation of the reservation would rest in their hands only.[32]

· · · · · ·

Dating back to World War II's aftermath, Native people had continuously called for their own Point IV program, which would compel the U.S. government to rebuild Indian Country as it had done for war-torn Europe.[33] But as this chapter has hopefully demonstrated, the rehabilitation of Indian Country proved incredibly difficult. The process at best unfolded in fits and starts, in no small part due to the fact that Indian people demanded a voice in the proceedings. Indeed, by 1970, Native people had embraced new economic strategies with such enthusiasm that the reliably perceptive Vine Deloria Jr. seemed mystified over whether or not the ever-evolving "Indian problem" and the contemporary meaning of "tribe" had become inextricably bound up in corporate culture. "Is [a tribe] a traditionally organized band of Indians following customs with medicine men and chiefs dominating the policies of the tribe," he wondered, "or is it a modern corporate structure attempting to compromise at least in part with modern white culture?"[34] Regardless of the answer, while portions of Native America's tribal base envisioned a future in urban metropolises, those who remained on reservations also sought economic and social regeneration.[35]

In 1980, influential anthropologist Alfonso Ortiz recalled how during the 1960s, Indians from the Southwest living in San Francisco and Los Angeles heard calls from back home for skilled professionals to help administer Great Society programs. The talented Indian people who answered the call effectively set in motion a process of reverse relocation. Ortiz's own San Juan Pueblo community's population, for example, expanded from 720 people in 1964 to 1,200 in 1980, and not because of natural increase. Rather, it was because several hundred of his people had concluded that the "California dream was dying."[36]

Writing in 1970, Vine Deloria Jr. witnessed a similar trend taking shape in Indian Country. Most at stake in his evaluation was Native people's right to exercise tribal self-determination away from the paternalistic gaze of BIA officials. "By 1967 there was a radical change in thinking on the part of many of us," he wrote. "Where non-Indians had been pushed out to make room for Indian people, they had wormed their way back into power and again controlled the major programs serving Indians." According to Deloria, the gains that Native individuals and tribal governments had made in recent years were being undermined by yet another intrusive cycle of non-Indian sociopolitical experts who refused to acknowledge Indians' capacity for managing their own affairs. The moment was ripe, then, for a new breed of Indian leadership—one that could beat federal bureaucrats at their own game—to emerge and retake control of tribal governance. "So, in large part, younger Indian leaders who had been playing with the national conference field began working at the local level to build community movements from the ground up," Deloria explained. Many of those younger Indian leaders emerged from urban metropolises.[37]

After a stint in the navy, Lester Chapoose landed not on his feet but down on his back in Los Angeles, where he ended up jobless and homeless, sleeping in parks and vacant buildings, and biding his time in the Indian bars at Third and Main Streets. Fortunately, he lived to tell about it. "The only way to [survive] is you don't take any shit from anybody and you don't give anybody a bad time," he declared. "There was no picnic out there for anybody

Lester Chapoose (Ute): "There was no picnic out there for anybody who didn't belong." Courtesy of the Denver Public Library, Western History Collection, call number X-30451.

who didn't belong." Chapoose eventually climbed his way back and gained admission to the University of Utah, where he earned an accounting degree that made him a viable candidate for tribal chair back home on his Ute reservation. Winning his first election in 1973, Chapoose's administration established a successful tannery, fabric factory, bowling alley, and cattle enterprise while lowering tribal unemployment to 14 percent, a remarkable figure for that time. Citing golf outings with Bob Hope and Gerald Ford, Chapoose credited much of his success to his talent for negotiating with non-Indians, a skill he developed away from the reservation. "[It's] not all that hard," he reasoned. "Because I've done it so damn many times. I could be an Indian here at the Fourth of July powwow and wear my boots and Levi's and talk to the Indian people. And I can be in the Governor's Ball the next night and be in an entirely different outfit, and an entirely different conversation."[38]

Former National Congress of American Indians representative, Brigham Young University political science graduate, and Muscogee Creek tribal member David Lester embraced a similar set of values. Having accepted the directorship of the Los Angeles Urban Indian Development Association shortly after its formation in 1970, he valued the city as a temporary training ground within which Indians could gain valuable experience to benefit their people back home on reservations. "You don't find the talent for development in rural areas in America; you find them in the cities," he asserted. "I think for too long the Bureau of Indian Affairs ignored that fact." Lester wanted to see the BIA "subsidize the qualified Indians, take him back to the reservation, because he's taking the unqualified Indian off the reservation to train him in the city and leave him there." Above all, Lester promoted what he termed "re-relocation," which involved "rekindling [Indians] desire to do something for their own people."[39]

Joseph Vasquez echoed David Lester's loyalty to reservations while promoting an entrepreneurial spirit. And like his larger emerging cohort of socioeconomically savvy leaders, he spoke from experience. Vasquez began working at the Los Angeles Indian center in 1937, and then bounced from aeronautics school to the navy to jobs in San Diego, El Paso, and Mexico before finally landing at Hughes Aircraft back in Los Angeles. His own travels notwithstanding, he agreed with David Lester that those who gained skills in mainstream society were obliged to make a meaningful contribution to their tribe. "The people who are running the programs on the reservations . . . are the people who have gone out, become urbans and got an education and have gone back," he explained. "I maintain, and I've said it time and again . . . the day of the bow and arrow is gone, the only way to fight the White man is to fight him with the white man's ways." The current weapons at Indians' disposal, Vasquez concluded, were "words, contracts, and money."[40]

Had the leaders of the Sac and Fox tribe read Vasquez's proclamation about the new trinity of contemporary Indian weaponry—words, contracts, and money—they likely would have agreed. They had learned that lesson the hard way. By 1980, the Sac and Fox tribe of Oklahoma had amassed $250,000 in debt, an overwhelming problem when taking into account their relatively meager $200,000 annual operating budget. The predicament proved so severe that the BIA stepped in and assumed control of the tribe's financial affairs. Despite the BIA's intervention, however, Sac and Fox leadership remained committed to crafting their own solution for their own misfortune. In his capacity as principal chief, forty-eight-year-old

Jack Thorpe, son of legendary athlete Jim Thorpe, attempted to rescue the nation from ruin. In his first move, he forfeited his own $18,000-a-year salary. Then, inspired by the capitalistic business strategies of H. Ross Perot, he embraced his executive power and designated responsibilities to a team of budgetary experts. "One of the main mistakes a lot of tribal leaders make is to try to run everything themselves when they don't have the expertise," he acknowledged.

Thorpe's leadership and business acumen proved successful. By 1986, the tribe had paid off its debts, was operating on a robust $3.2 million annual budget, and even boasted a modest cash surplus. Moreover, the tribe was making forays into the oil and gaming industries while simultaneously fashioning a plan to purchase and relocate a Tulsa-based textile factory to a small plot of land within the former Sac and Fox reservation.[41] The BIA, however, remained skeptical about the tribe's new financial prowess and dragged its feet on sanctioning the textile factory plan. Still, tribal general manager Gene Bread held out hope that BIA obstinacy would soften as it grew to understand the plan's value. "We've simply surpassed the ability of the BIA to deal with us," he reasoned. "Many of the things we're doing as a tribe are beyond the BIA bureaucrats' technical knowledge and background to understand." Responding to a journalist's inquiry about the implications that risky capitalist ventures held for tribal culture, tribal second chief Gaylon Franklin rejected cultural assumptions by asserting, "We're becoming more Indianized again. Instead of trying to assimilate ourselves to white America, we're taking what white America has to offer and assimilating it to us." Explicitly connecting capitalist entrepreneurship to tribal self-determination, Franklin elaborated, "The Sac and Fox tribe has decided to have a hand in its own destiny. . . . I call it the new Indian frontier."[42]

Some members of this new wave of tribal leadership strategically planted one foot in urban Indian America and the other in rural Indian America, maneuvering between the two for the mutual benefit of Native people in both vicinities. Consider, for example, Wah-Wah-Suk, a Haskell Institute graduate and citizen of the Potawatomie Nation who, during his thirties, juggled such a role when making regular pilgrimages from his family's home in Philadelphia's Mount Airy suburb to his reservation home in Mayetta, Kansas. Upon discharge from the U.S. Army, Wah-Wah-Suk settled in Philadelphia, where he first saw the Liberty Bell and concluded that it "held no liberty for me." He supported his family by driving a bleach truck around the Delaware Valley metro area. In his spare time, he practiced his true calling in life: providing legal counsel to his Potawatomie tribe back in Kansas, with whom he conferenced four to five times a year. Something of a legal autodidact, his Mount Airy home bulged with legal tomes and documents that he pored over each evening. On Sundays, he regularly met with roughly two dozen Indians who formed the United American Indians of the Delaware Valley social activist group. Regardless of which community he served, his mantra remained consistent: "What can I do for my people?"[43]

During a series of interviews in 1974 and 1977, Quechan tribal historian Lee Emerson spoke to a similar strategy of borrowing from mainstream America in order to strengthen Indian America when he suggested, "We ought to be progressive." Discussing the potential benefits of tribal hydroponic farming initiatives, he elaborated, "We have to get into the mainstream of the white society life." He insisted that his fellow tribespeople needed to begin using their own "initiative-ness" to establish more businesses like the new hotel the tribe was building at that time. "We are trying to emulate white citizens of Yuma, both in religion, development, and education," Emerson stated. He stressed that creating a thriving reservation economy was essential in keeping aspiring Indian professionals tied to their tribal land and culture. While he confessed that certain professions demanded proximity to urban America, he stressed that those in agriculture school, real estate, and business administration could "come back and use their expertise." After explaining that Quechan people had in recent decades dispersed "all over the states," Emerson proudly mentioned that when they returned home, they witnessed a growing reservation economy and, by extension, a changing Indian Country: "They come back through at times to see how we are and, every time they come back they notice the difference from when they left the reservation. We've increased our enterprises, increased our land development. We need more land."[44]

It might be fair to suggest that no tribal nation improved its economy and increased its enterprise portfolio as rapidly and extensively as the Choctaw Nation of Mississippi. When it did, the implications for urban relocated Choctaw people were significant. By 1990, Phillip Martin, "the architect of Choctaw development," had been a Mississippi Choctaw tribal leader for just over thirty years. This is interesting given his determination as a younger man to get as far away from Mississippi as possible. After graduating from boarding school in North Carolina, Martin joined the air force and accepted an assignment in postwar Europe, where he was inspired by Germany's determination to rebuild its economy. From there, the air force sent him to

Okinawa; San Francisco; and Bangor, Maine. Discharged in 1955, Martin briefly returned home, met his wife, and made plans to move away: "I thought maybe I'd find us something in Chicago or back in San Francisco— anywhere but the place I'd come from." At age thirty, he had already spent nineteen years away from his Choctaw tribe. He was not alone in his search for stable employment, anywhere and at virtually any cost. During the 1950s, the Mississippi Choctaw people suffered from unemployment rates that ranged from 50 to 80 percent. During that same decade, up to one- quarter of the Mississippi Choctaw people lived in Los Angeles, Chicago, or Cleveland. Martin's wife, however, convinced him to stay. He attended com- munity college in nearby Meridian, then in 1957 became a tribal council representative, before becoming tribal chief in 1959. When he led trips to Washington to meet with government officials to discuss Choctaw economic rehabilitation, he rejected BIA escorts: "I've been all over the world. I don't need to be *taken* to Washington."[45]

Beginning in 1966 with an Office of Economic Opportunity grant, Phil- lip Martin's administration guided what became known as the "Choctaw Miracle." This was no small achievement. During the 1960s, 90 percent of the Mississippi Choctaw tribe lived in poverty, with an average annual family income of less than $1,000. In 1969, Martin directed a Housing and Urban Development grant toward a Choctaw housing project to update the reservation's New Deal–era shacks. In 1975, these tribal initiatives were but- tressed by the Indian Self-Determination and Education Assistance Act, which finally allowed tribes to manage most of their own finances.[46]

By 1983, the tribe's economic prospects had grown so strong that Chief Martin began making pilgrimages to Los Angeles, Chicago, and Cleveland to bring his relocated people back home. Martin literally went door-to-door, promising that a return home would offer jobs, housing, drug counseling, and Choctaw public assistance. Even better, Martin assured them that they no longer needed to answer to "the Man" because back home, "the Man" was now a Choctaw.[47]

From 1983 to 1990, the Mississippi Choctaw tribal government oversaw the creation of fifteen hundred industrial jobs in and around Philadel- phia, Mississippi. In 1990, the tribal nation ranked as the State of Missis- sippi's fifteenth largest employer, and in the 2000s, moved all the way to number two. That year, referring to Mississippi's nationally low per capita income, the state's lieutenant governor, Brad Dye, said, "If the state could get caught up with the Choctaws in economic development, we'd get off the bottom."[48]

Choctaw business entrepreneurship did not necessarily come at the expense of tribal culture. The tribe used its profits to support language programs, stickball leagues, a tribal museum, community Thanksgiving feasts, the annual Choctaw Fair, and a 120-bed residential nursing home. By 1990, positive holistic health changes had unfolded too. Public assistance and suicide and alcoholism rates had declined, while life expectancy had risen. Virtually all tribal citizens had moved into homes with electricity and plumbing, and the number of Choctaw high school graduates had increased from 290 in 1975 to 1,000 in 1990. In addition, roughly 90 percent of the Mississippi Choctaw people demonstrated some fluency in the Choctaw language.[49]

In 1990, Mississippi Choctaw tribal secretary-treasurer Beasley Denson paused to reflect on the Choctaw Miracle and its distinction from the American dream: "We don't want what American society as a whole has. We like your television, we like your stereo, and we like your cars, but we don't want to be you. . . . I have no interest in alienating whites. I just don't want to live in their world. . . . Just because I don't want to be a white man doesn't mean I want to be some kind of mystical Indian either. Just a real human being." Denson's appraisal transcended binary thinking while challenging reductive assumptions about what it means to be Indian. For him, the "white" and "Indian" worlds could coexist, borrow from each other, and change over time, but preferably on their own terms and not at the behest of a colonizing nation.[50]

Finally, there is perhaps no better example of an urban Indian who eventually returned home to serve the tribe than Wilma Mankiller. She grew up in San Francisco, where her family went on the relocation program in 1956, and then returned home to her Cherokee community in Oklahoma in 1977. Given her impressive résumé, it is surprising that, after going on rural relocation to Oklahoma, she essentially had to demand that the Cherokee Nation give her a job. As an adult in the San Francisco Bay Area, Mankiller attended college at San Francisco State University, participated in the 1969 Alcatraz Occupation, served the San Francisco Indian center, developed an Indian adult education center, directed the Native American Youth Center in East Oakland, and volunteered for the Pit River Tribe on behalf of their legal battle against a gas and electric company. Through that latter experience, she learned about treaty rights and tribal sovereignty: "Based on all my experience with various tribes and Native American issues in California, it seemed so logical for me to finally do something on behalf of my own people."[51]

The Cherokee Nation hired Mankiller as an economic stimulus coordinator. Earning a decent salary and appreciating the contrast in cost of living between San Francisco and Oklahoma, she "felt a little bit rich." Reflecting on how her urban experiences made her a valuable asset to her Cherokee people, she recalled, "After all that time I had spent trying to raise money for various Native American causes and projects in Oakland and San Francisco, one thing I definitely knew how to do was write a fairly good grant proposal. . . . When folks at the Cherokee Nation discovered that I possessed some ability, I was kept very busy churning out proposals." Her success on that front earned the attention of Cherokee Nation principal chief Ross Swimmer. Wilma Mankiller would go on to succeed Swimmer as the first, and so far only, female principal chief of the Cherokee Nation.[52]

· · · · · ·

Notwithstanding numerous tribal leaders' fervent advocacy of tribal economic rehabilitation, some prominent Native people cautioned against placing too much value on any one strategy. Penning a guest editorial for Chicago Indian community newsletter the *Amerindian* in 1955, future commissioner of Indian affairs and current Ute agency superintendent Robert Bennett (Oneida) argued that economic advancement in rural Indian Country should not depend solely on developing "things" on reservations. Instead, he argued that the development of *people* should be the first order of business. "Many members of such a tribal group never participate in any of the benefits of tribal economy and are destitute," he wrote. Therefore, efforts at economic development of reservations would never succeed if investors and tribal leaders continued failing to create outlets for young Indian people to get involved. Everyone needed to play a substantive role in economic rehabilitation of reservations, Bennett implored. But his ultimate goal was not to see tribal homes evolve into gentrified American communities. Rather, he appreciated economic stability as the best strategy toward preserving "the remaining vestiges of our culture without sacrificing them to economic need." Bennett wanted Indians to succeed at the white man's game so they could remain *Indians*. He did not see "Indian" and "economic strength" as mutually exclusive.[53]

Similarly, in 1967, one year after he retired from his commissioner of Indian affairs post, Philleo Nash reflected on his administration's dual program for tribal resource development and Indian individual development. Nash argued that providing Indians choices on how and where to achieve economic stability was of vital importance. "The theory here," he expounded, "is that the individual should be put in the best possible position to take advantage of whatever opportunity he can find wherever he chooses to find it, so that if he chooses to find it in New York with the New York City Ballet, like Maria Tallchief, or in Beverly Hills as its mayor, which Will Rogers, Jr. did for a while, or in the oil fields of Los Angeles, as some people have done, or on a skyscraper in New York as some of the Iroquoian groups have done, this is their business, their right, and we have an obligation, I think, to maximize their opportunity for success." With these words, Nash neatly captured not only the general historical movement unfolding across Indian Country—both urban and rural—during the twentieth century but also the fact that Native people had been the real engines of that movement. Moreover, his sympathetic perspective encapsulated what truly mattered for Native people during this period: freedom of movement and choice, and an opportunity to become self-sufficient on their own terms. Moreover, Nash made sure to stipulate that freedom of choice needed to include the right to maintain connections to tribalism. "There will always be many Indian people who prefer rural life," he reasoned, "and the continuance of this rural life should not be at the price of a standard of living which is so much lower than the rest of us that it's a serious deprivation to the individual and an embarrassment." Simply put, Nash argued that the Indian bureau needed to make less demands on how and where Indians could belong in wider America, and instead support Indians' own creative visions for a happier future.[54]

That sentiment was shared by a new generation of ambitious young Indians who refused to allow past and contemporary assumptions about Indian potential to prevent them from attaining their individual goals, be they a life independent from the tribe or a life intimately devoted to the greater good of the tribe. By the late 1960s, numerous young Indians had roughly twenty years of history to reflect on when considering whether or not their parents had made the right decision in migrating away from reservations in search of jobs and social dignity. Needless to say, young Indians' attitudes toward their socioeconomic prospects were of vital importance when considering various tribes' intensifying efforts to secure a federal policy of tribal self-determination. As Standing Rock Sioux and Crow Creek Community Action Program administrator Floyd Taylor put it, "The success or failure of the Indian, or any race, lies in its youth—how well trained and experienced they are."[55]

Understanding that the future of their respective tribes rested on their shoulders, many Indian youths felt apprehensive about attaching their hopes to any one solution. Others seemed to be waiting for any window of opportunity to open on their behalf. Either way, most expressed mixed opinions on how and where to secure the most profitable future. For example, during an interview in 1968, a circle of Crow Creek Sioux girls projected a deep resentment toward tribal life, while maintaining that they were only waiting for an opportunity to transcend what they considered a stifling reservation existence. Sixteen-year-old Blossom insisted, "We just live here 'cause we have to." Her friend Sandy chimed in, "I hate it; I just maintain my cool." When the interviewer reminded the girls that the tribe was pursuing plans to bring industry to the reservation, a third girl named Carole, who was planning to spend the summer in Boston before entering medical school, scoffed, "So, what do you expect us to do, pack meat?"[56]

In stark contrast to the Crow Creek girls' statements, some young Crow Creek boys seemed both bewildered by expectations to live up to their parents' example and mired in a general state of ennui. When a journalist visited Joe Wounded Knee's home, the former Crow Creek tribal councilman sat at his kitchen table and proceeded to admonish his son Pat, who must have been in earshot from his position on the couch across the room. "The trend of young people seems to be to congregate to recreate," Joe lectured. "They have beer parties and stuff, and you can't get them interested in nothing. . . . Pat's 25 years old now, and he ain't got nothing other than the clothes he's wearing." Joe continued, "When I was his age I had horses and wagons and all kinds of stuff like that." This finally roused Pat from the couch. "It kind of gets me 'cause I can't get a job," he defended. "I've got to get away from here. . . . There just isn't anything here." Pat then explained that he was attaching his hopes to the relocation program, for which he would apply in the fall.[57]

At times, children's and parents' divergent perspectives on life undermined prevailing assumptions about where Indians should belong. Evelyn Prue, a Rosebud Sioux who migrated from South Dakota to Chicago, recalled how as a child she would dream about life away from her reservation: "Back in the 1930s I used to look across those sand hills on the reservation and wonder what it was like out there when I listened to the radio and heard all those big bands." Evelyn's dream came true, but by the mid-1970s, she and her son Mickey were struggling to bridge a generation gap. A Vietnam veteran who fought to kick a drug habit, and a staunch supporter of the American Indian Movement, Mickey wanted to return to Rosebud, where he felt he could make a real difference in his people's lives. Interestingly, it was his mother who insisted on remaining in the city. She believed that her children would be best served by embracing the non-Indian world. "You can't live in the past," she explained. "If you dwell on all the bad things that happened to us, you can't ever live with yourself."[58]

In addition to potential disconnects between young and old, some reservations became bitter battlegrounds between young urban Indians who returned home and those who never left. Echoing the experiences of Indian boarding school students around the turn of the century, Duane Birdbear, a freshman at Dartmouth College, mentioned that he felt alienated from his fellow tribespeople when he returned to his Mandan-Hidatsa-Arikara reservation in North Dakota. "I feel almost a total stranger coming back, and I just can't re-establish the same friendships we had before, because we think different thoughts," he explained. "My idea of what a good time is isn't their idea of what a good time is." In similar fashion, David Redhorse, a Navajo sophomore at Amherst College, theorized that exposure to current middle-class conveniences and technologies bred resentment toward reservations among young Indians who ventured off. For Redhorse, however, spending substantial time away from New Mexico resulted in an appreciation for tribal tradition and land that he would otherwise not have felt. "The farther you go away from the reservation, you strive harder to preserve it," he concluded.[59]

In 1969, Wallace Coffee, a twenty-three-year-old Cherokee and Choctaw, paused from his studies in business, psychology, and sociology at Northeastern State College in Tahlequah, Oklahoma, to reflect on urban relocation's implications for reservation life. Coffee considered relocation a distinct opportunity to practice self-sufficiency and gain a "sense of direction" that reservation life could not deliver. Interestingly, one specific benefit of relocation that he promoted was its capacity for separating ambitious young Indians from delinquent peers who preferred to "run off and get drunk." This sentiment is important to note in light of the fact that critics of relocation typically dismissed the program as a one-way ticket to poverty and alcoholism. Coffee worried not about such potential pitfalls. He confessed that relocated Indians might "be lost for quite a while," but he maintained that even that could result in a positive outcome in that it would force Indians to "work and think about work." Still, for all his enthusiasm for relocation, Coffee ultimately envisioned a life in which he would return home and help his people. He only felt that he needed to "learn more about the Indian and more about white ways first" and "realize what society is all about." Doing so, in his estimation, would not threaten tribalism. "More than likely the Indian will come back to Oklahoma," he predicted. "They love their home. They love their people. They can't stay away from the people."[60]

Whether or not young Indian urban sojourners would choose to one day return to their rural Indian Country roots ultimately depended on their own subjective experiences. Still, regardless of their competing visions for how and where to best achieve a most profitable future, one theme persisted among them: education and experience in the wider world were essential ingredients for success, both at home and abroad. During an interview in 2009, Father Peter Powell—whose St. Augustine's Center for American Indians has, for over five decades, operated on behalf of Chicago's Indian community—spoke to this fundamental assertion: "They took that practical savvy that they learned here in the city back to the reservation, remained certainly traditionally and spiritually as strong as ever, and yet at the same time have become tribal leaders today. The city experience gave them the practical know-how. It gave them the experience in working with other organizations and working with the government agencies that would not have been possible on the reservations. It has strengthened them in better serving their people back on the reservation."[61] Suggesting an important continuity across space and time, in 1970 William Wiley, who directed the Indian education program at Riverside City College in California, seemed to witness the end result of the process that Father Powell later delineated. Wiley noted how Native students who were interested in leading their tribes clearly recognized the significance of a college degree: "They do see, wherever they go on the reservation now, that people who are running things are Indians, white collar Indians, with a big hat."[62]

· · · · · ·

While it is important to understand the failures of the urban promise, it is also important to consider how Indians' urban experiences might have prepared them to positively influence tribal sovereignty and self-determination. Few relocated Indians completely abandoned reservation homes and tribal connections—not physically, emotionally, or intellectually. Understanding this provides an escape from a reductive assimilation–resistance binary that pits urban Indians against reservation Indians according to a divide-and-conquer strategy long practiced by the settler state. Yet while the Native protagonists discussed here may seem exceptional, they are merely representatives of a much larger generation of tribal leaders who aggressively pursued opportunities wherever they found them, including reservations that might have felt as exotic and intimidating as metropolitan life once felt to an earlier generation. Of course, most all endured misfortune. But those who eventually returned home often did so in spite of misfortune, not because of it.

On January 12, 1972, pointing to Indians' apparent refusal to be "melted down," the federal government officially renounced its relocation program. Between its formal introduction in 1952 and inconspicuous conclusion in 1972, more than 100,000 Indians had migrated through the program—a figure that does not account for tens of thousands more who relocated without benefit of Indian bureau support. According to the BIA's notoriously unreliable statistics, at least 40 percent of those who received government support eventually returned to reservations. In 1971 alone, roughly ten thousand Indians migrated through the program, and roughly half of them returned. In a grand stroke of situational irony, Mohawk businessman and Commissioner of Indian Affairs Louis R. Bruce announced that the government's annual $40 million training and job-assistance programs would now be relocated to reservations. "I want to see Indian economies where dollars move from Indian hand to Indian hand and are not drained out by those non-Indian cities that develop and grow and feed upon Indian reservations," Bruce explained. Reflecting the federal government's recent commitment to a policy of tribal self-determination, his plan was to immediately shift $7 million from the program's total budget to ten "Indian-Action Teams" that would prepare various tribal corporations for the management of reservation building trades and heavy construction jobs.[63]

To be sure, the Indian bureau promoted a useful, if problematic, agenda. By taking complete credit for it, however, it overlooked the essential role Native people played in the paradigmatic and programmatic transformation. What transpired amounted to less a matter of Indians' resistance to being "melted down" than a matter of Indians' insistence on freedom to exercise mobility and pursue opportunities wherever they could find them. The federal government officially sanctioned American Indian urban relocation in 1952, but Native people had by that point already been exploiting urban resources and "mainstreaming" for decades. Likewise, numerous Native visionaries had already refocused their attention on reservation rehabilitation long before the federal government officially sanctioned that process in 1972. In this respect, Indian initiative consistently outpaced Indian bureau indecision. Moreover, in direct opposition to the federal government's overarching agenda, Native people never had any intention of relinquishing reservation space. Numerous talented and ambitious young Indians demonstrated this throughout the postwar period while building from the ground up what historian and legal expert Charles Wilkinson terms an "Indian professional middle class."[64]

In a 1960 letter to the secretary of the interior, Mississippi Choctaw chief Phillip Martin expressed mixed feelings about the relocation program. He granted that the program was a "generous answer to the problems of some of our people," and that his local relocation officer was a "trustworthy man." Yet he ultimately saw his people's future at home in Choctaw country, where "most of the 3,000 will remain and multiply. . . . The numbers that relocate will never keep pace with the numbers that come home again, and the numbers that are born. For better or for worse, nothing will drive the Mississippi Choctaws from the place where they are."[65] During an interview in 1970, Navajo tribal councilman Howard Gorman echoed this distinct brand of loyalty to tribal homelands when, asked about urban Navajo people, he movingly repeated, "They always come back, they always come back, they always come back."[66]

Conclusion

A Place Made of Sorrow?

• •

Thomas Greenwood was born in 1908 to parents of Cherokee and Scottish descent residing in Hayti, Missouri. A village community nestled in the state's boot heel, Hayti was then experiencing an industrial-engineered transformation from swampy lowland to bristling wheat field. Growing up, Greenwood roamed the countryside hunting ducks alongside other boys from the community. In 1925, seeking opportunities beyond his rural confines, Greenwood, like the legendary bluesmen from the Mississippi delta, hopped on Highway 61 out of Hayti and headed five hundred miles north to the Midwest's mammoth metropolis: Chicago. There he found work as a blacksmith and boilermaker, and began forming bonds of friendship with fellow Native Chicagoans who regularly met at John Hunter's, an "Indian hang-out" located in one of the city's artist colonies.[1] Within one year, he had become something of a social ambassador for the city's Indian community. In this capacity, Greenwood befriended legendary Chicago mayor William "Big Bill" Thompson, who introduced him to heavyweight champion Jack Dempsey, Ojibwe star baseball pitcher Charles "Chief" Bender, and other celebrities who passed through the Second City.

In 1933, Greenwood put his political connections to productive use when he helped found Chicago's Grand Council Fire (later rechristened the Indian Council Fire), an Indian rights organization that represented twelve hundred Native people living in Chicago at that time. In 1935, he first gained experience as a job creator when he served as codirector of the New Deal Works Progress Administration (WPA) and Public Works Administration (PWA) projects in nearby Lyons and Berwyn Townships. His successful maneuvering within mainstream America did not, however, foreclose his commitment to preserving and teaching tribal culture. A central part of his WPA and PWA initiatives concerned the establishment of community Indian arts, crafts, and lore groups. He did not consider his dual roles of political mainstreamer and preserver of Indian culture as mutually exclusive endeavors. Rather, he expressed pride in blending the two seemingly opposed agendas. "I like to think my most satisfying experience was in actuating Whites and Reds as Brothers working to have a true and real relationship," he reflected in 1983.[2]

In early 1942, as America dove deeper into World War II, Greenwood hoped to advance his service to community and country when he visited his local navy office to enlist for service. They rejected him, however, because of blindness in his left eye sustained during an industrial accident several years prior. Still, the navy's rejection did not prevent him from contributing to the nation's war effort. In April 1942, Greenwood drew on his industrial labor experience and political connections to land a position as organizer of a new shipyard in quaint Seneca, Illinois, eighty miles southwest of Chicago along the Illinois and Michigan Canal. He rapidly climbed the ranks to become the chair of management and labor. Tasked with quickly amassing a team of energetic laborers, he recruited over two hundred fellow Cherokee and brought them to Seneca to help build not only a fleet of warships but also a small city where once stood a village.

After the war, Greenwood tirelessly persisted in his activism on behalf of not only the United States but also Indian country, which, as it came to include urban Indian communities, had unpredictably expanded as an idea while also changing size and shape as a literal geographic place.[3] In 1948, alongside fellow Chicago Indian community leader Albert Cobe, Greenwood organized both the Indian Service League of Chicago and a YMCA-sponsored Indian basketball team, which traveled throughout Illinois, Wisconsin, Minnesota, and Michigan to compete against regional opponents. In 1953, he helped found Chicago's American Indian Center, still in operation today. That same year, still maintaining a professional partnership with Cobe, Greenwood became active in the National Congress of American Indians, and in 1961, he helped organize the American Indian Chicago Conference (AICC), for which he served as chair of the ways and means committee. He also joined a team of AICC representatives that hand-delivered their final conference report and series of recommendations to President John F. Kennedy, whom Greenwood revered as the "Red Man's Moses."[4]

In the late 1960s, Greenwood finally and permanently retreated from the big city to a home he purchased in idyllic Willow Springs, Illinois—a village community in southwest Chicagoland that he had long cherished. His work was not done, however. In Willow Springs, he quickly impressed local mayor John Rust and landed a position on the town planning committee and board of trustees before advancing to chair of the police and fire commission, for which he helped erect a new firehouse. Meanwhile, he never surrendered what was important to him as an American Indian who cared about his people's culture. In Willow Springs, he worked as a conservationist, assisting a project to turn a landfill into a forest preserve, and in 1972 he served as chair of the local powwow committee. In 1976, he located spiritually significant sacred Indian stones in the healing waters around Willow Springs, which the Potawatomie used in ceremonies before they were forcibly removed from the area, and hosted a public ceremony to acknowledge and preserve the sacred stones.

Even in his twilight, Greenwood persisted in tying together the seemingly disparate strands of his dynamic life into a coherent statement. In 1984, he helped found the Isle a la Cache Museum on the Des Plaines River island near Romeoville. The museum commemorated Indian people's importance to the local history and included exhibit materials from the region's storied fur trade era.[5] Finally, in 1986, an august seventy-eight-year-old Thomas Greenwood continued his efforts at community restoration and historical preservation as he almost single-handedly led a local initiative to establish a park adjacent to the I and M Canal along Willow Springs. His primary agenda was to raze the dilapidated factories, junkyards, and tank farms that spoiled twenty-five miles of scenic river from Summit to Joliet. He continued working for the betterment of his Willow Springs community right up until his death in 1988.[6]

In 1983, considering the sum of his life experiences, Greenwood expressed genuine satisfaction: "I have lived to see poverty in its worst and progress unthought of 50 years ago. I've seen Indians become laborers, clerks, nurses, salespersons, business persons, owners of companies, doctors, lawyers, teachers, in the arts (actors, sculptors, artists, musicians), politicians, and yes beggars and thieves—entertainers."[7] Not unlike thousands of fellow Native American people, Greenwood's life meaningfully explored local and national activism and politics, conservation and industrial labor, and loyalty to both tribal and U.S. citizenship. Like so many others, he maneuvered not only within rural and urban space but also in the boundless physical and cultural terrains in between. Like hundreds of thousands of fellow Native Americans, he practiced an Indigeneity that is portable, pliable, perennial, and powerful.

Betraying no fundamental identity crisis, Greenwood's life wholly undermined the two-worlds trope. He had little use for those who believed that Native people had effectively become torn between two conflicting approaches to life ("white" and "Indian") and were therefore incapable of belonging in either. Ultimately, Greenwood represented a great, and greatly misunderstood, generation of Native people who resented the inherent limitations of "two worlds' bullshit," to quote influential Comanche activist LaDonna Harris, whose legacy also demonstrates an enthusiastic transgression against sociopolitical boundaries that continue to bar American Indians from meaningful participation in not only national but also global political affairs; culture making and remaking; and social, economic, military, and environmental decisions. Regardless of the federal government's vision for Indian assimilation through urban relocation, Native American people made urbanization into something more than an escape from a bad situation, caused by colonization and cured by seductive and coercive federal programs. It was about exercising presence and voice, body and spirit, beyond the relative and imposed boundaries around Indian Country.[8]

Thomas Greenwood's life perhaps seems exceptional. He certainly did cover an exceptional amount of ground. But as extraordinary as his life appears, he was not alone. There were thousands like him. And over the course of the twentieth century, those thousands gradually gave way to millions of Native people who rejected, and continue to reject, settler impositions on how and where they can belong in a global society that includes Indian nations and people. From boarding school students who advocated racial uplift to streetwise urban Indians who went home to help repair reservation communities and economies, Native people in the twentieth century sought to maneuver freely within their own sets of expectations. As Dakota writer Vine Deloria Jr. insisted, "Everyone doesn't have to do everything that the old Indians did in order to have a modern Indian identity. We don't have to have every male in the tribe do the Sun Dance. We need a larger variety of cultural expression today. I don't see why Indians can't be poets, engineers, songwriters or whatever. I don't see why we can't depart from traditional art forms and do new things."[9] Pointing to Deloria's rousing summons, anthropologist Thomas Biolsi concludes, "Such indigenous cosmopolitanism necessarily implies that Indians are at least as at home in cities, universities, the entertainment industry and mass media, and so on, as they are on reservations."[10] Throughout the twentieth century, Indians became more than sepia-toned relics of the past, bound in celluloid and denied a contemporary voice and presence. They increasingly emerged as a people whom the non-Indian American citizenry now needed to confront in the places where they walked, worked, and worshiped.[11]

Eventually, "urban" came to mean more than a location or a measurement of one's relative physical distance from their ancestral homes. "Urban" also measured one's relative remove from their culture and community. Yet many urban Indian people managed in their own way to carry their

"Junior relocatees waiting to depart," box 1, folder 4, Great Lakes Agency, BIA Relocation Records, Edward E. Ayer Manuscript Collection, Newberry Library, Chicago.

culture with them into new, often prohibitive, contexts. And they did so while finding creative ways to continue contributing to their people's causes. In a 2016 interview, celebrated Pawnee multimedia artist Bunky Echo-Hawk, who grew up in the Boulder and Denver metro area, shared his impressions of his father, the esteemed Native American Rights Fund lawyer Walter Echo-Hawk:

> So yeah, I grew up and he always made a point to bring us back to Oklahoma for our various ceremonial dances and funerals. It always struck me that my dad, to me, seemed like an artist and just a good Pawnee Citizen first. Once I got older, I found out all the stuff he was doing legally, in the world of law, and it just made me even more proud of him. When you see people out, away from the Native Community and they're successful, oftentimes, they're disconnected to their roots and their heritage. It always made me feel proud that my dad made it a point to keep us connected. Same thing with my mom. Living in Colorado, we'd go back and forth from Washington to Oklahoma.

"Our largest family unit—still successfully relocated," box 1, folder 4, Great Lakes Agency, BIA Relocation Records, Edward E. Ayer Manuscript Collection, Newberry Library, Chicago.

Bunky passed many hours at his father's law offices, witnessing the regular visits by Indigenous leaders and luminaries from an expansive Indian Country. Meanwhile, the Echo-Hawk family remained connected to their Pawnee community, while Walter used his legal talents to fight for Indian people everywhere.[12]

Because of Native people's sharp social ingenuity and collective resolve, federal policy makers who advocated a termination-relocation-assimilation policy never quite succeeded in their mission to end the Indian problem, nor, by extension, Indian people. As St. Augustine's Center for American Indians director Father Peter Powell recalled: "Native people on their own were able to maintain and attain lives of dignity and decency here in the city of Chicago. They did it without the Bureau of Indian affairs. For many it was long, and slow, and heartbreaking, but they made it. Now there are three generations of our people here, and, I would say, three generations who are still at heart very much committed to maintaining their Indianness, and they have done this on their own."[13] Powell's assessment rings true. The permanence and wider acceptance Native people achieved in urban America resulted primarily from a process they nurtured long before and long after the Bureau of Indian Affairs introduced a modicum of support. The transportation expenses, low-wage job leads, and meager weekly stipends that the relocation program briefly provided pale in comparison to what Indians provided for themselves across several decades in numerous American cities.

In 1953, a successful Mohawk-Sioux dairy farmer from upstate New York authored a guest editorial for the *Amerindian*, the Chicago Indian community's bimonthly newsletter. The author discussed how the nation's 400,000 American Indians in years past had "been skeptical of their chances of getting ahead in competition with the white man." Pointing to an inferiority complex among Native people who experienced "de-Indianization" in schools and on reservations, he regretted that Indian people who during previous decades succeeded in "the white man's sphere" would now only be labeled "unusual" at best. Championing that older generation, the author concluded, "Today, more and more Indian people have gone out into the world because of these trail-blazers" and, having learned self-reliance, were no longer bound to the patronage of the "great White Father." The author was none other than future commissioner of Indian affairs Louis Bruce, who in 1972 reluctantly carried out orders from above to terminate the relocation program.[14]

At an academic conference on urban Indians held at Chicago's Newberry Library, influential Pueblo anthropologist Alfonso Ortiz echoed Bruce's evaluation when he confessed in his opening remarks, "In the past it has been all-too-true that we, especially anthropologists, romantics that we are, followed Indians to the cities to find vestiges of 'tribal' life, concentrating almost exclusively on understanding how they managed to survive as culturally 'Indian' in the urban context." Ortiz then cited fellow conference presenter Ann Metcalf's argument that such scholarly pursuits denied the many examples of creative, dynamic, and successful adjustments that many relocated Native people made.[15]

Taking Bruce's, Ortiz's, and Metcalf's assertions one step further, cultural retention, adaptation, and incorporation achieved through spatial mobility reflect survival strategies that Native American people have practiced for millennia. Emphasizing how and where Native people maneuvered within the United States, and how they first transgressed and then remapped both reservation and urban social, cultural, and economic boundaries, facilitates a deeper understanding of and appreciation for Indian ingenuity and resolve in the twentieth century.

Certainly the effects of market capitalism, urbanization, and cultural mainstreaming manifested unevenly throughout Indian Country, which today ranges from economically impoverished Indian reservations situated within the poorest counties in the United States to the Florida Seminole Nation, which in 2006 purchased the Hard Rock international chain of casinos, restaurants, and entertainment complexes for $965 million. In addition, the period covered in this book contains both the brutal Wounded Knee Massacre of 1890 and the emergence of Native American political actors in the United Nations during the 1970s. The twentieth century witnessed extraordinary Indian population recovery, the federal embrace (however begrudgingly) of a self-determination policy, and new exercises in sovereignty and nationhood.[16] Did these developments happen in spite of or partly because of urban self-relocation and the federal urban relocation program? Does the BIA's midcentury relocation program sufficiently explain why, as of the 2010 census, over three-quarters of all Native American people live in urban areas? If the formation and exploitation of an urban Indian proletariat is the obvious and unavoidable effect of Indian urban relocation, then why did Indian people repeatedly fall for it, long after the program's conclusion?

The urban relocation program is one chapter of a larger story of Native American people moving through imagined geographies for imaginative reasons during the twentieth century. For some, relocation resulted in "a place made of sorrow" and "many, many lost lonely souls," as Indigenous rock band XIT put it in the title track to their 1977 album *Relocation*.[17] For others, relocation amounted to something less tragic, more transformative, and to some degree typical. "Man, we been doing the towns ever since Sitting Bull laid down the tools of his trade on the Little Big Horn and joined the touring Wild West Show of Buffalo Bill," a Sioux resident of San Francisco attested in 1968.[18] Decades later, that sentiment was echoed by Anishinaabe writer Gerald Vizenor, who, during the 1960s, worked first for Minneapolis's Waite Settlement House Indian community support center and then the American Indian Employment and Guidance Center. "Natives have always been on the move," he reasons, "by chance, necessity, barter, reciprocal sustenance, and by trade over extensive routes; the actual motion is a natural right, and the tribal stories of transmotion are a continuous sense of visionary sovereignty."[19]

Throughout the twentieth century, Native people seized opportunities to improve their lives through mobility and urbanity. Yet transgressing the boundaries of cultural expectations and accepting federal support for urban relocation could come at a real cost. This was born of a murky moment when a new colonial initiative paradoxically offered escape from an old one. Within these crosscurrents of colonization, it becomes difficult to tell if, when, and where, exactly, urban Indian people are being dragged along the mainstream's rock bottom or fancy dancing across the surface. Either way, while navigating the century that many concluded would be their last, most Native American people searched for the same ends, if not always through the same means.

Ultimately, the history of how and why Native people both collectively and individually reclaimed the reins of their own mobilities is more than a story of dislocation and even more than a meditation on Indian agency. It is a story about Indigenous peoples practicing a portable and pliable brand of tribal citizenship and Indigeneity that, as a result of their resolve, gained new meaning and wider application. Urban Indian people succeeded, against the odds, at expanding their worlds, and not embalming them. From the turn of the century forward, Native Americans—characterized by cosmopolitan histories, expansive understandings of cultural change and exchange, and economic and social ambitions all their own—employed cities for their own purposes, often transcending urban America's promises and pitfalls while forging new possibilities for Indigenous futures.

Notes

DDIOHC	Doris Duke Indian Oral History Collection, Western History Collections (WHC), University of Oklahoma
DDOHC	Doris Duke Oral History Collection, Marriott Library, University of Utah
DMP	Dillon S. Myer Papers, Government Agencies File, 1950–53, Harry S. Truman Presidential Library, Independence, Missouri
EACF	Employment Assistance Case Files, 1952–1956, National Archives and Records Administration, Southwest Region, Fort Worth, Texas
ECR	Elizabeth Clark Rosenthal Papers, Western History Collections, University of Oklahoma
FPP	Unpublished Papers of Father Peter J. Powell, St. Augustine's Center for American Indians, Chicago, Illinois
FPRO	Field Placement and Relocation Office Correspondence and Reports Relating to Employment of Indians, National Archives and Records Administration, Washington, D.C.
FPROEAP	Field Placement and Relocation Office Employment Assistance Records: Narrative Reports, compiled 1952–1960, National Archives and Records Administration, Washington, D.C.
GEP	Glenn Emmons Papers, Center for Southwest Research, University of New Mexico, Albuquerque
HIN	Haskell Indian Nations University Decimal Correspondence, National Archives and Records Administration, Central Plains Region, Kansas City
HSTP	Papers of Harry S. Truman: White House Central Files, Harry S. Truman Presidential Library, Independence, Missouri
KM	Correspondence and Reports of Kathryn Mahn, National Archives and Records Administration, Washington, D.C.
MAO	Minneapolis Area Office Employment Assistance Case Files, National Archives and Records Administration, Central Plains Region, Kansas City
NDPF	National Defense Program Files, National Archives and Records Administration, Southwest Region, Fort Worth, Texas
PA	Potawatomie Agency, Mayetta, Kansas, Decimal Correspondence (1883–1969), National Archives and Records Administration, Central Plains Region, Kansas City
PNP	Philleo Nash Papers, Harry S. Truman Presidential Library, Independence, Missouri
PSR	Placement and Statistical Reports, compiled 1949–1954, National Archives and Records Administration, Washington, D.C.
RKDP	Robert Kerr Departmental Papers, Carl Albert Center for Congressional Research, University of Oklahoma
RREAP	Records Relating to Employment Assistance Programs, compiled 1949–1973, National Archives and Records Administration, Washington, D.C.
SAP	Sophie Aberle Papers, Center for Southwest Research, University of New Mexico, Albuquerque

SLP	Stanley Lyman Papers, Marriott Library Special Collections, University of Utah
TGP	Thomas Greenwood Papers, Newberry Library, Chicago, Illinois
THP	Theodore Hetzel Papers, Center for Southwest Studies, Fort Lewis College, Durango, Colorado
TMP	Toby Morris Papers, Carl Albert Center for Congressional Research, University of Oklahoma
UII	Ute Indian Interviews, Marriott Library Special Collections, University of Utah, Salt Lake City
VV	Virgil J. Vogel Research and Personal Papers, Newberry Library, Chicago, Illinois
WA	Winnebago Agency Employee Assistance Decimal Correspondence, National Archives and Records Administration, Central Plains Region, Kansas City
WBP	William Brophy Papers, Harry S. Truman Presidential Library, Independence, Missouri
WZOF	William Zimmerman Office Files, National Archives and Records Administration, Washington, D.C.
WZP	William Zimmerman Papers, Center for Southwest Research, University of New Mexico, Albuquerque

Introduction

1. For further background on Tom Bee and XIT, see "The Musicology of Tom Bee," *Indian Country Today*, http://indiancountrytodaymedianetwork.com/2003/10/02/musicology-tom-bee-89383, accessed 10 September 2014.

2. I embrace historian Nicolas G. Rosenthal's study of how Native people carved out socioeconomic space in Los Angeles during the twentieth century and, in the process, expanded the scope and meaning of "Indian Country." See Rosenthal, *Reimagining Indian Country*.

3. XIT, "Relocation," *Relocation*.

4. "Native Son," *Spin Magazine*, December 1993.

5. XIT, "Relocation," *Relocation*.

6. Mankiller served as the first female principal chief of the Cherokee Nation. Mankiller and Wallis, *Mankiller*, 72.

7. Momaday, *House Made of Dawn*, 124.

8. N. Scott Momaday, interview with Leonard Maker, 12 August 1969, T-494, p. 4, University of Oklahoma, Western History Collections, Doris Duke Indian Oral History Collection (hereafter cited as DDIOHC).

9. Means and Wolf, *Where White Men Fear to Tread*, 68.

10. John Angaiak, "I'm Lost in the City," *I'm Lost in the City*.

11. Gerald Vizenor tells stories of "survivance over dominance," in which *survivance*, unlike *survival*, is a continuing phenomenon, not merely a historical one. See Vizenor, *Manifest Manners*, vii, 4.

12. Relocation Services Information Record, 14 November 1963, RG075, box 1, folder B1-59-18-R-De, Bureau of Indian Affairs, Billings Area Office: Mixed Vocational & Subject Files, 1939–1960 (hereafter cited as BAOMVSF). I emphasize Dennis Field's identification as "full-blood" in order to challenge any assumption that full-blood Indians were necessarily more traditional and therefore less amenable to leaving their reservations. Additionally, in all cases I have preserved grammatical mistakes that this study's Indian protagonists made in their applications and correspondence. Such imperfections suggest that Native people, rather than BIA agents, composed these statements themselves, which would mean that BIA agents did not corrupt such statements for their own purposes.

13. On Indian migratory labor patterns as a mode of economic survival and cultural persistence, see Bauer, *We Were All Like Migrant Workers Here*; Norrgard, *Seasons of Change*; Raibmon, *Authentic Indians*. Additionally, historian Joshua L. Reid illuminates Makah cultural persistence through participation in modern Pacific Northwest cultural, political, and economic transformations in *The Sea Is My Country*.

14. Lorde, "Master's Tools Will Never Dismantle the Master's House."

15. Joshua Reid, *Sea Is My Country*, 276.

16. Eric Hobsbawm, "Peasants and Politics," *Journal of Peasant Studies* 1, no. 1 (1973): 2–33, quoted in Scott, *Weapons of the Weak*, xv.

17. Gregory, *Southern Diaspora*, 10.

18. Handlin, *Uprooted*; Vecoli, "*Contadini* in Chicago."

19. Handlin, *Uprooted*, 4.

20. Blackhawk, "I Can Carry On from Here"; Thrush, "Iceberg and the Cathedral."

21. At the same time, Steiner quotes a Sioux man living in San Francisco who scoffed at a letter supposedly written by a fellow Sioux claiming that Indians who sold their land had nowhere else to go and could only descend into "Dantesque" urban ghettos and junkpile shantytowns on urban outskirts. "For one thing that's not how a Sioux thinks," he countered, refusing to believe the letter was anything more than a "put-on." "He can go home to his reservation any time. If he can crawl, they'll take him home." Steiner, *New Indians*, 175–76, 179.

22. Vine Deloria, "Urban Scene and the American Indian," 333.

23. Gregory, *Southern Diaspora*, 82.

24. Ibid., 8.

25. Thrush, *Native Seattle*, 7–9. This study draws significant inspiration from Blackhawk, "I Can Carry On from Here"; Buss and Genetin-Pilawa, *Beyond Two Worlds*; Philip Deloria, *Indians in Unexpected Places*; Harmon, *Rich Indians*; La-Grand, *Indian Metropolis*; O'Neill, "Rethinking Modernity and the Discourse of Development in American Indian History"; Ramirez, *Native Hubs*; Rosenthal, *Reimagining Indian Country*; Rosier, *Serving Their Country*; Shoemaker, "Urban Indians and Ethnic Choices."

26. Buss and Genetin-Pilawa, *Beyond Two Worlds*.

27. Biolsi, "Imagined Geographies," 240. On the concept of supratribalism, see Cornell, *Return of the Native*.

28. "Relocation Statistical Information Tables, Table 4 and 5," Association on American Indian Affairs Papers, Princeton University, Department of Rare Books and Special Collections, microfilm edition, reel 57 (hereafter cited as AAIA).

29. See, for example, LaGrand, *Indian Metropolis*; LaPier and Beck, *City Indian*; Straus and Arndt, *Native Chicago*; Rosenthal, *Reimagining Indian Country*; Weibel-Orlando, *Indian Country, L.A.*; Ramirez, *Native Hubs*; Blansett, "San Francisco, Red Power, and the Emergence of an 'Indian City'"; Danziger, *Survival and Regeneration*; Carpio, *Indigenous Albuquerque*; Guillemin, *Urban Renegades*; Thrush, *Native Seattle*; Thrush, *Indigenous London*.

30. For an excellent study that explores Indigenous peoples' relationship to race making in a major metropolis during the twentieth century, see Mays, "Indigenous Detroit."

31. See, for example, Child, *Boarding School Seasons*; Gram, *Education at the Edge of Empire*; Whalen, *Native Students at Work*; Stremlau, *Sustaining the Cherokee Family*.

32. According to anthropologist Raymond Fogelson, "Regarding Native Americans as hopeless victims may be yet a more subtle form of racism, since it strips them of certain attributes of humanity and denies them responsibility for their own actions and destiny. It has only recently become the new ethnohistorical orthodoxy to recognize that Indians were, if not kings, queens, or bishops, at least knights and castles on the colonial and post-colonial chessboard." See Fogelson, "Night Thoughts on Native American Social History," 78. Likewise, Richard White writes, "Seeing Indians as simply obstacles to expansion or victims of expansion is not very useful. Nor is the opposing tendency of condescending to them as yet another set of contributors to some American mosaic any more helpful." See Richard White, "Teaching Indian History and Social History," 94–95.

33. For an excellent study of tribal gaming's often positive, although complicated, impact on the Florida Seminole nation and surrounding community, see Cattelino, *High Stakes*.

34. Washington, D.C.'s National Coalition for the Homeless claims that despite making up only 1 percent of the nation's total population, Native American people constitute 8 percent of the national homeless population. "Minorities and Homelessness," July 2009, http://www.nationalhomeless.org/factsheets/minorities.html.

Chapter One

1. Here I suggest that regardless of land claims, the modern American state, as the geopolitical entity we imagine today, was not fully formed before its military conquest of sovereign tribal nations in the trans-Mississippi West. Interview with Lee Emerson (Quechan/Mojave–Quechan tribal historian), 1974, 1977, in Trafzer, ed., *Quechan Indian Voices*). On the negative discursive power of social, cultural, political, and economic expectations for Native people during the turn of the century, see Philip Deloria, *Indians in Unexpected Places*.

2. Salisbury, "Indians' Old World." On "the great Native American metropolis," see Young and Fowler, *Cahokia.* On the idea that nineteenth-century Chicago was made by its hinterlands, see Cronon, *Nature's Metropolis.*

3. Pauketat, *Cahokia.*

4. Rice, *The Rotinonshonni,* 167–72. This account is also supported by the author's conversation with Iroquois traditional knowledge keeper Doug George-Kanentiio in 2015.

5. Parmenter, *Edge of the Woods,* ix–xi.

6. Labelle, *Dispersed but Not Destroyed,* 5. Labelle succeeds in humanizing Wendat history by giving "considerable weight to the personal biographies of Wendat individuals as a means to offset the widespread 'faceless' history of Native North America." I aspire to the same in this study of Indian urban relocation.

7. Eiselt, *Becoming White Clay,* 6. In a second rich example concerning Indians in the Southwest, Robert Perez discusses how movement was essential for Apache and Comanche peoples' exercise of political and economic power during the eighteenth and nineteenth centuries. Perez quotes a Chemehuevi who explains how traveling was a central aspect of his tribe's culture, even in the presence of Spanish and Mexican colonial power. It was the denial of "traditional" movement, at the hands of the United States, that rendered his tribe's quality of life "totally diminished." By the end of the nineteenth century, Indian economies in the borderlands remained dependent on movement, but increasingly of the smuggling and underground variety. Meanwhile, regulating mobility and labor became a primary function of the Office of Indian Affairs. In the ensuing decades, however, Native people did not passively adhere to OIA directions. Whenever possible, they sought to regain control of their own labor and mobility. See Perez, "Confined to the Margins," 250–59.

8. Fisher, *Shadow Tribe.*

9. Norrgard, *Seasons of Change.*

10. Meyer, *White Earth Tragedy,* 9.

11. The phrase "infinity of nations" is a nod to Michael Witgen's recent masterful study of the dynamic and evolving social world that Native people fostered across centuries in the North American interior. See Witgen, *Infinity of Nations,* 364. On the vernaculars of conquest and erasing Indians from history, see O'Brien, *Firsting and Lasting.*

12. I define *Indigeneity* as Indigenous peoples' lived experiences belonging to tribal kinship communities and ancestral place(s). On the distinction between *Indigeneity* and *Indianness,* see Guzman, *Native and National in Brazil,* 13–15.

13. Robert White, *Tribal Assets,* 3.

14. Anthropologist Thomas Biolsi explains how, during the establishment of the reservation system, federal bureaucrats seeking to expand the state apparatus relied on four administrative processes that reflect the Foucauldian concept of "subjection": empropertiment, determination of "competence," blood quanta registration, and genealogy documentation. Through a process of surveillance and coercion, federal administrators undermined tribal kinship units and instead molded

Lakota people into knowable and legible "modern" individuals. Biolsi ultimately sees this as amounting to a centripetal shift in which Native people who formerly benefited from specialized, relatively powerful roles on the nation's periphery became caught in the gravitational pull of the nation's socioeconomic core. In a more cynical interpretation, Biolsi argues that to consider this a "civilization" project is to overstate its ambition. Rather, he asserts that federal policy makers' goals had more to do with individualizing Indian people in order to prepare them not for eventual meaningful citizenship but for limited, predetermined participation in metropolitan capitalism. The title of his article on this subject is most certainly a nod to Michel Foucault's "birth of the clinic" and "birth of the prison" analyses. See Biolsi, "Birth of the Reservation."

15. Ludlow, *Ten Years' Work for Indians*, 13. This volume is held within the Ayer Modern Manuscripts Collection, Newberry Library, Chicago.

16. Ibid., 1–12. For further background on Pratt's transition from Hampton to Carlisle, see Adams, *Education for Extinction*, 47–48. Adams points out that despite Pratt's initial assertion to the contrary, the retired colonel did eventually become concerned about the mingling of black and Indian students at Hampton.

17. Ludlow, *Ten Years' Work for Indians*, 24.

18. Ibid., 36.

19. Ibid., 37, 55.

20. Gravatt, *Record of Hampton's Returned Indian Pupils*. This book is held within the Ayer Modern Manuscripts Collection, Newberry Library, Chicago.

21. Ludlow, *Ten Year's Work for Indians*, 18, 44–45, 51.

22. Ibid., 61. According to historian David Wallace Adams, at the turn of the century, roughly two-thirds of all Indian children (21,568) were enrolled in boarding schools. Adams, *Education for Extinction*, 58.

23. See, for example, Child, *Boarding School Seasons*; Adams, *Education for Extinction*. In her dissertation "Warrior into Welder," historian Kathryn MacKay argues that federal Indian work programs created a system of dependency by limiting employment options for prospective Indian workers, thus reflecting the "dominant" society's control over a "minority" society. In contrast, I argue that Native people, despite such limitations, attempted to exploit these work programs for a greater degree of independence. I base this assertion on the idea that the reservation system had already produced a state of dependence for Native people, thereby rejecting the notion that deeper forays into settler economies necessarily resulted in deeper states of dependence. Moreover, the idea that the federal government consistently sought, from the turn of the century forward, to impoverish Indians into greater degrees of dependency does not correspond with its persistent reluctance to spend federal dollars on Indians. Still, MacKay and I likely agree that the salient point is that the context and meaning of "independence" changed, from independence as tribal nations to independence as citizen capitalists.

24. Cobe, *Great Spirit*, 8, 16, 24.

25. Ibid., 45; "I Must Step Up," *Chicago Tribune*, 30 May 1971.

26. Cobe, *Great Spirit*, 45.

27. Interview with Leroy Wesaw, 16 December 1982, box 2, folder 5, Chicago American Indian Oral History Project, Newberry Library, Chicago (hereafter cited as CAIOHP).

28. Kellogg, "Industrial Organization for the Indian," 9.

29. Historian Philip Deloria sees among four thousand initial invitations to join the SAI several tiers of Indian people classified according to their relative physical, intellectual, and cultural proximity to reservation Indian Country or, by contrast, to a mainstream American society typically located within urban space. As Deloria carefully critiques the implications of their stratification, one shared characteristic emerges: to varying degrees, and regardless of their primary, secondary, or tertiary sociocultural tiers within Indian Country, virtually all engaged with the non-Indigenous world, achieved visibility beyond their specific kin and tribal networks, and practiced both social and spatial mobility. Philip J. Deloria, "Four Thousand Invitations," *American Indian Quarterly* 37, no. 3 (Summer 2013): 25–43.

30. Carlos Montezuma, "The Reservation Is Fatal to the Development of Good Citizenship," *Quarterly Journal of the Society of American Indians* 2, no. 1 (January–March 1914): 69–71.

31. Carlos Montezuma, "United States, Now Free the Indians!" *Wassaja* 3, no. 8 (November 1918): 2–3.

32. Carlos Montezuma, "The Indian Reservation System," *Quarterly Journal of the Society of American Indians* 1, no. 4 (October–December 1913).

33. Carlos Montezuma, "What Indians Must Do," *Quarterly Journal of the Society of American Indians* 2, no. 4 (September–December 1914): 294.

34. Carlos Montezuma, "Light on the Indian Situation," *Quarterly Journal of the Society of American Indians* 1, no. 1 (January–April 1913): 52. On Carlos Montezuma generally, see Iverson, *Carlos Montezuma*. On the Society of American Indians, see Hertzberg's classic study *The Search for an American Indian Identity*.

35. Richard H. Pratt to Carlos Montezuma, 23 April 1920, box 3, folder 154, Carlos Montezuma Papers, Newberry Library, Chicago (hereafter cited as CMP). Sociologist Stephen Cornell discusses how "pan-Indianism," closely linked to assimilationists, yielded to a "supratribal" Indian political front that seemed more intent on achieving acculturation. See Cornell, *Return of the Native*.

36. Henry Roe Cloud, "Some Social and Economic Aspects of the Reservation," *Quarterly Journal of the Society of American Indians*, 1 no. 2 (April–June 1913): 151.

37. Sherman Coolidge, "The American Indian of Today," *Quarterly Journal of the Society of American Indians* 2, no. 1 (January–March 1914): 35.

38. Sherman Coolidge, "The Function of the Society of American Indians," *Quarterly Journal of the Society of American Indians* 2, no. 3 (March–June 1914): 187.

39. Charles H. Kealear, "What the Indian Can Do for Himself," *Quarterly Journal of the Society of American Indians*, 2, no. 1 (January–March 1914): 41.

40. Lucy E. Hunter, "Value and Necessity of Higher Academic Training for the Indian Student," 11–14.

41. Mary LeJeune, "What Indian Students Say about Education," *Quarterly Journal of the Society of American Indians* 1, no. 3 (July–September 1913): 295.

42. For an excellent volume on the two-worlds analytical trope, see Buss and Genetin-Pilawa, *Beyond Two Worlds.*

43. Leupp, *Indian and His Problem,* 221–23.

44. Ibid., 223.

45. Biolsi, "Birth of the Reservation," 35.

46. *Proceedings of the Twenty-Fifth Annual Meeting of the Lake Mohonk Conference of the Friends of the Indian and Other Dependent People,* 21–23. When the Ute people departed for Sioux country in South Dakota, their initial plan was to incorporate fellow Northern Plains Indian tribes along the way. The Ute people predicted that the Sioux would greet them with open arms and join their cause. This was not to be the case, however. Confronting their own substantial share of problems related to compulsory land allotment and Anglo encroachment, the Sioux not only refused to provide asylum for the Ute people but also insisted that their uninvited visitors pay a fee for grazing their ponies on Sioux land. See O'Neil, "Anguished Odyssey."

47. O'Neil, "Anguished Odyssey," 319.

48. *Proceedings of the Twenty-Fifth Annual Meeting of the Lake Mohonk Conference,* 21–23.

49. Emphasis added.

50. *Proceedings of the Twenty-Fifth Annual Meeting of the Lake Mohonk Conference,* 23.

51. Leupp, *Indian and His Problem,* 155.

52. On Native people working in the Indian service, see Cahill, *Federal Fathers and Mothers.*

53. *Proceedings of the Twenty-Fifth Annual Meeting of the Lake Mohonk Conference,* 24–25.

54. Leupp, *Indian and His Problem,* 156.

55. *Proceedings of the Twenty-Fifth Annual Meeting of the Lake Mohonk Conference,* 25.

56. Leupp, *Indian and His Problem,* vii–ix.

57. Ibid., 116, 125.

58. Ibid., 151.

59. "The Bureau of Indian Affairs Voluntary Relocation Services Program," box 34, folder 330: Relocation, VV; Meriam, *Problem of Indian Administration.*

60. Flandreau Interviews (1940), box 3, folder 8, Stanley Lyman Papers, Marriot Library Special Collections, University of Utah (hereafter cited as SLP).

61. Ibid.; Hobart J. Gates obituary, *Bismarck Tribune,* 6 November 1997. In anticipation of any potential confusion, it is important to note that this is *not* Hobart H. Gates, who served as Custer County's state's attorney during the American Indian Movement's takeover of the Custer County courthouse in 1973. I could not confirm whether Gates's job-counseling position in Cleveland was part of the Indian relocation program to that city, but that would not be surprising, in that I can find no other connection between Gates and Cleveland.

62. Letter to H. E. Bruce, 22 January 1936, RG75, box 122, folder: K.C. Employment, Students (Girls) in Government Service, PA.

63. Flora Goslire (last name is slightly illegible) to J. Preston Myers, 23 May 1935, RG75, box 122, folder: K.C. Employment, PA.

64. For recent scholarly studies of early-twentieth century urban Indian dynamism, see LaPier and Beck, *City Indian*; LaPier and Beck, "Crossroads for a Culture"; LaPier and Beck, "'One-Man Relocation Team'"; Rosenthal, *Reimagining Indian Country*.

65. The Columbia River Indians discussed in Fisher's *Shadow Tribe*, for example, fashioned a tribal identity inextricably linked to movement and a collective resistance against being corralled into one externally controlled space. On this, see Fisher, *Shadow Tribe*. See also Bauer, *We Were All Like Migrant Workers Here*; Harmon, *Indians in the Making* and *Rich Indians*; Hosmer, *American Indians in the Marketplace*; Raibmon, *Authentic Indians*.

66. On the subject of Indian visibility in Chicago, see LaPier and Beck, *City Indian*. On the turn-of-the-century Indian community that formed around the Hollywood industry in Los Angeles, see Rosenthal, *Reimagining Indian Country*.

67. Gober, *Metropolitan Phoenix*, 56–57.

68. *American Indian* (Newsletter of the Society of Oklahoma Indians) 5, no. 1 (November 1930): 4; Cowger, "Pan-Indian Movements," *Oklahoma Historical Society's Encyclopedia of Oklahoma History and Culture*.

69. On Arthur Watkins's advocacy of Indian "emancipation" and influence on federal Indian policy in the mid-twentieth century, see R. Warren Metcalf, *Termination's Legacy*.

70. *American Indian* (Newsletter of the Society of Oklahoma Indians) 5, no. 1 (November 1930): 4. Interestingly, historians Rosalyn LaPier and David Beck, in their research, locate Lee Harkins in Chicago in 1931, where he provided a keynote speech at the Chicago Art Institute's Indian Day celebration. See LaPier and Beck, *City Indian*, 128.

71. "Indians in the World War," *Six Nations* 2, no. 21 (January 1928): 12. For a chapter-length discussion of urban fraternal Indian societies that sprouted up during the 1920s, see Hertzberg, *Search for an American Indian Identity*, chap. 9. Hertzberg argues that for all their modern, progressive characteristics, these early urban Indian organizations actually reinforced Indian identity, allowing urban Indians to share their experiences and provide mutual support.

72. "Indians in the World War," *Six Nations* 2, no. 21 (January 1928): 12. For a general history of American Indians' role in World War I, see Britten, *American Indians in World War I*.

73. Tragically, Joseph Oklahombi, illiterate and unable to find work, descended into alcoholism, worked as a lumber loader for $2 per day, and eventually depended on a veteran's pension of $12 per month to stay alive. Britten, *American Indians in World War I*, 164–73.

74. On heterosocial leisure in Progressive Era New York City, see Peiss, *Cheap Amusements*. For boarding school students and graduates who went on outing programs, leisure culture provided an outlet for new freedoms after the restrictive boarding school experience, but it introduced new complications too. Historian Margaret Jacobs argues that "Indian women's paid work as domestic servants often

undermined their unpaid culturally reproductive work as mothers." Under pressure to remain a domestic servant and to care for rich white children, many Indian women were compelled to give their children up for adoption, board them, or send them to live with another family. This amounted to what feminist scholar Sau-ling Wong terms "diverted mothering." See Jacobs, "Diverted Mothering," 179.

75. "New York Indian Colony Now Has Its Own Club," *New York Times*, 6 February 1927; "Mrs. Mary Newell, Leader of Indians, Dies in Queens," *New York Times*, 29 October 1938; "New York City Indian Colony Reorganizes with a Membership of 200," *American Indian* (Newsletter of the Society of Oklahoma Indians), February 1927, found in box 18, folder 33, VV. Fascinatingly, in 1926, former Society of American Indians leader and Dakota intellectual Zitkala-Sa (Gertrude Bonnin) began investigating the authenticity of Mary Newell's claim of Indian identity. See Carpenter, "Detecting Indianness." Indeed, among the numerous challenges the first generation of urban Indians faced were urban swindlers, who sought to exploit Indian people directly or to exploit Indian identity for profit, typically by way of playing Indian. A group of urban Indians in Chicago created a comparable organization titled the Grand Council Fire (late renamed the Indian Council Fire) in 1923. The group's mission statement promised "to promote the advancement and protection of Indian rights and welfare; to assist the Indian in times of distress; to encourage the Indian in all educational and artistic pursuits; to strengthen and maintain the Indian character; and to cultivate friendlier relations between the Indian and White Race." See "The Indian Council Fire, 7 May 1944," box 18, folder 33, VV. For an insightful book on the history of Chicago's Indian community that includes extensive discussion of the Grand Council Fire, see LaPier and Beck, *City Indian*.

76. See, for example, Fixico, *Urban Indian Experience in America*, chap. 7.

77. Cory, *Within Two Worlds*, 64–65. Caughnawaga is an alternative spelling of Kahnawake. For an excellent documentary film about the Brooklyn Mohawks, see Reaghan Tarbell (director), *To Brooklyn and Back: A Mohawk Journey*. For a general study of high steel work during the twentieth century that includes ample discussion of the Mohawk workers, see Rasenberger, *High Steel*, especially chap. 6.

78. Mitchell, "Mohawks in High Steel," 21.

79. "Indians Live in Brooklyn!" *Los Angeles Times*, 2 September 1945.

80. Ibid.

81. Cory, *Within Two Worlds*; Mitchell, "Mohawks in High Steel," 27.

82. "Indians Live in Brooklyn!"

83. Mayor Bloomberg Mohawk Ironworkers Day Proclamation, Kanien'kehá:ka Onkwawén:na Raotitióhkwa Language and Cultural Center, Kahnawake, Quebec. Author visit, July 2015.

84. "Mohawk Ironworkers Help Raise Spire for Freedom Tower at One World Trade Center," *Indian Country Today*, 16 May 2013, https://newsmaven.io/indian countrytoday/archive/mohawk-ironworkers-help-raise-spire-for-freedom-tower-at -one-world-trade-center—XSmw9aHGkqfzs9iyPTYOg/.

85. Notes by author during visit to the Kahnawake Reserve, summer 2015.

86. I qualify this statement with the term "modern" because there have always been urban Indians in some discernible form. Consider the pre-Columbian

Mississippian city of Cahokia, which boasted the largest urban population in the history of the area that constitutes the present-day United States until the year 1800, when New York City and Philadelphia surpassed its peak population.

87. Historians Rosalyn LaPier and David Beck agree in their recent study on Chicago's early-twentieth-century Indian community. See LaPier and Beck, *City Indian*, 173.

88. In her study of First Nations women's community building efforts in Toronto during the mid-twentieth century, anthropologist Heather A. Howard argues that Indigenous people who ventured into Ontario's largest metropolis exploited the anonymity of mainstream urban space as a safe haven from government control and surveillance on tribal reserves. Essentially, assimilation in this case proved more of a push factor than a pull factor. Subsequently, through a process of acculturation, First Nations people in Toronto mastered the "tools of the oppressors" and deployed them as a strategy toward strengthening tribalism. Howard's analysis also applies to countless American Indians who mostly sought through a similar process of acculturation to add layers to their being, rather than reduce them. See Howard, "Women's Class Strategies as Activism in Native Community Building in Toronto."

89. Thomas, "Colonialism: Classic and Internal," 37–44.

90. As historian Steven Conn explains, cities encourage cosmopolitanism—a product of economic or social, and casual or intimate, interactions dependent on population density. "In the main, however," Conn writes, "cities have been the places where we have first and most fully confronted the task of living alongside people who do not necessarily belong to our own tribe." Conn uses the term "tribe" generally, but its more specific meaning for the study at hand is evident. See Conn, *Americans Against the City*, 4.

91. Deloria ultimately challenges us to locate within progressive era Indian communities "an incredibly complex Indian world, one full of priests and teachers, schemers and con artists, athletes, artists and singers, people who stayed engaged with Indian politics, education, law, and culture; and people who melted into reservation communities, small towns, and big cities as dentists, clerks, farmers, and mechanics." Deloria, "Four Thousand Invitations," 37–39.

92. On *postcolonial resistance*, see Bruyneel, *Third Space of Sovereignty*, 19–24.

93. Kellogg, "Industrial Organization for the Indian," 140.

Chapter Two

1. "A Pasture Turns into a Shipyard in Just 8 Months!" *Chicago Daily Tribune*, 24 January 1943; "Boat-a-Week Keeps Seneca Yard Hustling," *Chicago Tribune*, 6 June 1943.

2. "A Pasture Turns into a Shipyard in Just 8 Months!"; "Seneca Builds 157 LST's for Yank Invasions," *Chicago Tribune*, 29 May 1945; Thomas Greenwood letter to Brian G. Bardy, 22 February 1983, box 1, folder 19, Thomas Greenwood Papers, Newberry Library, Chicago, Illinois (hereafter cited as TGP); "Restoring Prairie Shipyard's Crucial Role in D-Day, WWII," *Chicago Tribune*, 7 June 2014.

3. "A Pasture Turns into a Shipyard in Just 8 Months!"; "Seneca Builds 157 LST's for Yank Invasions"; Thomas Greenwood letter to Brian G. Bardy, 22 February 1983, box 1, folder 19, TGP; "Restoring Prairie Shipyard's Crucial Role in D-Day, WWII." For background on Chicago's American Indian community between the 1893 and 1934 world's fairs, see LaPier and Beck, *City Indian*.

4. The "Double-V" term typically refers to wartime black civil rights activism that called for victory over fascism abroad and victory over racism and segregation at home.

5. Rosier, *Serving Their Country*, 2, 9, 73. For further background on America's competing visions of homogeneous and pluralistic society in the aftermath of World War II, see Wall, *Inventing the "American Way."* Likewise, historian Gary Gerstle argues that World War II and the Cold War provided excuses for federal policy makers and the general American public alike to "sharpen American national identity" while attempting to transform "millions of Americans whose loyalty was uncertain into ardent patriots." See Gerstle, *American Crucible*, 9. On decolonization in Cold War Indian Country, see Cobb, *Native Activism in Cold War America*. On decolonization and Third World liberation in a global Cold War context, see Westad, *Global Cold War*.

6. Bernstein, *American Indians and World War II*, 64–88, 168–69. See also Townsend, *World War II*.

7. U.S. Department of the Interior, *Annual Report of the Secretary of the Interior*, 237. Statistics on the number of Indians who labored in war industries and off-reservation agricultural projects during the war are somewhat unreliable. Collier claimed that roughly twenty-five thousand Native people enlisted for overseas military service, and that roughly forty thousand more labored in the domestic war industry. In contrast, sociologist Alan Sorkin claimed that forty-six thousand Indians left the reservation for war industries in 1943 alone, and that forty-four thousand more left in 1944. See Sorkin, *American Indians and Federal Aid*, 104–5.

8. Vine Deloria, "This Country Was a Lot Better Off When the Indians Were Running It."

9. "Report from the Great Lakes," *Indians at Work* 11, no. 3 (September–October 1943): 16.

10. The 1940 U.S. census counted 12,528 total American Indians residing in the State of Minnesota. U.S. censuses are notoriously problematic when it comes to counting American Indians, but even when allowing for a degree of unreliability, this figure is remarkable.

11. Kent Fitzgerald, "Indians in the Twin Cities," 1954, box 90, folder 17, Elizabeth Clark Rosenthal Papers, Western History Collections, University of Oklahoma (hereafter cited as ECR). Fitzgerald was director of placement for the Bureau of Indian Affairs.

12. Broker, *Night Flying Woman*, 5.

13. Kent Fitzgerald, "Indians in the Twin Cities," 1954, box 90, folder 17, ECR.

14. "Eastern Band of Cherokee in North Carolina Contribute to War Effort," *Indians at Work* (July–August–September 1942): 12–13.

15. A "MacArthur shift," otherwise known as a "graveyard shift," was a midnight-to-8 A.M. shift that patriotic workers served in honor of General Douglas MacArthur, commander of U.S. forces in World War II's Pacific theater. See "On the Night Shift," *Popular Mechanics*, November 1942, 168; "Indian Women Harness Old Talents to New War Jobs," *Indians at Work* 10, no. 2–6 (September 1942): 25–26. The degree to which Native women in this article exhibited national patriotism is not clear. Because the Department of Interior created and distributed *Indians at Work* during wartime, it is not surprising but important to note that contributing authors generally framed their protagonists as patriots. We should be careful not to assume that desire for work necessarily reflected patriotic fervor, or vice versa.

16. Peters, "Continuing Identity," 121–22.

17. "Indians Live in Brooklyn!"

18. For this section, I reviewed Indian service reports from 1942 that contain job placement figures for fifty reservations. Reservation Superintendent Employment Survey Responses, box 1, folder: Correspondence and Reports of Kathryn Mahn re: Indian Employment Opportunities in 1942, RG75, Correspondence and Reports Relating to the Employment of Indians, National Archives and Records Administration, Washington, D.C. (hereafter cited as CRREI).

19. Beulah Head (Tohono O'odham Reservation Superintendent) to Fred Daiker (Director of Indian Welfare), 3 October 1942, box 1, folder: Early 1940s, RG75, CRREI.

20. "American Indians Fight Axis," *New York Times*, 30 August 1942.

21. Employment questionnaires submitted to Kathryn Mahn, 1942, box 1, folder: Correspondence and Reports of Kathryn Mahn re: Indian Employment Opportunities in 1942, RG75, CRREI.

22. Ibid.

23. Ibid.

24. Ibid.

25. Reservation Superintendent Employment Survey Responses, box 1, folder: Correspondence and Reports of Kathryn Mahn re: Indian Employment Opportunities in 1942, RG75, CRREI.

26. Survey responses, box 1, folder: Response to June 1944 Circular re: Indian Employment Collected by F.H. Daiker, RG75, CRREI.

27. Ibid.

28. Tom White to John Collier, 29 July 1944, box 1, folder: Response to June 1944 Circular re: Indian Employment Collected by F.H. Daiker, RG75, CRREI.

29. Interview with Carl Kickingbird, 6 August 1968, T-302, 3, DDIOHC; Carl Kickingbird Obituary, *Oklahoman*, 10 July 2005.

30. "Indian Schools Adjust Schedules to Aid War Work," *Indians at Work*, April 1942, 29.

31. There is a robust historiography on Indian boarding schools. See, for example, Adams, *Education for Extinction*; Child, *Boarding School Seasons*.

32. "National Defense Training Program," 30 June 1942, box 1, folder: "Memorandums," RG75, Records of the Chilocco Indian School, National Archives and Records Administration, Southwest Region, Fort Worth, Texas (hereafter cited as CIS);

"From the Defense Course," *Indian School Journal*, 19 March 1943, Chilocco Indian School Collection, Oklahoma Historical Society Research Center, Oklahoma City (hereafter cited as CISC).

33. A. Durant, "Ship Building," *Indian School Journal*, 27 November 1942, CISC.

34. "Hints on Getting a Job," *Indian School Journal* 42, no. 20 (February 1942); "Getting a Job," *Indian School Journal* 42, no. 21 (February 1942), CISC.

35. "Another Instructor for Defense Course," *Indian School Journal* 42, no. 28 (March 1942), CISC.

36. L. E. Correll to Chilocco Staff, 16 February 1943, RG75, box 3, folder: Department of Interior Correspondence, CIS.

37. Stella Norman to L. E. Correll, 19 August 1941, RG75, box 3, folder: General Correspondence, CIS.

38. Mrs. Benge to L. E. Correll, 1941 (month and day indiscernible), RG75, box 3, folder: General Correspondence, CIS.

39. "War Effort" brochure, RCIS, Records of the Superintendent, National Defense Program Files, 1941–1943, General Administration Files, RG75, box 2, folder: "Aircraft," CIS.

40. "Haskell Institute—Information about War Production Courses," 26 October 1942, RCIS, Records of the Superintendent, National Defense Program Files, 1941–1943, General Administration Files, RG75, box 2, folder "Aircraft," CIS.

41. "From Needles to Battleships," *Indians at Work*, October 1941, 9.

42. "From the Mailbag," *Indians at Work*, July–August–September 1942, 31.

43. Lloyd D. Weir, "A Yakima Indian Boy in a War Job," *Indians at Work*, April 1942, 19–20.

44. "Indians Prove Expert Workers in Air Factories," *Wichita Beacon*, 29 March 1942, found in RG75, box 2, folder: Aircraft, CIS. In the 1970s, McDonnell Douglas introduced its Tomahawk missile. The U.S. Armed Forces has long appropriated Indian terms, from "Geronimo" to "Indian Country." To the best of my knowledge, it has yet to employ "Tepee" as a nom de guerre.

45. Ella Deloria, *Speaking of Indians*, 144, 148.

46. James Earle Fraser's famous *End of the Trail* sculpture portrays an Indian warrior slumped forward on his halted horse, thereby suggesting that Indians would not participate in history's forward march.

47. "The Navajos Consider Their Future," *Indians at Work* 12, no. 1 (May–June 1944): 23. Colleen O'Neill discusses how, during the midcentury period, the Navajo nation developed a mixed economy that blended modern and traditional work patterns both at home and beyond. Meanwhile, cultural kinship ties kept them bound together during this transformation. See O'Neill, *Working the Navajo Way*.

48. Vogt, *Navaho Veterans*, 109–12.

49. Ibid.

50. Underhill, *Red Man's America*, 239; Underhill, *The Navajos*, 243–53.

51. Ibid.

52. Burnette and Koster, *Road to Wounded Knee*, 157.

53. "Displaced Indians," *American Indian* (newsletter of the Association on American Indian Affairs) 3, no. 2 (Spring 1946): 9–11.

54. "Employment of Indians Off Reservation, Circular No. 3426," John Collier to Superintendents, 22 September 1941, box 1, folder 1 (Early 1940s), RG75, CRREI.

55. Ibid.

56. On Collier's vision of a "Red Atlantis," see Philp, *John Collier's Crusade for Indian Reform*, 1–25. For wider background on Collier's ideas about Indians, see Collier's memoir, *From Every Zenith*.

57. John Rockwell (Field Representative in Charge, Sacramento Indian Agency) to John Collier, 4 January 1942, box 1, folder: Early 1940s, RG75, CRREI.

58. "When the Indian Comes to the City," *American Indian* 1, no. 2 (Winter 1944): 9.

59. Haven Emerson, "Freedom or Exploitation!" *American Indian* 2, no. 4 (Fall 1945): 4.

60. Willard Beatty, "The Indian in the Postwar Period," *American Indian* 3, no. 1 (Winter 1946): 2–7, emphasis added. In a study of Navajo and Pueblo World War II veterans, graduate student ethnologist John Adair argued that alcohol prohibition back home on the reservation was especially offensive to discharged servicemen who appreciated drinking with white compatriots during military furloughs as a sign of equality and acceptance. Coupled with state laws denying them the franchise and trouble securing loans they were promised as part of the GI Bill, Navajo and Pueblo veterans felt acute discrimination and that their non-Indian fellow Americans were dismissing their brave efforts abroad. See "The Navajo and Pueblo Veteran: A Force for Culture Change," *American Indian* 4, no. 1 (1947): 5–11.

61. For example, the Colorado River Indian Reservation received twenty thousand Japanese evacuees from the West Coast. The evacuees were tasked with improving ninety thousand acres of reservation land for irrigated farming. See, for example, "First Japanese Evacuee Colony Is on Colorado River Indian Lands," *Indians at Work* 9, no. 6 (February 1942): 12.

62. Fred Daiker to William Zimmerman, 7 September 1943, box 1, folder: Early 1940s, RG75, CRREI.

63. Minutes of Staff Meeting, United Pueblos Agency, 12 August 1944, box 1, folder: Early 1940s, RG75, CRREI.

64. Ibid.

65. Ibid.

66. William Zimmerman (Assistant Commissioner of Indian Affairs) to Fred Daiker (Director of Welfare), 5 September 1944, box 1, folder: Early 1940s, RG75, CRREI. On wartime discussions about a postwar termination policy, see David Lewis, "Termination of the Confederated Tribes of the Grand Ronde Community of Oregon."

67. Fred Daiker to Paul Fickinger, 18 September 1944, box 1, folder: Early 1940s, RG75, CRREI.

68. Officer, "American Indian and Federal Policy," 46–49.

69. For analysis of Myer's advocacy for termination and relocation, see Drinnon, *Keeper of Concentration Camps*; Fixico, *Termination and Relocation*; and Philp, *Termination Revisited*.

70. For insightful scholarship on the termination policy, see Metcalf, *Termination's Legacy*. Metcalf argues that the termination policy emerged from confusion,

neglect, and willful ignorance and arrogance. He emphasizes the influence of Senator Arthur V. Watkins (R-Utah), who, informed by his Mormon faith's teachings about Native American people, called for an "emancipation program" for Native people.

71. "The Indian Who Never Got Home," published by UAW-CIO Fair Practices and Anti-Discrimination Department in Detroit, box 11a, folder 5, Theodore Hetzel Papers, Center for Southwest Studies, Fort Lewis College, Durango, Colorado (hereafter cited as THP); Hewitt, "The Indian Who Never Got Home."

72. Ella Deloria, *Speaking of Indians*, 136–38.

73. Pursuant to the 1924 Snyder Act, Congress extended United States citizenship over all Native American people. "Relocation Statistical Information Tables 4 and 5," AAIA; Richard Freeman (*Dallas Morning News* writer): "Rebuttal to Form Letter Written by Ass't Secretary of the Interior Roger Ernst to Various Members of the Congress and Senate concerning My Letter of Recent Date and News Clippings Concerning Relocation," March 1959, box 12, folder 29: Interior: Indian Affairs: General (Mar. 1959), Robert Kerr Departmental Papers, Carl Albert Center for Congressional Research, University of Oklahoma (hereafter cited as RKDP).

74. Rotella, *October Cities*, 57.

Chapter Three

1. George T. Barrett to Paul L. Fickinger, Placement Officer's Report, 18 March 1952, box 17, folder: Reports and Correspondence, FY 1952, 8NS-075-97-270, Bureau of Indian Affairs, Billings Area Office: Vocational and Subject Case Files, 1951–1960, National Archives and Records Administration, Rocky Mountain Region, Denver, Colorado (hereafter cited as BAOVSCF).

2. Ibid.

3. George Barrett to James Crawford, 6 March 1956, box 16, folder: Reports (Ft. Belknap) F.Y. 1956, RG75, BAOMVSF.

4. On Cold War cultural consensus versus pluralism, see Wall, *Inventing the "American Way."*

5. See, for example, Norrgard, *Seasons of Change*.

6. See, for example, Genetin-Pilawa, *Crooked Paths to Allotment*; Stremlau, *Sustaining the Cherokee Family*; Child, *Boarding School Seasons*; Whalen, *Native Students at Work*; R. Warren Metcalf, *Termination's Legacy*.

7. Relocation Brochure, box 34, folder 330: Relocation, Virgil J. Vogel Research and Personal Papers, Newberry Library, Chicago, Illinois (hereafter cited as VV).

8. "The Public Share in Indian Assimilation," *American Indian* (newsletter of the American Association on Indian Affairs) 4, no. 3 (1948): 4.

9. *Report on Urban and Rural Non-Reservation Indians*, 28.

10. "Truman Urges Aid for Needy Navajos," *New York Times*, 3 December 1947.

11. Statement by Harry S. Truman on the Navajo Crisis, 2 December 1947, HSTP. Secretary of the Interior Julius Krug prepared this statement on Truman's behalf. For general background on the Truman administration's legacy in Indian affairs, see Hosmer, *Native Americans and the Legacy of Harry S. Truman*.

12. "The Bureau of Indian Affairs Voluntary Relocation Services Program," box 34, folder 330: Relocation, VV; Navajo Placements for Calendar Year 1949 and January 1950 to September 30, 1950, box 1, folder: Stats: General Placement and Relocation (General Correspondence), 1950, RG75, Placement and Statistical Reports, compiled 1949–1954, National Archives and Records Administration, Washington, D.C. (hereafter cited as PSR).

13. "The Bureau of Indian Affairs Voluntary Relocation Services Program," box 34, folder 330: Relocation, VV. Historian Donald L. Fixico, whose work is foundational in relocation historiography, points to the Navajo rehabilitation program as the primary model for the subsequent national Voluntary Relocation Program. See Fixico, *Termination and Relocation*, 134–35. In his subsequent study of Indian urbanization, Fixico emphasizes the War Relocation Authority as BIA commissioner Dillon S. Myer's central model for a national Indian relocation program. See Fixico, *Urban Indian Experience in America*, 10.

14. "Planning in Action on the Navajo-Hopi Reservations," Report Number 11 (Department of Interior), box 1, folder 9, Glenn Emmons Papers, Center for Southwest Research, University of New Mexico, Albuquerque (hereafter cited as GEP).

15. "The Indian Enters Business," box 1, folder 13, GEP.

16. Stanley Lyman interview with Floyd O'Neil, Doris Duke Number 1029, box 17, folder 40, and Stanley Lyman interview with Floyd O'Neil, Doris Duke Number 1030, box 17, folder 41, American Indian History Project, SLP.

17. "'Great Mover of People' Title Given to Miller" (unidentified newspaper story), box 15, folder 20, SLP.

18. Stanley Lyman interview with Floyd O'Neil, Doris Duke Number 1029, box 17, folder 40, American Indian History Project, SLP.

19. Interview with Philleo Nash, 5 June 1967, 695–96, Harry S. Truman Presidential Library, Independence, Missouri.

20. Concerning termination, I am referring to Warren Metcalf's emphasis on Republican Utah senator Arthur V. Watkins's forceful advocacy of an Indian "emancipation proclamation." See R. Warren Metcalf, *Termination's Legacy*.

21. Toby Morris to Harry S. Truman, 19 October 1951, box 9, folder 88, Toby Morris Papers, Carl Albert Center for Congressional Research, University of Oklahoma (hereafter cited as TMP).

22. Toby Morris to Angie Debo, 7 May 1951, box 9, folder 88, TMP; Debo, *Five Civilized Tribes of Oklahoma*.

23. Dr. George B. Roop to Toby Morris, 15 June 1951, box 9, folder 92, TMP.

24. Reservation Conditions Summary, box 1, folder 1: Cheyenne River Agency, Bureau of Indian Affairs Indian Relocation Records, Newberry Library, Chicago, Illinois (hereafter cited as BIAIRR).

25. "How Fare the Indians?" box 9, folder 74, TMP.

26. "The Overprotected Indian," *American Indian* (newsletter of the American Association on Indian Affairs) 6, no. 1 (Summer 1951): 1–2.

27. On the influence of late-nineteenth-century "friends of the Indian" advocates, see historian Frederick Hoxie's seminal work *A Final Promise*.

28. "A Way Out for the Navajos," *American Indian* (newsletter of the American Association on Indian Affairs) 6, no. 1 (Summer 1951): 14. On the Cold War's impact on ideas that linked Indian cultural and political tribalism with communism, see Rosier, "'They Are Ancestral Homelands'"; Cobb, "Talking the Language of the Larger World: Politics in Cold War (Native) America"; Cobb, *Native Activism in Cold War America*.

29. "In the Hands of Its Users," *American Indian* 6, no. 3 (Spring 1952): 38. On America's postwar obsession with material wealth and status, see Marcuse, *One-Dimensional Man*. On Collier, Dodge, and Lawrence, see Kelly, *Assault on Assimilation*; Philp, *John Collier's Crusade for Indian Reform*; Smith, *Reimagining Indians*. On citizen consumers, see Lizabeth Cohen, *Consumer's Republic*.

30. Elizabeth Clark Rosenthal to Theodore Hetzel, 24 June 1957, box 28, folder 11, THP.

31. *The Reservation Indian Comes to Town*. On discursive power exercises that shaped expectations for Indian behavior in the early twentieth century, see Philip Deloria, *Indians in Unexpected Places*. During this same period, anthropologist Oscar Lewis began developing his "culture of poverty" theory, which suggests that those who dwell in poverty suffer from provincialism, suspicion of outsiders, rivalry along the bottom rung, and general ignorance about the encompassing world and how it functions. For the most part, according to Lewis, they lack class-consciousness and remain mystified by government and politics. Moreover, they lack both a sense of history and a sense of the future, thus rendering their beliefs and behaviors predictable. Finally, they tend to be superstitious in their attitudes toward sickness and death, and they suffer from general lifelong feelings of help-lessness, inferiority, and worthlessness. Such attitudes, according to Lewis, translate into a distorted value system that accepts—encourages, even—misogyny, domestic abuse, and substance abuse. Because attempts at adaptation often only reify the cycle, physical escape and socioeconomic uplift often prove impossible to achieve. See Oscar Lewis, *Five Families* and *The Children of Sanchez*.

32. *Flandreau Spirit*, senior souvenir edition, vol. 26, no. 11, 9 May 1956, box 2, folder 2: Sisseton Agency, BIAIRR.

33. *Indian Leader* 56, no. 15 (May 1953), published by the Haskell Institute, Lawrence, Kansas.

34. "Notes and Impressions from the Superintendents' and Principals' Meeting, Oklahoma City, November 20–22, 1944," 1925–1959, RG075, box 41, folder: Memo—Notices, 1948–1956, Haskell Indian Nations University Decimal Correspondence, National Archives and Records Administration, Central Plains Region, Kansas City (hereafter cited as HIN).

35. On the limited and racially formative nature of turn-of-the-century educational and vocational training for Native people, see Hoxie, *Final Promise*.

36. Between 1940 and 1950, the total urban Indian population increased from roughly twenty-four thousand to about fifty-six thousand. Neils, *Reservation to City*, 17.

37. Consolidated Chippewa Agency, Placement Narrative Report, October 1951, Field Placement and Relocation Office Employment Assistance Records: Narrative (hereafter cited as FPROEAP).

38. Reports on Trips to Prairie Island Community, 20 November 1951 and 18–19 December 1951, FPROEAP.

39. Narrative Report—January 1952 (MPLS Area Office), FPROEAP.

40. Monthly Reports, August–November 1951, box 1, folder: Reports-Narrative, Juneau, 1952, FPROEAP.

41. Ibid.

42. Marie Street (San Jose Field Office) to Charles F. Miller (Chief, Branch of Relocation Services), 17 July 1958, box 102, folder: Counseling Relocatees, RG75, Records Relating to Employment Assistance Programs, compiled 1949–1973, National Archives and Records Administration, Washington, D.C. (hereafter cited as RREAP).

43. August Placement Report, 1953, box 3, folder: Reports—Narrative, Juneau, 1954, FPROEAP.

44. George LaVatta (Portland Area Placement Officer) to Allan Harper (Area Director, Window Rock, Arizona), 29 October 1951, and Monthly Summary Report, October 1951, box 1, folder: Narrative Reports, Portland, 1952, FPROEAP.

45. January Narrative Report, 1952, Mary Nan Gamble (Acing Field Placement Officer) to Selene Gifford (Chief Relocation Officer), box 1, folder: Reports—Narrative, Chicago, 1952, FPROEAP.

46. Mary Nan Gamble to Selene Gifford, 10 January 1952, box 1, folder: Reports—Narrative, Chicago, 1952, FPROEAP.

47. June 1952 Monthly Statistical Report Summary, box 2, folder: Reports—Narrative, Salt Lake City, 1952, FPROEAP. For wider background and a dynamic analysis of Navajo labor during the twentieth century, see O'Neill, *Working the Navajo Way*.

48. Minutes from Standing Rock tribal leaders' meeting with Indian affairs commissioner Glenn Emmons, 20 July 1956, box 3, folder 1, GEP.

49. February Placement Report, 1953, box 3, folder: Reports—Narrative, Portland, 1953, RG75, FPROEAP.

50. Consolidated Chippewa Agency, Placement Narrative Report, December 1951, box 3, folder: Reports—Narrative, Minneapolis, 1952, FPROEAP. Interestingly, although the tribal committee's resolution benefited his efforts, Fitzgerald explained that it would not be binding until the secretary of the interior approved it.

51. Guest editorial by Louis Bruce Jr., *Amerindian* 1, no. 6 (July–August 1953); guest editorial by Robert L. Bennett, *Amerindian* 3, no. 6 (July–August 1955).

52. "The Federal Government and the States in Indian Administration: An Address by Commissioner of Indian Affairs Dillon S. Myer before the Western Governors' Conference at Phoenix, Arizona," 9 December 1952, box 2, folder: 1950–1953, Dillon S. Myer Papers, Government Agencies File, 1950–53, Harry S. Truman Presidential Library, Independence, Missouri (hereafter cited as DMP).

53. Travel Notebook Five, entry: 2 May 1960, box 1, RG1, THP. Woodenlegs is referring to the "Cheyenne Exodus" from Indian Territory to their Northern Plains homelands during 1877–1879. On this topic, see Monnet, *Tell Them We Are Going Home*; Powell, *Sweet Medicine*.

54. "The Federal Government and the States in Indian Administration: An Address by Commissioner of Indian Affairs Dillon S. Myer before the Western Governors' Conference at Phoenix, Arizona," 9 December 1952, box 2, folder: 1950–1953, DMP.

55. Interview with Stanley Lyman, 1972, box 17, folder 41, SLP.

Chapter Four

1. Congress's Public Law 959 created the AVT in 1956. Employment Assistance Case File, folder: Myron E. Miller, Jr., RG75, selected files from boxes 390, 393, 398 (All Subjects Are Deceased), Minneapolis Area Office Employment Assistance Case Files, National Archives and Records Administration, Central Plains Region, Kansas City (hereafter cited as MAO). By 1969, there were 125 occupational training schools operating in 26 states. Most of them were in urban areas and demanded that Indians leave the reservation for training. See Fay, *Developing Indian Employment Opportunities*, 38.

2. Myron Miller case file, MAO.

3. "Few Hunters Would Get Lost in the Woods If Myron Miller Were a Member of Party," *Milwaukee Journal*, 3 February 1953.

4. Myron Miller case file, MAO.

5. Statistical Summary of Activities from Inception of the Individual Program through June 30, 1965, RG75, box 102, folder: Community Living, RREAP.

6. Child, *Boarding School Seasons*. For excellent volumes containing useful statistical data on Indian urban relocation, see Neils, *Reservation to City*; Sorkin, *Urban American Indian*.

7. "Summary of History—Nationwide," Report on Branch of Relocation Services, 18 October 1957, box 10, folder 9, Sophie Aberle Papers, Center for Southwest Research, University of New Mexico, Albuquerque (hereafter cited as SAP); Madigan, *American Indian Relocation Program*.

8. Narrative Report for Fiscal Year Ending June 30, 1955 (MPLS Area Office), box 13, folder: Narrative and Statistical Records, 1955–1958, and Monthly Narrative Reports (May–June 1955), box 13, folder: Superintendent's Narrative Reports, 1955, RG75, Records of the Bureau of Indian Affairs, 1793–1999, Consolidated Chippewa Agency, Cass Lake, Minnesota, Annual Reports 1942–1946, National Archives and Records (hereafter cited as CCA).

9. Assisted Navajo Relocation, 1952–1956, prepared by Gallup Area Relocation Specialist Robert M. Cullum for Gallup Area Relocation Director W. Wade Head (October 1957), box 10, folder 9, SAP.

10. Box 2, folders 24 and 26, BIAIRR.

11. "Navaho Program Newsletter," 1 May 1953, AAIA.

12. BIA Billings Area Office Relocation Information Pamphlet, box 17, folder: "Reports, 1951," 8NS-075-97-270, BAOVSCF.

13. "Information about Relocation Services," box 27, folder 13, SAP.

14. Ibid. Thomas Biolsi discerns a similar Foucauldian subjection of Indian people in "Birth of the Reservation."

15. Bold and capitalized text is true to the original document.

16. "Information about Relocation Services," box 27, folder 13, SAP.

17. St. Louis City Attractions Brochure, box 3, folder 36: St. Louis Field Office, Education, Entertainment, BIAIRR.

18. Thrush, "Iceberg and the Cathedral."

19. Jack Womeldorf (Intermountain School Relocation Officer) to Rudolph Russell (field relocation officer, Joliet, IL office), 3 December 1957, box 1, folder 6: Intermountain School, 1957, BIAIRR.

20. "Why We Left Our Reservation Homes," newspaper clipping from unidentified source (responses range from years 1956 to 1960), box 5, folder 14, GEP.

21. On the role of women in Cold War American marriages, see Coontz, *Way We Never Were*; May, *Homeward Bound*; Meyerowitz, *Not June Cleaver.*

22. "Suggestions for Counseling Prospective Relocation Applicants," 12 March 1952, box 1, folder: Reports—Narrative, Chicago, 1952, RG75, FPROEAP.

23. Ibid.

24. Goodner, *Indian Americans in Dallas*, 9.

25. "Manual Supercessions and Additions, 1960," box 1, folder 11, Bureau of Indian Affairs Records, University of Utah, Marriott Library Special Collections (hereafter cited as BIAR).

26. "Relocation Information Record," 1958, box 1, RG75, BAOMVSF. I omit the folder number for this source to protect the subject's identity.

27. Home Visit Report, Carson Family, Cincinnati, Ohio, 21 April 1961, box 102, folder: Community Living Home Visits, RG75, RREAP. This family's name has been changed to protect their privacy.

28. Home Visit Report, Whitehorse Family, Cincinnati, Ohio, 21 April 1961, box 102, folder: Community Living Home Visits, RG75, RREAP. This family's name has been changed to protect their privacy.

29. Letter to Charles Penoi, Concho Area Field Office, 18 March 1957, RG75, E.216, Employment Assistance Case Files, 1952–1956, National Archives and Records Administration, Southwest Region, Fort Worth, Texas (hereafter cited as EACF). "Arnold Conrad" is not the real name of this correspondent. I have elected to change this person's name and omit the folder number in an effort to protect the person's identity. This is true for all personal correspondence materials I used from RG75, E.216, EACF.

30. Letter to Charles Penoi, 7 October 1957, RG75, E.216, box 1, EACF.

31. Letter to Charles Penoi, 15 November 1957, RG75, E.216, box 1, EACF.

32. George Wolf to Relocation Services, 6 March 1959, box 25, folder "Relocation Correspondence, FY 1957–1959," 8NS-075-97-270, BAOVSCF.

33. Letter to relocation officer, 10 September 1955, RG75, E.216, box 1, EACF.

34. Arends, "Socio-Cultural Study of the Relocation of American Indians to Chicago," 49–51.

35. Charles Willing to AAIA, 28 October 1956, AAIA.

36. Albert Allard Jr. to Denver Indian Office, date unknown, AAIA.

37. Willie C. Jones to Angie Debo, 25 September 1959, AAIA.

38. Letter to relocation officer, 22 February 1961, RG75, E.216, box 1, EACF.

39. Lewis Carter to Mrs. King, 15 February 1959, RG75, box 25, folder: Relocation Correspondence, FY 1957–1959, Bureau of Indian Affairs, Billings Area Office Papers, National Archives and Records Administration, Rocky Mountain Region, Denver, Colorado (hereafter cited as BAOP). "Lewis Carter" is not this person's real name. I have elected to change his name in order to protect his privacy. I have tried whenever possible to piece together such individuals' ultimate fate. Alas, the historical record for individuals such as "Lewis Carter" presents unbridgeable gaps.

40. Nathaniel Johnson Relocation Subject File, box 2, RG75, EACF. This individual's name has been changed to protect his identity.

41. Neils, *Reservation to City*, 109.

42. Ibid., 152.

43. O. K. Armstrong and Marjorie Armstrong, "The Indians Are Going to Town," *Reader's Digest*, January 1955, 42.

44. Ivy Coffey, *The Urban Indian* (a reprint from the *Sunday Oklahoman* and the *Oklahoma City Times*), WHC.

45. "Navajos Lead Movement from Wilds to City Life," *Los Angeles Examiner*, 1953 (month and day unknown), AAIA.

46. Alfred and Mary Sue Boneshirt, interview with Herbert T. Hoover, 10 July 1970, American Indian History Research Project, Northern State College, Aberdeen, South Dakota (hereafter cited as AIHRP-NSC).

47. John S. Painter, "Benjamin Reifel: Transitional Sioux Leader," included within Carl Whitman Jr. interview with John S. Painter, 3 June 1982, AIHRP-NSC.

48. Home Counselor's Report, Los Angeles, 2 July 1957, box 19, folder: Assistance to Individuals (Crow, N. Cheyenne, Wind River), 8NS-075-97-270, BAOVSCF. I have elected to change this family's name in an effort to protect their identity. This is true of all vocational and subject case files that I viewed at the NARA Rocky Mountain branch.

49. Wilbur Peacock (Field Relocation Officer, San Francisco Office) to Reuben Fuhrer (Flathead Agency Relocation Officer), 21 May 1958, box 20, folder: Assistance to Individuals—Blackfeet, FY 1958, 8NS-075-97-270, BAOVSCF.

50. Gary Lawrence to Mr. Maggart (Sisseton Area Field Office Relocation Officer), 20 March 1957, box 2, folder 2: Sisseton Agency, BIAIRR.

51. Arends, "Socio-Cultural Study of the Relocation of American Indians to Chicago," 52–54.

52. George Barrett to Paul Fickinger (Area Director), 5 March 1954; Monthly Report 1 February 1954 and Monthly Report 31 December 1953, box 17, folders: Area Relocation Reports, FY 1954 and Monthly Reports from Agencies, FY 1954, RG75, BAOMVSF.

53. Folder: Earl F. Sargent, RG75, Selected Files from Boxes 390, 393, 398 (All Subjects Are Deceased), MAO.

54. Ibid.

55. Ibid.

56. "Bridging the Gap: The Twin Cities Native American Community," report conducted by the Minnesota State Advisory Committee under the auspices of the

United States Commission on Civil Rights, United States Department of Health, Education, and Welfare (Washington: Government Printing Office, 1975).

57. "Placement Narrative Report 1952, Chicago Field Office," box 1, folder: Reports—Narrative, Chicago, 1952, RG75, FPROEAP.

58. "Chicago Field Placement Office Report, April 1952," box 1, folder: Reports—Narrative, Chicago, 1952, RG75, FPROEAP.

59. Metropolitan School of Business Student Guide Addendum and Chicago Field Employment Assistance Office Memo, 22 July 1963, box 151, folder: Chicago Field Employment Assistance Office, Philleo Nash Papers, Harry S. Truman Presidential Library, Independence, Missouri (hereafter cited as PNP).

60. Ibid.

61. Interview with Stanley Lyman (1972), box 17, folder 41, SLP.

62. "Denver Field Relocation Office, 201 Old Custom House, Denver, CO: Office Policy and Procedure," box 14, folder 19, SLP.

63. Relocation Subject File, folder: Randolph Lussier, RG75, Selected Files from Boxes 390, 393, 398 (All Subjects Are Deceased), MAO.

64. Ibid.

65. "Denver Field Relocation Office, 201 Old Custom House, Denver, CO: Office Policy and Procedure," box 14, folder 19, SLP.

66. "Integrating the Indian in Big City Life," *St. Louis Post Dispatch*, 28 February 1958.

67. "Narrative of Incidents Relating to Assignment of Joe La Salle to Chicago Field Relocation Office, 20 November 1959," box 14, folder 20, SLP. On stereotypes about Native Americans' supposed propensity for "squandering money," see Philip Deloria, *Indians in Unexpected Places,* 151; Harmon, *Rich Indians*, especially chap. 5.

68. "U.S. Trains Eskimos for Large City Jobs," *New York Times*, 6 January 1969.

69. Interestingly, these are precisely the reasons why Kennedy administration associate commissioner of Indian affairs James E. Officer argued that historians are mistaken when they suggest that relocation should be understood as a key component of the termination policy. If relocation provided the primary economic safety net for terminated Indians, why, then, was the program so consistently underfunded, understaffed, and mismanaged? See Officer, "American Indian and Federal Policy," 45–47.

70. Interview with Marlene Strouse (Pima), 18 July 1983, box 2, folder 10, CAIOHP.

71. Ibid.

72. Goodner, *Indian Americans in Dallas*, 2.

73. Ibid., 8.

74. Assisted Navajo Relocation, 1952–1956, prepared by Gallup Area Relocation Specialist Robert M. Cullum for Gallup Area Relocation Director W. Wade Head (October 1957), box 10, folder 9, SAP.

75. Profile of Carl Larson Family, 1964, box 151, folder: Chicago Field Employment Assistance Office, PNP.

76. Home Visit Report, Miller Family, St. Louis, Missouri, 12 April 1961, box 102, folder: Community Living Home Visits, RG75, RREAP. This family's name has been changed to protect their privacy.

77. For an in-depth analysis of the discursive power of expectations about and for Native people, see Philip Deloria, *Indians in Unexpected Places*.

78. Goodner, *Indian Americans in Dallas*, 6.

79. *The Valley Breeze: Fox Valley Manufacturers' Association Newsletter* 2, no. 4 (May 1958), RG75, box 6, folder: Joliet Field Relocation Office Narrative Reports for Relocation Services Prior to July 1, 1958, FPROEAP.

80. Adam Martinez (San Ildefonso Pueblo Governor) to AAIA, 4 June 1956, AAIA.

81. Torres-Martinez (Desert Cahuilla) to AAIA, 25 May 1956, AAIA.

82. Ennis Moon (Skull Valley Goshute Reservation, Utah) to AAIA, no date, AAIA.

83. Sac and Fox Tribe of Oklahoma to AAIA, no date, AAIA.

84. "Relocation for the Indian," letter to the editor, *Minneapolis Tribune*, 6 March 1956.

85. W. W. Keeler to Sophie Aberle and William Brophy, 15 October 1960, box 22, folder: Keeler, 1957–1959, William Brophy Papers, Harry S. Truman Presidential Library, Independence, Missouri (hereafter cited as WBP).

86. The eight tribal presidents represented the Affiliated Tribes of the Northwest. Helen Peterson, "NCAI Looks at Relocation," 20 June 1956, AAIA.

87. Recommendations, 13 December 1956, box 10, folder 5: Indian Affairs, Bureau of (1958), TMP. The tribal nations that formed the committee included the Cherokee, Chickasaw, Seminole, Oklahoma Choctaw, Creek, Eastern Shawnee, Mississippi Choctaw, Quapaw, Iowa, Seneca-Cayuga, Kaw, Sac and Fox, and Osage.

88. "Winnebago Meeting with Commissioner Glenn Emmons," 20 July 1956, box 3, folder 1, GEP.

89. Ibid.

90. Minneapolis Area Indian Affairs Conference (held in Des Moines, IA), 15 October 1956, box 3, folder 7, GEP.

91. *Smoke Signals: Colorado River Indian Tribes*, newsletter printed in Parker, Arizona, July 4, 1956.

92. *Smoke Signals: Colorado River Indian Tribes*, December 1957.

93. Department of the Interior Internal Memo, 25 October 1955, box 28, folder 14, THP.

94. Assisted Navajo Relocation, 1952–1956, prepared by Gallup Area Relocation Specialist Robert M. Cullum for Gallup Area Relocation Director W. Wade Head (October 1957), box 10, folder 9, SAP.

95. Ibid.

96. Travel Notebook Zero, entry: 26 June 1955, box 1, RG1, THP.

97. Assisted Navajo Relocation, 1952–1956, prepared by Gallup Area Relocation Specialist Robert M. Cullum for Gallup Area Relocation Director W. Wade Head (October 1957), box 10, folder 9, SAP. On the Navajo "Long Walk," see Iverson, *Diné*, chap. 2.

98. "Navajo Tribe Memorandum on Relocation Committee visit to San Francisco, Bay Area, and Los Angeles between March 10–24, 1962," box 148, folder: San Francisco Bay Area Branch Employment Assistance, PNP.

99. Ibid.

100. El Reno Federal Reformatory Inmate to Jim Huff, 11 July 1968, box 170, folder: Parolee Release Program, El Reno, Oklahoma Federal Reformatory, RG75, RREAP. The BIA also negotiated an American Indian parolee release program with the Federal Youth Center in Englewood, Colorado.

101. In her study of Native people in California's Silicon Valley, anthropologist Renya Ramirez imagines urban Indians as people who maneuver through a central metropolitan hub, which nurtures "unbounded connections" to their tribal homelands. Her urban Indian protagonists embrace urban space as venues within which to gain new sociopolitical insights on their way to becoming transmitters of knowledge. See Ramirez, *Native Hubs*.

Chapter Five

1. "Narrative," 7 January 1960, box 14, folder 20, SLP.

2. Ibid.

3. It is interesting to consider whether those who self-relocated tended to experience an easier adjustment process. They likely migrated to cities where they could exploit some previous relationship—possibly stemming from prior military service or war-industry work—for employment and housing arrangements. By contrast, those who relocated through the Indian bureau placed an uncertain degree of fate and faith in the program's hands. Frustratingly, the BIA at best kept insufficient records on relocated Indians and did not track the movement of self-relocated Indians in any meaningful capacity. Such an evaluation would perhaps need to be conducted through oral history.

4. In sum, I reviewed sixty-seven subject case files from the NARA Rocky Mountain Branch in Denver, Colorado; twenty-five from the NARA Great Plains Branch in Kansas City, Missouri; and roughly twenty to thirty from the NARA Southwest Branch in Fort Worth, Texas.

5. *Smoke Signals: Colorado River Indian Tribes* (undated, but must be between 1 December 1956 and 12 December 1956, and is likely vol. 1, no. 6).

6. Travel Notebook Four: entry 26 July 1959, box 1, RG1, THP.

7. Fort Belknap Consolidated Agency Relocation Officer's Monthly Report, 1 July 1955, box 17, folder: Monthly Reports from Agencies, FY 1954, 8NS-075-97-270 BAOVSCF.

8. On Lake Superior Ojibwe people's seasonal work patterns, see Norrgard, *Seasons of Change*; on Round Valley Indian labor migrations, see Bauer, *We Were All Like Migrant Workers Here*.

9. Raibmon, *Authentic Indians*, 114.

10. Land-Bar Chart, 1867–1956, and Primary Sources of Income on Sisseton reservation, 1957, box 2, folder 2: Sisseton Agency, BIAIRR.

11. *A Program for Indian Citizens: A Summary Report*, prepared by the Commission on the Rights, Liberties, and Responsibilities of the American Indian (p. 16), box 1, folder 4, TGP. Authors of this piece included W. W. Keeler (Cherokee Nation Principal Chief), Karl Llewellyn (law professor at the University of Chicago), Arthur M. Schlesinger (professor emeritus, Harvard), Charles Sprague (editor and publisher of the *Oregon Statesman*), and Meredith Wilson (president of the University of Minnesota).

12. Arends, *Socio-Cultural Study of the Relocation of American Indians to Chicago*, 48–49.

13. Father Peter Powell, interview with author, 9 December 2009. Transcript in author's possession.

14. "A Policy to Meet Indian Needs Today," *Indian Truth* (published by the Indian Rights Association, Philadelphia) 36, no. 1 (January–April 1959): 2.

15. "Winnebago Meeting with Commissioner Glenn Emmons," 20 July 1956, box 3, folder 1, GEP.

16. On urban Indian centers, see, for example, LaGrand, *Indian Metropolis*; Fixico, *Urban Indian Experience*. On St. Augustine's Center for Indians, see Douglas Miller, "Dignity and Decency."

17. Interview with Jim Olquin, 1971, box 26, UII. Various sources on the duration of relocation financial support put it anywhere from two weeks to ninety days.

18. "Special Message to the Congress on Indian Affairs," 8 July 1970, *Public Papers of the President of the United States: Richard Nixon*, 564–76.

19. "Chicago Field Placement Office Report, April 1952," RG75, box 1, folder: Reports—Narrative, Chicago, 1952, FPROEAP.

20. "Humboldt Park," Chicago Historical Society, Encyclopedia of Chicago History, accessed 12 March 2014, www.encyclopedia.chicagohistory.org/pages /617.html. The neighborhood was in fact just beginning to receive a substantial influx of Puerto Rican migrants during this period, which might explain some of the ignorant Caucasian residents' confusion about the Bearskin family's race.

21. "Bigotry Here—an Indian Home Is Stoned," *Chicago Sun-Times*, 16 May 1960.

22. "Bearskin Family to Move from W. Side," *Chicago Sun-Times*, 26 May 1960; "Indian Family Hunting Home After Eviction," *Chicago Tribune*, 26 May 1960.

23. Leigh Hubbard to Charles Rovin (Acting Chief, Branch of Training, Placement and Relocation), 12 September 1952, box 2, folder: Reports—Narrative, Denver 1953, RG75, FPROEAP.

24. "Bridging the Gap: The Twin Cities Native American Community." American Indian Movement leader Dennis Banks worked for Honeywell as a job recruiter during the late 1960s. See Banks, *Ojibwa Warrior*, 346.

25. Harold E. Fey, "Our American Indian Neighbors" (address to 73rd Annual Meeting of IRA, on 2 February 1956), *Indian Truth* (published by the Indian Rights Association, Philadelphia, PA) 33, no. 1 (January–February 1956).

26. "When Our Grandfathers Carried Guns," *Gallup Independent*, 11 September 1969, found in box 11A, folder 3, THP.

27. Biolsi characterizes antagonistic relationships between reservation-based Indians and local non-Indians on and adjacent to the Rosebud reservation as a "zero-sum game," in which each side becomes increasingly intent on restricting each other's power, but neither side ever gets ahead. In the process, Native people ultimately lose sight of their true "deadliest enemy": the U.S. government. See Biolsi, *Deadliest Enemies*.

28. Saint Augustine's Center Annual Report, 1962, Unpublished Papers of Father Peter J. Powell, St. Augustine's Center for Indians, Chicago, Illinois (hereafter cited as FPP).

29. "The Urban Indian: He Has Become a Stranger in His Native Land," *Chicago Tribune*, 22 August 1971.

30. Frost, *"An Interracial Movement of the Poor,"* 56.

31. Field Employment Assistance Office Questionnaire, Los Angeles (1965), box 102, folder: Relocatee Progress Evaluation, RG75, RREAP. Charles Munson is not this individual's real name. The questionnaire to which he responded did not specify his tribal designation.

32. "Father Peter Powell: A White Man They Can Trust," *Sunday Herald*, 18 November 1979.

33. *Episcopal Church News*, 3 March 1957.

34. *Urban Indians: Proceedings of the Third Annual Conference on Problems and Issues concerning American Indians Today.*

35. Ibid. Further demonstrating the tendency among critics to characterize relocation as a "one-way ticket," former Indian affairs commissioner Philleo Nash, who worked to improve the program when he took over during the Kennedy administration, stated, "Myer's relocation program was essentially a one-way bus ticket from rural to urban poverty." See Philp, *Indian Self-Rule*, 166.

36. Interview with Paul Harrison, 28 July 1968, AIRP 0051, AIHRP-NSC.

37. Jobs for Minnesota Indians: In Cooperation with the Minnesota Labor Committee for Human Rights and the Governor's Human Rights Commission, box 148, folder: June 4–10, 1962—Minneapolis Trip—Correspondence (3 of 4), PNP.

38. Fort Belknap Consolidated Agency Superintendent J. W. Wellington to Paul Plummage, 16 December 1953, box 17, folder: Monthly Reports from Agencies, FY 1954, RG75, BAOVSCF.

39. "The Uprooted Americans," *Sunday Herald*, 18 November 1979.

40. Ibid.

41. Interview with Darrell Gardner, 18 October 1986, box 1, folder 9, Ute Indian Interviews, Marriott Library Special Collections, University of Utah, Salt Lake City (hereafter cited as UII).

42. Relocation Memo, 10 July 1959, box 7, folder 40, SAP.

43. "Relocation Not Full Answer," *Devils Lake Journal*, 23 November 1956, found in box 13, folder 12, William Zimmerman Papers, Center for Southwest Research, University of New Mexico, Albuquerque (hereafter cited as WZP). In 1960, Minneapolis's total population of 482,872 people included 2007 American Indians. See Sorkin, *Urban American Indian*, 11.

44. Relocation Survey Questionnaires (1959), box 6, folder 8, SAP.

45. Ibid.

46. "Chicago, It Was a Jungle," *Chicago Tribune*, 13 September 1976.

47. Meeting Minutes, Tribal Council Conference with BIA Commissioner Glenn Emmons, Omaha, Nebraska, 19–21 July 1956, box 3, folder 1, GEP.

48. Survey of Reasons for Return, box 19, folder: Special Study of Returnees, FY 1959, RG75, BAOMVSF.

49. Goodner, *Indian Americans in Dallas,* 4.

50. Stanley Lyman (Chicago Field Relocation Officer) to Crow Agency Superintendent, 3 April 1959, box 1, folder (anonymous), RG 75, BAOMVSF.

51. Ibid.

52. *Smoke Signals: Colorado River Indian Tribes* 1, no. 7 (January 11, 1957).

53. Telesfore Romero to Sophie Aberle, 1 December 1959, box 6, folder 8, SAP. In his evaluation, Romero also felt compelled to share with Aberle that relocatees were "classified as *color race* would be classified. And some are actually live amongs them [*sic*]."

54. "Emmons Cites Evidence of Indian Success in Relocation," Bureau of Indian Affairs Internal Memo, 29 February 1960, box 10, folder 9, SAP. Emmons specifically cited 1955 as the most "successful" year, claiming that 76 percent of all relocatees had achieved urban independence during that period. In 1968, vice president Hubert Humphrey claimed that the relocation program "has lured 50,000 Indians into successful urban living." See Steiner, *New Indians*, 180.

55. Richard Freeman: "Rebuttal to Form Letter Written by Ass't Secretary of the Interior Roger Ernst to Various Members of the Congress and Senate concerning My Letter of Recent Date and News Clippings Concerning Relocation," March 1959, box 12 folder 29: Interior: Indian Affairs: General (Mar. 1959), RKDP.

56. "Cheyenne Warrior," *Chicago Tribune Magazine*, 2 May 1982.

57. Annual Report, 1958, RG75, box 6, folder: Joliet Field Relocation Office Narrative Reports for Relocation Services Prior to July 1, 1958, FPROEAP.

58. Stanley Lyman Interview with Floyd O'Neil, Doris Duke Number 1030, American Indian History Project, box 17, folder 41, SLP.

59. Rapid City Conference Meeting Minutes, 2–3 December 1957, box 28, folder: Meetings and Reports (Conferences Attended), 1957–1958, RG75, BAOMVSF.

60. Ibid.

61. "The Urban Indian: He Has Become a Stranger in His Native Land," *Chicago Tribune*, 22 August 1971.

62. Jacob Ahtone to K. W. Bergen, Coordinator, State of Montana, Dept. of Indian Affairs, 15 October 1958, box 3, folder: Relocation Correspondence, FY 1957–1959, BAOMVSF.

63. "Chicago Field Placement Office Report, April 1952," box 1, folder: Reports— Narrative, Chicago, 1952, RG75, FPROEAP.

64. Kurt Dreifuss to Charles Rovin (Assistant Chief, Placement Section), 17 June 1952, box 1, folder: Reports—Narrative, Chicago, 1952, RG75, FPROEAP.

65. Hemingway, *Ira Hayes, Pima Marine*, 149–56; "Ira Hayes, 32, Iwo Jima Hero, Is Found Dead," *Chicago Tribune*, 25 January 1955.

66. Glenn Emmons to *Harper's* editor, 8 March 1956, AAIA.

67. "In the suburb one might live and die without marring the image of an innocent world, except when some shadow of evil fell over a column in the newspaper," Mumford wrote. "Thus the suburb served as an asylum for the preservation of illusion. Here domesticity could prosper, oblivious of the pervasive regimentation beyond. This was not merely a child-centered environment; it was based on a childish view of the world, in which reality was sacrificed to the pleasure principle." Mumford, *City in History*, 464.

68. During the 1950s, as the old northern industrial cities contracted, the GDP actually expanded by 80 percent. Conn, *Americans Against the City*, 149.

69. For postwar Chicago manufacturing statistics, see Squires et al., *Chicago*, 25–27. On the "white flight" phenomenon, see Kruse, *White Flight* and Jackson, *Crabgrass Frontier*.

70. Vizenor, *Everlasting Sky*, 126.

71. Here, I am building on Paul Rosier's *Serving Their Country*, which focuses on patriotism and how Indians became *American* Indians during the twentieth century.

72. Philleo Nash notes from meeting with tribal leaders, Pierre, South Dakota, 27 March 1961, box 147, folder: March 5–7, 1962, PNP.

Chapter Six

1. Excerpts from *Indian Youth*, 22 September 1968, published biweekly in Philadelphia by United Church Press, box 3, folder 10, THP. A Vietnam veteran and esteemed poet in Indian Country and abroad, Phillip William George was born in Seattle in 1946 and died in October 2012. Vincent Price once read his more famous poem, "Proviso," on Johnny Carson's *Tonight Show*. See George's obituary, *Lewiston Tribune*, 10 October 2012, http://lmtribune.com/obituaries/article_5d4ef97c-9417-55e2-b7ec-679ab6f32ada.html?mode=jqm.

2. Philp, *Indian Self-Rule*, 171. In a study of the relocation program that the AAIA published in 1965, LaVerne Madigan reported that numerous tribal leaders had complained that the program robbed tribes of potential leadership and in its place left behind "irredeemable misfits." See *The American Indian Relocation Program* (New York: Association of American Indian Affairs, 1965), WHC. In a third example, Potawatomie agency superintendent Harold E. Bruce explained in his commencement speech to the Haskell Institute graduating class of 1941 that "it has been our observation that relatively few Haskell graduates remain long in their reservation communities. Usually they must go away from home to find employment in the fields for which they have been trained. Thus on our reservation we have been deprived of valuable, potential trained leadership." See *The Indian Leader*, Commencement, 23 May 1941 (Lawrence, KS: Haskell Institute, 1941), box 31, folder 5, SLP. In a final example, the Winnebago tribal chair complained to Indian affairs commissioner Glenn Emmons during a meeting in 1956 that the "better qualified" Winnebago people were "going out by natural process" and, as a result, leaving "not the best quality part of the tribe" behind on the reservation. See "Winnebago Meeting with Commissioner Glenn Emmons," 20 July 1956, box 3, folder 1, GEP.

3. Vine Deloria, "Urban Scene and the American Indian," 336.

4. My use of the term "reimagined" is a reference to historian Nicolas Rosenthal's impressive study of how Native people in twentieth-century Los Angeles actively reimagined Indian Country as a place that included urban space. See Rosenthal, *Reimagining Indian Country*. I am attempting to build on Rosenthal's work by arguing that Native people also reimagined old, rural-reservation Indian Country as a place that could benefit from and support metropolitan and cosmopolitan socioeconomic strategies while providing opportunities for a new generation of college-educated Indians. American Indians were not alone in seeking retreat to greener pastures after becoming exhausted or disenchanted with urban living during the postwar period. The "white flight" phenomenon, for example, is well documented. See, for example, a foundational study on this topic: Jackson, *Crabgrass Frontier*. There was nothing uniquely "Indian" about shifting away from life in mammoth metropolises, just as gravitating toward them during the first half of the twentieth century was also not uniquely Indian.

5. Vine Deloria, "Urban Scene and the American Indian," 334.

6. See, for example, Fixico, *Urban Indian Experience in America*; LaGrand, *Indian Metropolis*; Rosenthal, *Reimagining Indian Country*. Rosenthal makes important strides in focusing on Red Power at the local grassroots level in Los Angeles. He posits a needed social history of the Red Power phenomenon. The essays in Daniel Cobb and Loretta Fowler's anthology *Beyond Red Power* collectively argue for scholarly inquiries that look beyond the Red Power watershed moment of the late 1960s and early 1970s in order to highlight other modes and examples of Indigenous sociopolitical activism otherwise obscured by militant Red Power's gravitational pull. I seek to build on Cobb, Fowler, et al., by arguing that it is important to see beyond militant urban activism as the overarching and most salient outcome of Indian urban relocation. See Cobb and Fowler, *Beyond Red Power*. Scholars of the Red Power movement correctly cite urban crises and disappointments as primary motives for Red Power's coalescence. See, for example, Smith and Warrior, *Like a Hurricane*; Nagel, *American Indian Ethnic Renewal*. While the history of Indian urbanization and the rise of Red Power are inextricably entangled, exclusive focus on angry activists denies the importance of other outcomes of the urbanization phenomenon and perhaps even overlooks causes of the Red Power movement.

7. Minneapolis Area Indian Affairs Conference, Des Moines, Iowa, 16 October 1956, box 3, folder 7, GEP; "Bender Digs Up Another Indian for Connie Mack," *Toronto Sunday World*, 15 February 1914; Verna Graves obituary, https://www.olsonschwartzfuneralhome.com/notices/Reverend-Graves accessed 5 August 2013.

8. Minneapolis Area Indian Affairs Conference, Des Moines, Iowa, 16 October 1956, box 3, folder 7, GEP.

9. Pueblo of Taos Council meeting minutes, 6 October 1959, box 7, folder 40, SAP.

10. Interview with Howard Gorman (Navajo Tribal Councilman), 25 October 1968, American Indian Oral History Project, Center for Southwest Research, University of New Mexico, Albuquerque (hereafter cited as AIOHP).

11. Matthew Pilcher, interview with author, 12 July 2012, Winnebago, Nebraska; Matthew Pilcher, "American Indian Scholarships: A Primary Concern for 1971," *Cross and the Calumet*, Winter 1970.

12. Ibid. In my interview with Pilcher, he mentioned that he always thought of Winnebago as "home" and that he was only "*living*" in Chicago.

13. Vine Deloria, "Urban Scene and the American Indian," 337.

14. "Reservation Lures Urban Indian," *Chicago Tribune*, 27 August 1971.

15. "Stranger in His Native Land," *Chicago Tribune*, 22 August 1971; "Indian Country Mourns Passing of S. Timothy Wapato," 28 April 2009, https://www.indianz.com/News/2009/014289.asp.

16. "Stranger in His Native Land," *Chicago Tribune*, 22 August 1971.

17. For some tribal nations, "rehabilitate" is an erroneous term. Some had yet to ever enjoy the benefits of a thriving economy within reservation boundaries.

18. Glenn Emmons to Theodore Hetzel, 2 December 1955, box 28, folder 14, THP.

19. At the same time, it is important to avoid painting too rosy a picture of Navajo tribal business pacts with outside corporations, which often proved capable of exploiting asymmetrical power relations to Indian people's detriment. Dakota scholar Vine Deloria Jr., for example, did not necessarily think big corporations were the answer to tribal economic woes. Rather, he suggested that Indians would be better off consolidating and expanding their land base while purchasing small businesses along highways around reservations. "They could train Indians to keep books and run these," he proposed. Deloria also suggested that rather than play bit parts in the amusement of tourists, Indians could take over the tourist industries that exploited Indians and reaped a majority of the profits. During the 1960s, the Indian bureau had repeatedly tried to lure large-scale corporations within reservation limits, mostly failing in that endeavor. Deloria, by contrast, concluded that businesses of more manageable size and stature were what small tribes truly needed: "They don't need those million-dollar showcases." See Steiner, *New Indians*, 173. Likewise, according to historians Sherry Smith and Brian Frehner, during the 1960s, when resource extraction expanded onto Navajo lands, the Navajo people suffered because they lacked "sufficient expertise or knowledge to negotiate in their people's best interest." I argue that such experiences only fueled Native people's conviction that in order to compete in a changing world, they had to meaningfully experience that changing world. Indeed, Smith and Frehner argue that over time, Navajo and Hopi energy initiatives evolved "from exploitation to opportunity." See Smith and Frehner, *Indians and Energy*, 11–12.

20. Department of Interior Internal Memo, 17 December 1956, Bureau of Indian Affairs website document archive, http://www.bia.gov/cs/groups/public/documents/text/idc016179.pdf; Department of Interior Internal Memo, 9 August 1955, Bureau of Indian Affairs website document archive: http://www.bia.gov/cs/groups/public/documents/text/idc016256.pdf; "Notes on a Conversation with Neal Jensen, Relocation Officer, United Pueblos Agency" (by William Brophy), 30 November 1957, box 10, folder 9, SAP; Glenn Emmons, "Industry Moves to Indian Country," *Industrial Development*, June 1957, box 10, folder 32, TMP.

21. "Indian Territory: Tribes Draw Industry to Reservations with Cheap Labor, Financing," *Wall Street Journal*, 13 August 1964; "Plant Will Help Jobless Indians," *New York Times*, 25 September 1966.

22. Ibid.

23. Ibid.

24. Box 47, folder 35: Tribes, Chippewa, Minnesota, VV. This folder also contained several tourism brochures from other reservations and tribes, including Mille Lacs, Leech Lake, and Cass Lake in Minnesota; Lac du Flambeau in Wisconsin; Okmulgee (Creek) in Oklahoma; and Crow in Montana.

25. Box 1, folder 3: Fort Peck Agency Facts, 1963, BIAIRR.

26. Box 50, folder: Tribes—Oneida, VV.

27. "Documentation of Record," 12 April 1966, Select Files, box 3, folder: Contracts, Golden Eagle Arts and Crafts, Winnebago Agency Employee Assistance Decimal Correspondence, National Archives and Records Administration, Central Plains Region, Kansas City (hereafter cited as WA).

28. "A Living Dream for Pine Ridge Indians," *Dakota*, 15 August 1963, box 15, folder 22, SLP. To cite a second example, the Fort Peck Tribes of Montana engaged in a similar housing development project at Poplar and Wolf Point. The project employed more than forty Fort Peck Indians in the construction of forty homes outfitted with electricity and modern plumbing. See "Fort Peck Tribes to Dedicate Homes," *Billings Gazette*, August 1963, box 15, folder 22, SLP.

29. "Plant Closing Deepens Navajo Plight," *Washington Post*, 17 March 1975.

30. Lisa Nakamura, "Indigenous Circuits: Navajo Women and the Racialization of Early Electronic Manufacture," *American Quarterly* 66, no. 4 (December 2014): 933–35.

31. "Plant Closing Deepens Navajo Plight," *Washington Post*, 17 March 1975.

32. "Monthly OJT Narrative report, 31 December 1962"; "Monthly OJT Narrative Report, 5 April 1963"; "Monthly OJT Narrative Report, 8 August 1963"; "Chairs Unlimited, On-the-Job Training Program, 1962," RG75, box 3, folder: Contracts, WA.

33. See, for example, Rosier, *Serving Their Country*.

34. Vine Deloria, "This Country Was a Lot Better Off When the Indians Were Running It."

35. Several scholars have argued that Native people were not merely victims of, or reliably resistant to, capitalist markets. See, for example, Harmon, *Indians in the Making* and *Rich Indians*; Hosmer, *American Indians in the Marketplace*; Hosmer and O'Neill, *Native Pathways*; O'Neill, *Working the Navajo Way*; Raibmon, *Authentic Indians*; Usner, *Indian Work*.

36. *Urban Indians: Proceedings of the Third Annual Conference on Problems and Issues concerning American Indians Today*, 178. For an in-depth study of the impact of "Great Society" programs on Indian Country, see Cobb, *Native Activism in Cold War America*.

37. Vine Deloria, "This Country Was a Lot Better Off When the Indians Were Running It."

38. Lester Chapoose interview, 25 October 1986, UII.

39. David Lester interview (1971), 19–21, box 26, item no. 1008, Doris Duke Oral History Collection, Marriott Library, University of Utah (hereafter cited as DDOHC).

40. Interview with Joseph C. Vasquez (unspecified tribe) (1971), box 26, item no. 1009, DDOHC.

41. Tragically, as a legacy of the 1887 Dawes Act, the Sac and Fox reservation of Oklahoma was essentially allotted out of existence.

42. "No Land, No Money, but a Tribe Rebounds," *Insight*, 1 September 1986, box 34, folder 331: Reservations, VV. Jack Thorpe was born in Hawthorne, California, in 1937. He entered the army after high school in Kansas; after his discharge, he migrated to Oklahoma in 1970, where he entered the University of Oklahoma for one year. He became tribal councilman in 1971 and tribal chief in 1980. He died in 2011. See Al Zagofsky, "Jim Thorpe's Son Jack Dies," *Times News*, 24 February 2011, http://www.tnonline.com/2011/feb/24/jim-thorpes-son-jack-dies.

43. "Philadelphia's Indians Return to the Warpath," *Philadelphia Inquirer*, 30 January 1972; "Indian in Mt. Airy Tells of Bigotry and Poverty," *Philadelphia Evening Bulletin*, 3 March 1970.

44. Interview with Lee Emerson (Quechan/Mojave–Quechan tribal historian), 1974/1977, in Trafzer, ed., *Quechan Indian Voices*.

45. White, *Tribal Assets*, 67, 70–73.

46. Ibid., 76.

47. Ibid., 89.

48. Ibid., 56–57; Debbie Elliott, "Mississippi Choctaws Find Economic Success," *All Things Considered*, 17 July 2004, www.npr.org/templates/story/story.php?storyId=3465024.

49. White, *Tribal Assets*, 67, 99, 104.

50. Ibid., 112.

51. Mankiller and Wallis, *Mankiller*, 217–19.

52. Ibid.

53. Guest editorial, *Amerindian* 3, no. 6 (July–August 1955), WHC.

54. Interview with Philleo Nash, 5 June 1967, Harry S. Truman Presidential Library, Independence, Missouri.

55. *Indian Youth* (published biweekly in Philadelphia by the United Church Press), 22 September 1968, box 3, folder 10, THP.

56. Ibid.

57. Ibid.

58. "Between Chicago and the Reservation Is a Generation Gap," William Mullen, *Chicago Tribune*, 15 September 1976, 12.

59. *Indian Youth*, 22 September 1968, box 3, folder 10, THP.

60. Interview with Wallace Coffee (T-484), 31 July 1969, DDIOHC.

61. Father Peter Powell, interview with author, 9 December 2009. Transcript in author's possession.

62. Interview with William Wiley, item no. 1019, DDOHC.

63. "U.S. Shifts Indian Focus from City to Reservation," *Chicago Sun-Times*, 13 January 1972, box 19, folder 50: Urban Indians, VV.

64. Wilkinson, *Blood Struggle*, 85.

65. Martin, "Mississippi Choctaws Are Not Going Anywhere," 112.

66. Interview with Howard Gorman (Navajo Tribal Councilman), 10 July 1970, AIOHP.

Conclusion

1. I have been unable to determine the precise location of John Hunter's, or even the artist colony in question, but it is likely that the location was in either Old Town or Hyde Park, which hosted the most prominent artist colonies during the era.

2. Thomas Greenwood to Brian G. Bardy, 22 February 1983, box 1, folder 19: Correspondence, TGP.

3. On the incorporation of urban Indian communities into Indian Country cultural networks, see Rosenthal, *Reimagining Indian Country*.

4. The AICC marked a watershed moment in Native people's movement toward national political unity and advocacy of a self-determination policy. For a discussion of the AICC's importance, see Cobb, *Native Activism in Cold War America*, chaps. 2–3.

5. "Tribute Recalls Significance of Waterways," *Chicago Tribune*, 6 January 1984.

6. "Parade Is 1st Step in Rescuing Canal from Stagnation," *Chicago Tribune*, 29 August 1986.

7. Thomas Greenwood to Brian G. Bardy, 22 February 1983, box 1, folder 19: Correspondence, TGP.

8. LaDonna Harris, quoted in Daniel M. Cobb, "'Born in the Opposition': The Intellectual Life of D'Arcy McNickle According to his Diary," paper delivered at the Annual Meeting of the American Society for Ethnohistory Ottawa, Canada, October 2010. In this paper, Cobb provides a critical ethnobiography of legendary Flathead activist D'Arcy McNickle, who, similar to Greenwood, consistently added complex layers of meaning to "Indian," as that term applied to his own life. Interestingly, Greenwood worked closely with McNickle at the 1961 American Indian Chicago Conference and most likely in other capacities as well. On LaDonna Harris's remarkable life and legacy, see her autobiography, *LaDonna Harris*.

9. Vine Deloria, *Behind the Trail of Broken Treaties*, 93; quoted in Biolsi, "Imagined Geographies," 249.

10. Biolsi, "Imagined Geographies," 249.

11. As James Gregory asserts in his study of southern plains people who migrated to California before, during, and after the Dust Bowl, "success" should be measured not only in terms of economic impact but also according to cultural impact. Gregory, *American Exodus*, 246.

12. Bunky Echo-Hawk interview with Julie Pearson Little-Thunder, 26 January 2016, Spotlighting Oklahoma Oral History Project, Edmon Low Library, Oklahoma State University.

13. Father Peter Powell, interview with author, 9 December 2009. Transcript in author's possession.

14. Guest Editorial, *Amerindian* 1, no. 6 (July–August 1953), WHC.

15. *Urban Indians: Proceedings of the Third Annual Conference on Problems and Issues concerning American Indians Today.*

16. For an excellent study on Indian population recovery, see Shoemaker, *American Indian Population Recovery in the Twentieth Century.* For a critical analysis on how and why more people became comfortable identifying as "Indian" during recent decades, see Sturm, *Becoming Indian.*

17. XIT, "Relocation," *Relocation.*

18. Steiner, *New Indians,* 176.

19. Vizenor, *Manifest Manners,* ix. See also Vizenor, "The Unmissable."

Bibliography

Archival Manuscript Collections

Bureau of Indian Affairs Digital Document Archive
Carl Albert Center for Congressional Research, University of Oklahoma
    Toby Morris Papers
    Robert Kerr Departmental Papers
Center for Southwest Research, University of New Mexico, Albuquerque
    Glenn Emmons Papers
    Sophie Aberle Papers
    William Zimmerman Papers
Center for Southwest Studies, Fort Lewis College, Durango, Colorado
    Theodore Hetzel Papers
Harry S. Truman Presidential Library, Independence, Missouri
    Dillon S. Myer Papers, Government Agencies File, 1950–53
    Papers of Harry S. Truman: White House Central Files
    Philleo Nash Papers
    William Brophy Papers
National Archives and Records Administration, Central Plains Region,
    Kansas City
    Haskell Indian Nations University Decimal Correspondence
    Minneapolis Area Office Employment Assistance Case Files
    Potawatomie Agency, Mayetta, Kansas, Decimal Correspondence (1883–1969)
    Winnebago Agency Employee Assistance Decimal Correspondence
    Records of the Bureau of Indian Affairs, 1793–1999, Consolidated Chippewa
        Agency, Cass Lake, Minnesota, Annual Reports 1942–1946
National Archives and Records Administration, Rocky Mountain Region, Denver
    Bureau of Indian Affairs, Billings Area Office: Mixed Vocational and Subject
        Files, 1939–1960
    Bureau of Indian Affairs, Billings Area Office: Vocational and Subject
        Case Files, 1951–1960
    Bureau of Indian Affairs, Billings Area Office Papers
National Archives and Records Administration, Southwest Region, Fort Worth, TX
    Employment Assistance Case Files, 1952–1956
    National Defense Program Files
    Records of the Chilocco Indian School
National Archives and Records Administration, Washington, DC
    Correspondence and Reports of Kathryn Mahn

Correspondence and Reports Relating to the Employment of Indians

Field Placement and Relocation Office Correspondence and Reports Relating to Employment of Indians

Placement and Statistical Reports, compiled 1949–1954

Field Placement and Relocation Office Employment Assistance Records: Narrative Reports, compiled 1952–1960

Records Relating to Employment Assistance Programs, compiled 1949–1973

William Zimmerman Office Files

Newberry Library, Chicago, Illinois

    Bureau of Indian Affairs Indian Relocation Records

    Carlos Montezuma Papers

    Thomas Greenwood Papers

    Virgil J. Vogel Research and Personal Papers

Oklahoma Historical Society Research Center, Oklahoma City

    Chilocco Indian School Collection

Princeton University, Department of Rare Books and Special Collections

    Association on American Indian Affairs Papers

St. Augustine's Center for American Indians, Chicago, Illinois

    Unpublished Papers of Father Peter J. Powell

University of Oklahoma, Western History Collections

    Elizabeth Clark Rosenthal Papers

University of Utah, Marriott Library Special Collections

    Bureau of Indian Affairs Records

    Stanley Lyman Papers

Collected Interviews

Center for Southwest Research, University of New Mexico, Albuquerque. American Indian Oral History Project.

    Gorman, Howard. 22 October 1968.

    Gorman, Howard. 10 July 1970.

Harry S. Truman Presidential Library, Independence, Missouri.

    Nash, Philleo. 5 June 1967.

Newberry Library, Chicago, Illinois. Chicago American Indian Oral History Project.

    Strouse, Marlene. 18 July 1983.

    Wesaw, Leroy. 16 December 1982.

Northern State College, Aberdeen, South Dakota. American Indian History Research Project.

    Boneshirt, Alfred, and Mary Sue Boneshirt. 10 July 1970.

    Harrison, Paul. 28 July 1968.

Oklahoma State University. Spotlighting Oklahoma Oral History Project. Edmon Low Library.

    Echo-Hawk, Bunky. 26 January 2016.

University of Oklahoma, Western History Collections. Doris Duke Indian
    Oral History Collection.
    Coffee, Wallace. 31 July 1969.
    Kickingbird, Carl. 6 August 1968.
    Momaday, N. Scott. 12 August 1969.
University of Utah, Marriott Library. Doris Duke Oral History Collection.
    Lester, David. 1971.
    Lyman, Stanley. Interviewed by Floyd O'Neil. Number 1029.
    Lyman, Stanley. Interviewed by Floyd O'Neil. Number 1030.
    Vasquez, Joseph C. 1971.
    Wiley, William. Undated.
University of Utah, Marriott Library. Ute Indian Interviews.
    Chapoose, Lester. 25 October 1986.
    Gardner, Darrell. 18 October 1986.
    Olquin, Jim. 1971.

Published Interviews

Emerson, Lee. 1974 & 1977. By Clifford E. Trafzer. *Quechan Indian Voices: Lee
    Emerson and Patrick Miguel*. Riverside: California Center for Native Nations,
    2012.

Uncollected Interviews

Deer, Ada. Interview with the author, Fitchburg, Wisconsin. October 2012.
Pilcher, Matthew. Interview with the author, Winnebago, Nebraska. 12 July 2012.
Powell, Father Peter. Interview with the author, Chicago, Illinois. 9
    December 2009.

Community, Tribal, and Institutional Publications

American Indian (Association on American Indian Affairs)
American Indian (Newsletter of the Society of Oklahoma Indians, Tulsa, OK)
American Indian Magazine (Society of American Indians)
Amerindian
Cross and the Calumet: Newsletter of the Committee on American Indian Work
    (St. Augustine's Center for American Indians, Chicago, IL)
Dakota Magazine
Episcopal Church News
Flandreau Spirit
Indian Country Today
Indian Leader (Haskell Institute, Lawrence, KS)
Indian School Journal (Chilocco Indian School, Newkirk, OK)
Indian Truth (Indian Rights Association, Philadelphia, PA)

Indian Youth (United Church Press, Philadelphia, PA)
Proceedings of the Twenty-Fifth Annual Meeting of the Lake Mohonk Conference of the Friends of the Indian and Other Dependent People (Lake Mohonk Conference, 1907)
Quarterly Journal of the Society of American Indians (Society of American Indians)
Reservation Indian Comes to Town (New York: National Social Welfare Assembly, 1953)
Rosebud Sioux Herald
Six Nations (Iroquois Confederacy)
Smoke Signals: Colorado Indian River Tribes (Parker, Arizona)
Wassaja

Government Publications

Bureau of Indian Affairs, U.S. Department of the Interior. *Indians at Work.* Washington, DC: Government Printing Office, 1934–45.

Fay L. Keith *Developing Indian Employment Opportunities* (study commissioned by the U.S. Department of the Interior). Washington, DC: GPO, 1976.

Public Papers of the President of the United States: Richard Nixon, 1970. Washington, DC: GPO, 1970.

Report on Urban and Rural Non-Reservation Indians. Task Force Eight: Urban and Rural Non-Reservation Indians, Final Report to the American Indian Policy Review Commission. Washington, DC: GPO, 1976.

U.S. Department of Health, Education, and Welfare. "Bridging the Gap: The Twin Cities Native American Community" (report conducted by the Minnesota State Advisory Committee). Washington, DC: GPO, 1975.

U.S. Department of the Interior. *Annual Report of the Secretary of the Interior.* Washington, DC: GPO, 1944.

Newspapers and Magazines

Billings Gazette
Bismarck Tribune
Chicago Sun-Times
Chicago Tribune
Chicago Tribune Magazine
Devils Lake Journal
Gallup Independent
Industrial Development Magazine
Insight Magazine
Los Angeles Examiner
Los Angeles Times
Minneapolis Tribune
New Yorker

New York Times
Oklahoma City Times
Philadelphia Evening Bulletin
Philadelphia Inquirer
St. Louis Post Dispatch
Spin Magazine
Sunday Herald
Sunday Oklahoman
Toronto Sunday World
Wall Street Journal
Washington Post
Wenatchee Daily World
Wichita Beacon

Albums

John Angaiak. *I'm Lost in the City.* Vinyl LP, original copyright 1971, reissued by
  Future Days Recording/Light in the Attic Records, 2015.
XIT. *Silent Warrior.* Vinyl LP. Rare Earth Records, 1973.
XIT. *Relocation.* Vinyl LP. Canyon Records, 1977.

Films

MacKenzie, Kent, dir. *The Exiles.* Milestone Films, 2008.
Riffe, N. Jed, dir. *Rosebud to Dallas.* Jed Riffe Films, 1977.
Tarbell, Reaghan, dir. *To Brooklyn and Back: A Mohawk Journey.*
  Visionmaker Video, 2009.

Podcasts

"Philip J. Deloria on Family, Scholarship, and Politics." *Indigenous Politics,*
  hosted by J. Kehaulani Kauanui for Wesleyan University radio.

Books, Articles, and Dissertations

Ablon, Joan. "Relocated American Indians in the San Francisco Bay Area." *Human
  Organization* 24 (1964): 296–304.
Adams, David Wallace. *Education for Extinction.* Lawrence: University of Kansas
  Press, 1995.
Arends, Wade B. "A Socio-Cultural Study of the Relocation of American Indians to
  Chicago." MA thesis, University of Chicago, 1958.
Banks, Dennis. *Ojibwa Warrior: Dennis Banks and the Rise of the American Indian
  Movement.* With Richard Erdoes. Norman: University of Oklahoma Press,
  2004.

Baudelaire, Charles. "The Painter of Modern Life." *The Painter of Modern Life and Other Essays.* London: Phaidon, 1964.

Bauer, William J. *We Were All Like Migrant Workers Here: Work, Community and Memory on California's Round Valley Reservation, 1850–1941.* Chapel Hill: University of North Carolina Press, 2009.

Bernstein, Alison R. *American Indians and World War II: Toward a New Era in Indian Affairs.* Norman: University of Oklahoma Press, 1991.

Biolsi, Thomas. "The Birth of the Reservation: Making the Modern Individual among the Lakota." *American Ethnologist* 22, no. 1 (February 1995): 28–53.

——. *Deadliest Enemies: Law and the Making of Race Relations on and off the Rosebud Reservation.* Berkeley: University of California Press, 2001.

——. "Imagined Geographies: Sovereignty, Indigenous Space, and American Indian Struggle." *American Ethnologist* 32, no. 2 (May 2005): 239–59.

——. *Organizing the Lakota: The Political Economy of the New Deal on the Pine Ridge and Rosebud Reservations.* Tucson: University of Arizona Press, 1992.

Bishop, Joan. "From Hill 57 to Capitol Hill: 'Making the Sparks Fly,'" *Montana: The Magazine of Western History* 43, no. 3 (Summer 1993): 16–29.

Blackhawk, Ned. "I Can Carry On from Here: The Relocation of American Indians to Los Angeles." *Wicazo Sa Review* 11 (1995): 16–30.

Blanchard, David. *Seven Generations: A History of the Kanienkehaka.* Kahnawake, Quebec: Kahnawake Survival School, 1980.

Blansett, Kent. "San Francisco, Red Power, and the Emergence of an 'Indian City.'" In *City Dreams Country Schemes: Community and Identity in the American West,* edited by Kathleen A. Brosnan and Amy L. Scott. Reno: University of Nevada Press, 2011.

Britten, Thomas A. *American Indians in World War I: At Home and at War.* Albuquerque: University of New Mexico Press, 1997.

Broker, Ignatia. *Night Flying Woman: An Ojibway Narrative.* St. Paul: Minnesota Historical Society Press, 1983.

Bruyneel, Kevin. *The Third Space of Sovereignty: The Postcolonial Politics of U.S.-Indigenous Relations.* Minneapolis: University of Minnesota Press, 2007.

Burnette, Robert. *The Tortured Americans.* Englewood Cliffs, NJ: Prentice-Hall, 1971.

Burnette, Robert, and John Koster. *The Road to Wounded Knee.* New York: Bantam Books, 1974.

Burt, Larry W. *Tribalism in Crisis: Federal Indian Policy, 1953–1961.* Albuquerque: University of New Mexico Press, 1982.

Buss, James Joseph, and C. Joseph Genetin-Pilawa, eds. *Beyond Two Worlds: Critical Conversations on Language and Power in Native North America.* Albany, NY: SUNY Press, 2015.

Cahill, Cathleen D. *Federal Fathers and Mothers: A Social History of the United States Indian Service, 1869–1933.* Chapel Hill: University of North Carolina Press, 2011.

Calloway, Colin G. *One Vast Winter Count: The Native American West before Lewis and Clark.* Lincoln and London: University of Nebraska Press, 2003.

Carpenter, Cari M. "Detecting Indianness: Gertrude Bonnin's Investigation of Native American Identity." *Wicazo Sa Review* 20, no. 1 (Spring 2005): 139–59.

Carpio, Myla Vicenti. *Indigenous Albuquerque*. Lubbock: Texas Tech University Press, 2011.

Cattelino, Jessica. "The Double Bind of American Indian Need-Based Sovereignty." *Cultural Anthropology* 25, no. 2 (2010): 235–62.

———. *High Stakes: Florida Seminole Gaming and Sovereignty*. Durham, NC: Duke University Press, 2008.

Child, Brenda. *Boarding School Seasons: American Indian Families, 1900–1940*. Lincoln: University of Nebraska Press, 1998.

Clark, Blue. "Bury My Heart in Smog: Urban Indians." In *The American Indian Experience: A Profile, 1524 to the Present*, edited by Philip Weeks, 278–91. Arlington Heights, IL: Forum Press, 1988.

Clow, Richmond L. "Robert Burnette: A Postwar Lakota Activist." In *The Human Tradition in the American West*, edited by Benson Tong and Regan A. Lutz, 193–208. Lanham, MD: Rowan and Littlefield, 2001.

Cobb, Daniel M. *Native Activism in Cold War America: The Struggle for Sovereignty*. Lawrence: Kansas University Press, 2008.

———, ed. *Say We Are Nations: Documents of Politics and Protest in Indigenous America since 1887*. Chapel Hill: University of North Carolina Press, 2015.

———. "Talking the Language of the Larger World: Politics in Cold War (Native) America." In *Beyond Red Power: American Indian Politics and Activism since 1900*, edited by Daniel M. Cobb and Loretta Fowler, 161–77. Santa Fe, NM: School for Advanced Research Press, 2007.

Cobb, Daniel M., and Loretta Fowler, eds. *Beyond Red Power: American Indian Politics and Activism since 1900*. Santa Fe, New Mexico: School for Advanced Research Press, 2007.

Cobe, Albert. *Great Spirit*. Chicago: Children's Press, 1970.

Cohen, Lizabeth. *A Consumer's Republic: The Politics of Mass Consumption in Postwar America*. New York: Vintage Books, 2003.

Collier, John. *From Every Zenith: A Memoir; and some Essays on Life and Thought*. Denver, CO: Sage Books, 1963.

Conn, Steven. *Americans Against the City: Anti-Urbanism in the Twentieth Century*. New York: Oxford University Press, 2014.

Coontz, Stephanie. *The Way We Never Were: American Families and the Nostalgia Trap*. New York: Basic Books, 1992.

Cornell, Stephen. *Return of the Native: American Indian Political Resurgence*. New York: Oxford University Press, 1988.

Cory, David M. *Within Two Worlds*. New York: Friendship Press, 1955.

Cowger, Thomas W. "Pan-Indian Movements." *Oklahoma Historical Society's Encyclopedia of Oklahoma History and Culture*, accessed 27 August 2018, http://www.okhistory.org/publications/enc/entry.php?entry=PA010.

Cronon, William. *Nature's Metropolis: Chicago and the Great West*. New York: W. W. Norton, 1991.

Danziger, Edmund. *Survival and Regeneration: Detroit's American Indian Community.* Detroit: Wayne State University Press, 1991.

Debo, Angie. *The Five Civilized Tribes of Oklahoma: Report on Social and Economic Conditions.* Philadelphia: Indian Rights Association, 1951.

Deloria, Ella. *Speaking of Indians.* Lincoln: University of Nebraska Press, 1998. Originally published in 1944.

Deloria, Philip J. "Four Thousand Invitations," *American Indian Quarterly* 37, no.3 (Summer 2013).

———.*Indians in Unexpected Places.* Lawrence: University Press of Kansas, 2004.

———. *Playing Indian.* New Haven, CT: Yale University Press, 1998.

Deloria, Vine, Jr. *Behind the Trail of Broken Treaties: An Indian Declaration of Independence.* Austin: University of Texas Press, 1985. Originally published in 1974.

———. "This Country Was a Lot Better Off When the Indians Were Running It." In *Red Power: The American Indians' Fight for Freedom*, edited by Alvin M. Josephy Jr., 240–41. New York: American Heritage Press, 1971.

———. "The Urban Scene and the American Indian." *Indian Voices: The First Convocation of American Indian Scholars.* San Francisco: The Indian Historian Press, 1970.

Deloria, Vine, Jr., and Clifford M. Lytle. *The Nations Within: The Past and Future of American Indian Sovereignty.* Austin: University of Texas Press, 1988.

Dreiser, Theodore. *Sister Carrie.* New York: Doubleday, Page, 1900.

Drinnon, Richard T. *Keeper of Concentration Camps: Dillon S. Myer and American Racism.* Berkeley: University of California Press, 1987.

Eiselt, B. Sunday. *Becoming White Clay: A History and Archaeology of Jicarilla Apache Enclavement.* Salt Lake City: University of Utah Press, 2012.

Fisher, Andrew H. *Shadow Tribe: The Making of Columbia River Indian Identity.* Seattle: University of Washington Press, 2010.

Fixico, Donald L. *Termination and Relocation: Federal Indian Policy, 1945–1960.* Albuquerque: University of New Mexico Press, 1986.

———. *The Urban Indian Experience in America.* Albuquerque: University of New Mexico Press, 2000.

Fogelson, Raymond. "Night Thoughts on Native American Social History." Paper delivered at The Impact of Indian History on the Teaching of United States History, McNickle Center Chicago Conference, 1984, Sessions V–VI, Newberry Library, 1985.

Frost, Jennifer. *"An Interracial Movement of the Poor": Community Organizing and the New Left in the 1960s.* New York: NYU Press, 2001.

Gaines, Kevin K. *Uplifting the Race: Black Leadership, Politics, and Culture in the Twentieth Century.* Chapel Hill: University of North Carolina Press, 1996.

Genetin-Pilawa, Joseph. *Crooked Paths to Allotment: The Fight over Federal Indian Policy After the Civil War.* Chapel Hill: University of North Carolina Press, 2012.

Gerstle, Gary. *American Crucible: Race and Nation in the Twentieth Century.* Princeton, NJ: Princeton University Press, 2002.

Gilmore, Glenda Elizabeth. *Gender and Jim Crow: Women and the Politics of White Supremacy in North Carolina, 1896–1920.* Chapel Hill: University of North Carolina Press, 1996.

Gober, Patricia. *Metropolitan Phoenix: Placemaking and Community Building in the Desert.* Philadelphia: University of Pennsylvania Press, 2005.

Goodner, James. *Indian Americans in Dallas: Migrations, Missions, and Styles of Adaptation.* Minneapolis: Center for Urban and Regional Affairs, University of Minnesota, 1969.

Gram, John R. *Education at the Edge of Empire: Negotiating Pueblo Identity in New Mexico's Indian Boarding Schools.* Seattle: University of Washington Press, 2015.

Gravatt, Reverend J. J. *The Record of Hampton's Returned Indian Pupils.* Philadelphia: Indian Rights Association, 1885.

Gregory, James. *American Exodus: The Dust Bowl Migration and Okie Culture in California.* New York: Oxford University Press, 1991.

———. *The Southern Diaspora: How the Great Migrations of Black and White Southerners Transformed America.* Chapel Hill: University of North Carolina Press, 2005.

Guillemin, Jeanne. *Urban Renegades: The Cultural Strategy of American Indians.* New York: Columbia University Press, 1975.

Guzman, Tracy Devine. *Native and National in Brazil: Indigeneity after Independence.* Chapel Hill: University of North Carolina Press, 2013.

Handlin, Oscar. *The Uprooted: The Epic Story of the Great Migrations That Made the American People.* New York: Grosset and Dunlap, 1951.

Harmon, Alexandra. *Indians in the Making: Ethnic Relations and Indian Identities around Puget Sound.* Berkeley: University of California Press, 1998.

———. *Rich Indians: Native People and the Problem of Wealth in American History.* Chapel Hill: University of North Carolina Press, 2010.

Harris, LaDonna. *LaDonna Harris: A Comanche Life.* Edited by H. Henrietta Stockel. Lincoln: University of Nebraska Press, 2007.

Hemingway, Albert. *Ira Hayes, Pima Marine.* Lanham, MD: University Press of America, 1988.

Hertzberg, Hazel W. *The Search for an American Indian Identity: Modern Pan-Indian Movements.* Syracuse, NY: Syracuse University Press, 1971.

Hewitt, William L. "The Indian Who Never Got Home: The Burial of Sergeant John R Rice." *Nebraska History* 77 (1996): 12–20.

Hogue, Michael. *Metis and the Medicine Line: Creating a Border and Dividing a People.* Chapel Hill: University of North Carolina Press, 2015.

Holm, Tom. *The Great Confusion in Indian Affairs: Native Americans and Whites in the Progressive Era.* Austin: University of Texas Press, 2005.

Hosmer, Brian C. *American Indians in the Marketplace: Persistence and Innovation among the Menominees and Metlakatlans, 1870–1920.* Lawrence: University of Kansas Press, 1999.

———, ed. *Native Americans and the Legacy of Harry S. Truman.* Kirksville, MO: Truman State University Press, 2010.

Hosmer, Brian C., and Colleen O'Neill, eds. *Native Pathways: American Indian Culture and Economic Development in the Twentieth Century.* Boulder: University of Colorado Press, 2004.

Howard, Heather A. "Women's Class Strategies as Activism in Native Community Building in Toronto, 1950–1975." In *Keeping the Campfires Going: Native Women's Activism in Urban Communities,* edited by Susan Applegate Krouse and Heather A. Howard, 105–24. Lincoln: University of Nebraska Press, 2009.

Hoxie, Frederick E. *A Final Promise: The Campaign to Assimilate the Indians, 1880–1920.* Lincoln: University of Nebraska Press, 1984.

———. "From Prison to Homeland: The Cheyenne River Reservation before World War I." In *The Plains Indians of the Twentieth Century,* edited by Peter Iverson, 55–75. Norman: University of Oklahoma Press, 1985.

Indian Voices: The First Convocation of American Indian Scholars. San Francisco: Indian History Press, 1970.

Iverson, Peter. *Carlos Montezuma and the Changing World of American Indians.* Albuquerque: University of New Mexico Press, 1982.

———. *Diné: A History of the Navajos.* Albuquerque: University of New Mexico Press, 2002.

Jackson, Kenneth T. *The Crabgrass Frontier: The Suburbanization of the United States.* New York: Oxford University Press, 1985.

Jacobs, Margaret D. "Diverted Mothering among American Indian Domestic Servants, 1920–1940." In *Indigenous Women and Work: From Labor to Activism,* edited by Carol Williams, 179–92. Chicago: University of Illinois Press, 2012.

Kellogg, Laura Cornelius. "Our Democracy and the American Indian." In *Our Democracy and the American Indian and Other Works,* edited by Kristina Ackley and Cristina Stanciu. Syracuse, NY: Syracuse University Press, 2015.

Kelly, Lawrence C. *The Assault on Assimilation: John Collier and the Origins of Indian Policy Reform.* Albuquerque: University of New Mexico Press, 1983.

Krouse, Susan Applegate, and Heather A. Howard, eds. *Keeping the Campfires Going: Native Women's Activism in Urban Communities.* Lincoln: University of Nebraska Press, 2009.

Kruse, Kevin M. *White Flight: Atlanta and the Making of Modern Conservatism.* Princeton, NJ: Princeton University Press, 2005.

Labelle, Kathryn Magee. *Dispersed but Not Destroyed: A History of the Seventeenth-Century Wendat People.* Vancouver: University of British Columbia Press, 2013.

LaGrand, James. *Indian Metropolis: Native Americans in Chicago, 1945–75.* Urbana: University of Illinois Press, 2002.

LaPier, Rosalyn R., and David R. M. Beck. *City Indian: Native American Activism in Chicago: 1893–1934.* Lincoln: University of Nebraska Press, 2015.

———. "Crossroads for a Culture: American Indians in Progressive Era Chicago." *Chicago History* 38, no. 1 (Spring 2012): 22–43.

———. "'One-Man Relocation Team': Scott Henry Peters and American Indian Urban Migration in the 1930s." *Western Historical Quarterly* 45, no. 1 (Spring 2014): 17–36.

Leupp, Francis E. *The Indian and His Problem*. New York: Charles Scribner's Sons, 1910.

Lewis, David G. "Termination of the Confederated Tribes of the Grand Ronde Community of Oregon: Politics, Community, Identity." PhD diss., Department of Anthropology, University of Oregon.

Lewis, Oscar. *The Children of Sanchez: Autobiography of a Mexican Family*. New York: Vintage Books, 1961.

——. *Five Families: Mexican Case Studies in the Culture of Poverty*. New York: Basic Books, 1959.

Lorde, Audre. "The Master's Tools Will Never Dismantle the Master's House." In *This Bridge Called My Back: Writings by Radical Women of Color*, edited by Cherríe Moraga and Gloria Anzaldúa, 94–98. New York: Kitchen Table Press, 1983.

Ludlow, Helen, ed. *Ten Years' Work for Indians at Hampton Institute*. Hampton, VA: Hampton Institute Press, 1888.

MacKay, Kathryn. "Warrior into Welder: A History of Federal Employment Programs for American Indians, 1878–1972." PhD diss., University of Utah, 1987.

Madigan, Laverne. *The American Indian Relocation Program*. New York: Association on American Indian Affairs, 1965.

Mankiller, Wilma, and Michael Wallis. *Mankiller: Chief of Her People*. New York, 1993.

Marcuse, Herbert. *One-Dimensional Man*. Boston: Beacon Press, 1964.

Martin, Phillip. "The Mississippi Choctaws Are Not Going Anywhere." In *Say We Are Nations: Documents of Politics and Protest in Indigenous America since 1887*, edited by Daniel M. Cobb, 111–14. Chapel Hill: University of North Carolina Press, 2015.

May, Elaine Tyler. *Homeward Bound: American Families in the Cold War Era*. New York: Basic Books, 1988.

Mays, Kyle T. "Indigenous Detroit: Indigeneity, Modernity, and Racial and Gender Formation in a Modern American City, 1871–2000." PhD diss., University of Illinois at Urbana Champaign, 2015.

McNickle, D'Arcy. *The Surrounded*. New York: Quality Paperback Book Club, 1998. Originally published in 1936.

Means, Russell. *Where White Men Fear to Tread*. With Marvin J. Wolf. New York: St. Martin's Press, 1995.

Meeks, Eric. *Border Citizens: The Making of Indians, Mexicans, and Anglos in Arizona*. Austin: University of Texas Press, 2007.

Meriam, Lewis. *The Problem of Indian Administration: Report of a Survey Made at the Request of Honorable Hubert Work, Secretary of the Interior, and Submitted to Him, February 21, 1928/Survey Staff: Lewis Meriam . . . [et al.]*. Baltimore, MD: Johns Hopkins Press, 1928.

Metcalf, Ann. "Navajo Women in the City: Lessons from a Quarter-Century of Relocation." *American Indian Quarterly* 6 (1982): 71–89.

Metcalf, R. Warren. *Termination's Legacy: The Discarded Indians of Utah.* Lincoln and London: University of Nebraska Press, 2002.

Meyer, Melissa L. *The White Earth Tragedy: Ethnicity and Dispossession at a Minnesota Anishinaabe Reservation.* Lincoln: University of Nebraska Press, 1999.

Meyerowitz, Joanne, ed. *Not June Cleaver: Women and Gender in Postwar America, 1945–1960.* Philadelphia: Temple University Press, 1994.

Miller, Douglas K. "Dignity and Decency: Father Peter Powell and American Indian Relocation to Chicago." In *Harry S. Truman and Native Americans and the Legacy of Harry S. Truman,* edited by Brian Hosmer, 25–46. Kirksville, MO: Truman State University Press, 2010.

———. "Willing Workers: Urban Relocation and American Indian Initiative, 1940s–1960s." *Ethnohistory* 60, no. 1 (Winter 2013): 51–76.

Miller, Robert J. *Reservation "Capitalism": Economic Development in Indian Country.* Westport, CT: Praeger, 2012.

Mitchell, Joseph. "The Mohawks in High Steel." Reprinted in *Apologies to the Iroquois,* edited by Edmund Wilson, 3–36. New York: Farrar, Straus, and Cudahy, 1960. Originally published in the *New Yorker,* 1949.

Momaday, N. Scott. *House Made of Dawn.* New York, 1966.

Monnet, John H. *Tell Them We Are Going Home: The Odyssey of the Northern Cheyennes.* Norman: University of Oklahoma Press, 2001.

Morgan, Lewis H. *Ancient Society.* New York: H. Holt, 1877.

Mumford, Lewis. *The City in History: Its Origins, Its Transformations, and Its Prospects.* San Diego, CA: Harcourt, 1961.

Nabokov, Peter, ed. *Native American Testimony: A Chronicle of Indian-White Relations from Prophecy to the Present, 1492–2000.* New York: Penguin Books, 1999.

Nagel, Joane. *American Indian Ethnic Renewal: Red Power and the Resurgence of Identity and Culture.* New York: Oxford University Press, 1996.

Needham, Andrew, and Allen Dieterich Ward. "Beyond the Metropolis: Metropolitan Growth and Regional Transformation in Postwar America." *Journal of Urban History* 35, no. 7 (2009): 943–69.

Neils, Elaine M. *Reservation to City: Indian Migration and Federal Relocation.* Chicago: Department of Geography, University of Chicago, 1971.

Norrgard, Chantal. *Seasons of Change: Labor, Treaty Rights, and Ojibwe Nationhood.* Chapel Hill: University of North Carolina Press, 2014.

O'Brien, Jean M. *Firsting and Lasting: Writing Indians Out of Existence in New England.* Minneapolis: University of Minnesota Press, 2010.

O'Neil, Floyd A. "An Anguished Odyssey: The Flight of the Utes, 1906–1908." *Utah Historical Quarterly* 36, no. 4 (1968).

O'Neill, Colleen. "Rethinking Modernity and the Discourse of Development in American Indian History." In *Native Pathways: American Indian Culture and Economic Development in the Twentieth Century,* edited by Brian Hosmer and Colleen O'Neill, 1–24. Boulder: University of Colorado Press, 2004.

———. *Working the Navajo Way: Labor and Culture in the Twentieth Century.* Lawrence: University of Kansas Press, 2005.

Officer, James E. "The American Indian and Federal Policy." In *The American Indian in Urban Society*, edited by Jack O. Waddell and O. Michael Watson, 9–65. Boston: Little, Brown, 1971.

Parman, Donald. *The Navajos and the New Deal.* New Haven, CT: Yale University Press, 1976.

Parmenter, Jon. *The Edge of the Woods: Iroquoia, 1534–1701.* East Lansing: Michigan State University Press, 2010.

Pauketat, Timothy R. *Cahokia: Ancient America's Great City on the Mississippi.* New York: Viking, 2009.

Peiss, Kathy. *Cheap Amusements: Working Women and Leisure in Turn-of-the-Century New York.* Philadelphia: Temple University Press, 1986.

Perez, Robert. "Confined to the Margins: Smuggling among Native Peoples of the Borderlands." In *Land of Necessity: Consumer Culture in the United States-Mexico Borderlands*, edited by Alexis McCrossen, 248–73. Durham, NC: Duke University Press, 2009.

Peters, Kurt M. "Continuing Identity: Laguna Pueblo Railroaders in Richmond, California." In *American Indians and the Urban Experience*, edited by Susan Lobo and Kurt Peters, 117–26. Walnut Creek, CA: Altamira Press, 2001.

———. "Watering the Flower: Laguna Pueblo and the Santa Fe Railroad, 1880–1943." In *Native Americans and Wage Labor: Ethnohistorical Perspectives*, edited by Alice Littlefield and Martha C. Knack, 177–97. Norman: University of Oklahoma Press, 1996.

Philp, Kenneth R., ed. *Indian Self-Rule: First-Hand Accounts of Indian-White Relations from Roosevelt to Reagan.* Logan: Utah State University Press, 1995.

———. *John Collier's Crusade for Indian Reform, 1920–1954.* Tucson: University of Arizona Press, 1997.

———. "Stride toward Freedom: The Relocation of Indians to Cities, 1952–1960." *Western Historical Quarterly* 16 (1985): 175–90.

———. *Termination Revisited: American Indians on the Trail to Self-Determination, 1933–1953.* Lincoln: University of Nebraska Press, 1999.

Powell, Peter J. *Sweet Medicine: The Continuing Role of the Sacred Arrows, the Sun Dance, and the Sacred Buffalo Hat in Northern Cheyenne History.* Vol. 1. Norman: University of Oklahoma Press, 1969.

Raibmon, Paige. *Authentic Indians: Episodes of Encounter from the Late-Nineteenth Century Northwest Coast.* Durham, NC: Duke University Press, 2005.

Ramirez, Renya K. *Native Hubs: Culture, Community, and Belonging in Silicon Valley and Beyond.* Durham, NC: Duke University Press, 2007.

Rasenberger, Jim. *High Steel: The Daring Men Who Built the World's Greatest Skyline, 1881 to the Present.* New York: Harper Perennial, 2005.

Reid, Gerald F. "Illegal Alien? The Immigration Case of Mohawk Ironworker Paul K. Diabo." Sociology Faculty Publications, Paper 4, Sacred Heart University, 2007. http://digitalcommons.sacredheart.edu/sociol_fac/4.

Reid, Joshua L. *The Sea Is My Country: The Maritime World of the Makahs.* New Haven, CT: Yale University Press, 2015.

Rice, Brian. *The Rotinonshonni: A Traditional Iroquoian History Through the Eyes of Teharonhia:Wako and Sawiskera.* Syracuse, NY: Syracuse University Press, 2013.

Richter, Daniel K. *Facing East from Indian Country: A Native History of Early America.* Cambridge, MA: Harvard University Press, 2003.

Riffe, Jed, ed. *Rosebud to Dallas: The Reservation Indian Relocates to the Urban Environment: A Humanities and Public Policy Handbook.* Dallas: American Indian Center and Southern Resource Center, 1977.

Rosenthal, Nicholas G. *Reimagining Indian Country: Native American Migration and Identity in Twentieth-Century Los Angeles.* Chapel Hill: University of North Carolina Press, 2012.

Rosier, Paul C. *Serving Their Country: American Indian Politics and Patriotism in the Twentieth Century.* Cambridge, MA: Harvard University Press, 2009.

———. "'They Are Ancestral Homelands': Race, Place, and Politics in Cold War Native America." *Journal of American History* 92 (2006): 1300–26.

Rotella, Carlo. *October Cities: The Redevelopment of Urban Literature.* Berkeley: University of California Press, 1998.

Salisbury, Neal. "The Indians' Old World: Native Americans and the Coming of Europeans." *William and Mary Quarterly* 53, no. 3 (July 1996): 435–58.

Scott, James C. *Weapons of the Weak: Everyday Forms of Peasant Resistance.* New Haven, CT: Yale University Press, 1987.

Shoemaker, Nancy. *American Indian Population Recovery in the Twentieth Century.* Albuquerque: University of New Mexico Press, 1999.

———. "Urban Indians and Ethnic Choices: American Indian Organizations in Minneapolis, 1920–1950." *Western Historical Quarterly* 19 (1988): 431.

Smith, Paul Chaat, and Robert Allen Warrior. *Like a Hurricane: The Indian Movement from Alcatraz to Wounded Knee.* New York: New Press, 1996.

Smith, Sherry L. "Francis LaFlesche and the World of Letters." *American Indian Quarterly* 25, no. 4 (Fall 2001).

———. *Hippies, Indians, and the Fight for Red Power.* Oxford: Oxford University Press, 2012.

———. *Reimagining Indians: Native Americans through Anglo Eyes, 1880–1940.* Oxford: Oxford University Press, 2000.

Smith, Sherry L., and Brian Frehner, eds. *Indians and Energy: Exploitation and Opportunity in the Southwest.* Santa Fe: School for Advanced Research Press, 2010.

Sorkin, Alan L. *American Indians and Federal Aid.* Washington, DC: Brookings Institute, 1971.

———. *The Urban American Indian.* Lexington, MA: Lexington Books, 1978.

Squires, Gregory D., Larry Bennett, Kathleen McCourt, and Philip Nyden. *Chicago: Race, Class, and the Response to Urban Decline.* Philadelphia: Temple University Press, 1987.

Stabler, Hollis D. *No One Ever Asked Me: The World War II Memoirs of an Omaha Indian Soldier.* With Victoria Smith. Lincoln: University of Nebraska Press, 2005.

Steiner, Stan. *The New Indians.* New York: Dell, 1968.

Straus, Terry, and Grant P. Arndt, eds. *Native Chicago.* Chicago: Native Chicago Independent Press, 1998.

Stremlau, Rose. *Sustaining the Cherokee Family: Kinship and the Allotment of an Indigenous Nation.* Chapel Hill: University of North Carolina Press, 2011.

Sturm, Circe. *Becoming Indian: The Struggle over Cherokee Identity in the Twenty-First Century.* Santa Fe, NM: School for Advanced Research Press, 2011.

Taylor, Graham D. *The New Deal and American Indian Tribalism: The Administration of the Indian Reorganization Act, 1934–45.* Lincoln: University of Nebraska Press, 1980.

Thomas, Robert K. "Colonialism: Classic and Internal." *New University Thought* 4, no. 4 (1966/1967): 37–44.

Thrush, Coll. "The Iceberg and the Cathedral: Encounter, Entanglement, and Isuma in Inuit London." *Journal of British Studies,* Winter 2013.

———. *Indigenous London: Native Travelers at the Heart of Empire.* New Haven, CT: Yale University Press, 2016.

———. *Native Seattle: Histories from the Crossing Over Place.* Seattle: University of Washington Press, 2007.

Townsend, Kenneth William. *World War II and the American Indian.* Albuquerque: University of New Mexico Press, 2000.

Troutman, John W. *Indian Blues: American Indians and the Politics of Music, 1879–1934.* Norman: University of Oklahoma Press, 2009.

Underhill, Ruth M. *The Navajos.* Norman: University of Oklahoma Press, 1956.

———. *Red Man's America: A History of Indian in the United States.* Chicago: University of Chicago Press, 1953.

Urban Indians: Proceedings of the Third Annual Conference on Problems and Issues concerning American Indians Today. Chicago: Newberry Library, 1981.

Usner, Daniel H., Jr. *Indian Work: Language and Livelihood in American History.* Cambridge, MA: Harvard University Press, 2009.

Vecoli, Rudolph J. "*Contadini* in Chicago: A Critique of *The Uprooted.*" *Journal of American History* 51, no. 3 (December 1964): 404–17.

Vizenor, Gerald. *The Everlasting Sky: Voices of the Anishinabe People.* St. Paul: Minnesota Historical Society Press, 2000. Originally written in 1972.

———. *Manifest Manners: Narratives on Postindian Survivance.* Lincoln: University of Nebraska Press, 1994.

———. "The Unmissable: Transmotion in Native Stories and Literature." *Transmotion* 1, no. 1 (2015).

———. *Wordarrows: Indians and Whites in the New Fur Trade.* Minneapolis: University of Minnesota Press, 1978.

Vogt, Evon Z. *Navaho Veterans: A Study of Changing Values.* Reports of the Rimrock Project Value Series, No. 1. Cambridge: Peabody Museum, 1951.

Wall, Wendy L. *Inventing the "American Way": The Politics of Consensus from the New Deal to the Civil Rights Movement*. Oxford: Oxford University Press, 2008.

Weibel-Orlando, Joan. *Indian Country, L.A.: Maintaining Ethnic Community in Complex Society*. Champaign: University of Illinois Press, 1999.

Westad, Odd Arne. *The Global Cold War: Third World Interventions and the Making of Our Times*. Cambridge: Cambridge University Press, 2006.

Whalen, Kevin. *Native Students at Work: American Indian Labor and Sherman Institute's Outing Program, 1900–1945*. Seattle: University of Washington Press, 2016.

White, Richard. "Teaching Indian History and Social History: Comments and Reflections." Paper delivered at The Impact of Indian History on the Teaching of United States History, McNickle Center Chicago Conference, 1984, Sessions V–VI, Newberry Library, 1985.

White, Robert H. *Tribal Assets: The Rebirth of Native America*. New York: Henry Holt, 1990.

Wilkinson, Charles *Blood Struggle: The Rise of Modern Indian Nations*. New York: W. W. Norton, 2005.

Witgen, Michael. *An Infinity of Nations: How the Native New World Shaped Early North America*. Philadelphia: University of Pennsylvania Press, 2012.

Young, Biloine Whiting, and Melvin L. Fowler. *Cahokia: The Great Native American Metropolis*. Urbana: University of Illinois Press, 2000.

Index

Note: Figures are indicated by page numbers in *italics*.

"Public Share in Indian Assimilation, The" (Warne), 70–71
Public Works Administration (PWA), 187
PWA. *See* Public Works Administration (PWA)

racial uplift, 6–7, 22, 24, 35, 51, 106, 190
racism, 34, 57, 60, 62, 65, 132, 138–140
Raibmon, Paige, 134
Ramirez, Renya, 222n101
Rapid City, South Dakota, 30, 75, 143, 153–54, 166
Red Cap, 27
Redcloud, William, 131
Redhorse, David, 183
Red Lake Agency, 49, 85
Red Lake Chippewa Reservation, 113, 162
Red Power movement, 158, 161, 170–171, 227n6
Red Wing, Minnesota, 81
Reid, Joshua, 5
Reid, Thomas, 85–86, 124
Reifel, Benjamin, 110, 147–48
Relocation (XIT), 1–2
reservations, 22–23, 26–27, 71–72, 202n14, 204n29
reverse relocation, 7, 161, 173
Rice, John Raymond, 65
Richmond, California, 47, 51
Roberts, Virginia, 154
Rochester, Minnesota, 82
Rockwell, John, 59
Rogers, Will, Jr., 181
Romero, Telesfor, 145, 150, 225n53
Roop, George B., 74–75
Roosevelt, Theodore, 28
Rosebud Sioux, 126
Rosenthal, Betty Clark, 78
Rosenthal, Nicolas G., 199n2
Rosier, Paul, 44
Rotella, Carlo, 67
Rovin, Charles, 155

Russell, Rudolph, 102, 152
Rust, John, 188

Sac and Fox tribe, 122, 175–76
Sacramento Indian Agency, 59
SAI. *See* Society of American Indians (SAI)
St. Augustine's Center for Indians (Chicago), 141, 151, 163, 184
St. Louis, Missouri, 99–100, 117, 120
St. Paul, Minnesota, 45–46, 139
Salt Lake City, 72, 85, 152
Saluskin, Joe, 53–54
San Diego, 47, 175
San Francisco, 2, 10, 38, 51, 110, 140, 173, 179–80, 194
San Ildefonso Pueblo Tribal Council, 122
San Jose, California, 83, 93, 128
Santa Fe railroad, 29–30
Santiago, Irvin, 167
Sargent, Earl, 112–13
Savage, W. D., 124–25
Schmidt, Josephine, 39
Schurz, Carl, 17
seasonal employment, 133–34
Seattle, 12, 48, 50–51, 53, 118, 226n1
Seattle Orientation Center, 118
self-relocation, 10, 89, 109, 123, 127, 139, 194, 222n2
Seminole, 126, 194
Seneca, Illinois, 42–43, 188
September 11 attacks, 39
Shane, LeRoy, 82
Sherman Institute, 47
Shiprock, New Mexico, 129
Shoemaker, Alice, 77–78
Shoshone-Bannock, 126
Sioux, 27–28, 205n46
Sioux City, Iowa, 65, 123
Sisseton Dakota reservation, 111, 134
Sitting Bull, 13
Smith, Sherry, 228n19
Snyder Act, 213n73
social mainstreaming, 13, 40–41, 132